'Never be lied to by statistics again: this book will teach you everything you need to know to combat dodgy data, spot shoddy stats, and to start constructing your own robust and reliable statistics.'

—Jude Towers, Lancaster University, UK

'This book provides a straightforward and timely tutorial in how to make informed decisions regarding which statistics are to be trusted. This is precisely the type of book needed to empower the public to disentangle the valid from the invalid in the information age.'

—Jennie E. Brand, UCLA, USA

'This book is a must for those taking introductory statistics courses. Rather than being a dry, technical textbook, it provides real-world every day examples of the use of statistics in everyday life.'

—John Jerrim, University College London, UK

'This book provides a welcome complement to the wide range of "how to do statistics" books that are available. It takes students in measured steps, providing useful exercises along the way.'

—Gillian Whitehouse, University of Queensland, Australia

'*Critical Statistics* provides an accessible and entertaining tour through the ways that statistics can be used to mislead us. It's a thorough introduction for people who shudder at the thought of data, but people who see themselves as experts will learn something from this too.'

—Mark Taylor, University of Sheffield, UK

'This is a highly readable introduction to the ways numbers are manufactured and misrepresented in today's society, teaching the importance of thinking critically about statistics and showing how to do better in our own learning and research. In the age of fake news, this is essential reading for all students of the social sciences.'

—Richard Harris FAcSS, University of Bristol, UK

'This is the perfect statistics book in an era in which it is so difficult to navigate the numbers and data we are exposed to in our everyday life. It helps the reader – anyone, from students to more expert readers – understand how difficult it is to interpret and utilize statistics in the news, and it teaches how to make better use of the incredible amount of data available today.'

—Maria Sironi, University College, London, UK

'This is a most impressive teaching resource. De Vries adopts an embedded approach to introduce students to statistical reasoning, guaranteed to increase student engagement with quantitative methods and to encourage a much-needed critical eye to quantitative evidence.'

—Stella Chatzitheochari, University of Warwick, UK

CRITICAL STATISTICS: SEEING BEYOND THE HEADLINES

Robert de Vries

'Darrell Huff's *How to Lie with Statistics* is rightly a classic but after over 60 years is inevitably showing its age. Robert de Vries "seeing beyond the headlines" is a much needed Huff for our times. It takes the reader skilfully through the essentials of statistics by taking apart the way in which numbers are routinely misused by the media. The result is not only an engaging introduction to statistics but an essential guide in the "post truth" era of "alternative facts" and "fake news".'

—John MacInnes, University of Edinburgh, UK

First published 2019 by
RED GLOBE PRESS

Red Globe Press in the UK is an imprint of Springer Nature Limited, registered in England, company number 785998, of 4 Crinan Street, London N1 9XW.

Red Globe Press® is a registered trademark in the United States, the United Kingdom, Europe and other countries.

ISBN 978–1–137–60980–9 hardback
ISBN 978–1–137–60979–3 paperback

This book is printed on paper suitable for recycling and made from fully managed and sustained forest sources. Logging, pulping and manufacturing processes are expected to conform to the environmental regulations of the country of origin.

A catalogue record for this book is available from the British Library.

A catalog record for this book is available from the Library of Congress.

Don't take anyone's word for it.
— Motto of the Royal Society
(roughly translated)

CONTENTS

LIST OF FIGURES AND TABLES

Figures

Tables

ABBREVIATIONS

ASHE	Annual Survey of Hours and Earnings
BSA	British Social Attitudes survey
CDC	Centers for Disease Control (US)
CSGC	Center for the Study of Global Christianity
GSS	General Social Survey (US)
HMRC	Her Majesty's Revenue and Customs (UK)
IFOP	Institut Francais d'Opinion Publique (French Institute of Public Opinion)
IPCC	Intergovernmental Panel on Climate Change
IPSO	Independent Press Standards Organisation (UK)
LFS	Labour Force Survey (UK)
MHRA	Medicines and Healthcare Regulatory Authority (UK)
NEA	National Education Association (US)
NGO	Non-Governmental Organisation
NHS	National Health Service (UK)
ONS	Office for National Statistics (UK)
PR	Public Relations
RCT	Randomised Controlled Trial
SIC	Standard Industrial Classification
UNDP	United Nations Development Programme
UNODC	United Nations Office on Drugs and Crime

PREFACE

As a psychology undergraduate (back in the mists of the early 2000s) I had to take a statistics course every year. I didn't really mind – I was pretty good at it, so it helped counteract the downward pressure on my grades exerted by alcohol and computer games. But I must confess that, at the time, I didn't really see the point. The attraction of psychology for me was grappling with the knotty problems of language, consciousness, personality, and self-esteem – not columns of averages and percentages. It didn't occur to me until much later that many of the insights researchers had gleaned into the subjects I cared so much about came from the painstaking application of statistics: from experiments based on carefully calibrated quantitative measurements and statistical comparisons.

What finally opened my eyes to the power and necessity of numbers was not a university class, but a column in a newspaper – specifically Ben Goldacre's 'Bad Science' column in *The Guardian*. A medical doctor by training, Goldacre used his column to skewer misleading science wherever he found it, from the British media's anti-vaccination campaigns, to the pharmaceutical industry's distortion of evidence from drug trials. His columns combined clear, straightforward explanations of seemingly complex statistical concepts with caustic takedowns of the incompetence and mendacity of homeopaths, anti-vaxxers, science journalists, and Big Pharma pill-peddlers. His articles woke me up to how little of what appeared in the media could be taken on trust. The message was clear: if I wanted to understand what was going on in the world, I needed to approach the 'facts' in the news with a much more critical eye. I needed to look behind the headlines to find out where these facts and figures were coming from, how they were produced, and what they really meant.

When I became an academic, and it was my turn to induct the next generation of social scientists into the mysteries of statistics, it was therefore natural that I would turn to 'Bad Science' for inspiration – as well as to the work of the other great critics of misleading numbers, like Darrel Huff (author of the classic *How to Lie With Statistics*), Sir Andrew Dilnot (former Chair of the UK Statistics Authority and author of *The Tiger That Isn't*), and Tim Harford (economist and host of the BBC's flagship statistics programme *More or Less*). Their work taught me that the best way to learn how something works is often to see how it breaks. And that is the approach I've taken in this book. The chapters that follow contain numerous striking examples of the statistical mistakes and deceptions that are all too common in the media, in politics, and in many other spheres of life. My hope is that by looking in depth at what went wrong in each case, we can also figure out how to make things go right.

Chapter 1 begins with an illustration of why statistical literacy is essential for understanding the world around us and why we need to think critically about the statistics we encounter in our everyday lives. **Chapter 2** goes on to discuss where the statistics in the news come from, and why the job of checking their veracity ultimately falls to us. **Chapters 3 to 7** introduce and explain the five fundamental concepts that lie behind almost all the statistics you'll see in the news and in the social sciences: sampling, measurement, averages, percentages, and causal inference (working out when one thing causes another). **Chapter 8** focuses on how statistics are displayed visually using graphs and charts. **Chapter 9** illustrates the importance of context to understanding what a number really means. And finally, **Chapter 10** demonstrates how to put it all together to answer real questions about the social world.

Each chapter closes with a 'Seeing Beyond the Headlines' toolbox, a practical guide to using the lessons of the chapter to spot dodgy statistics. After each chapter, there is also a set of exercises, intended to help solidify your understanding of what has been covered. These exercises are intended mainly for social science students who are reading this book to help with their degree courses. But even if that's not you, there's nothing stopping you from giving them a try just for the personal satisfaction!

Together, these chapters represent my attempt to distil into a manageable form the statistical knowledge I wish I'd had as an undergrad – and that now, faced with a world of fake news and dodgy numbers, I'm deeply glad to have at my disposal.

TOUR OF THE BOOK

The book includes a range of features which help you to apply and further explore the concepts discussed in the text:

Headlines
Throughout the text, I use real-world examples, taken from a wide range of media sources, to demonstrate how ubiquitous numbers are in today's society, where they come from, and how we can go about analysing and critiquing them.

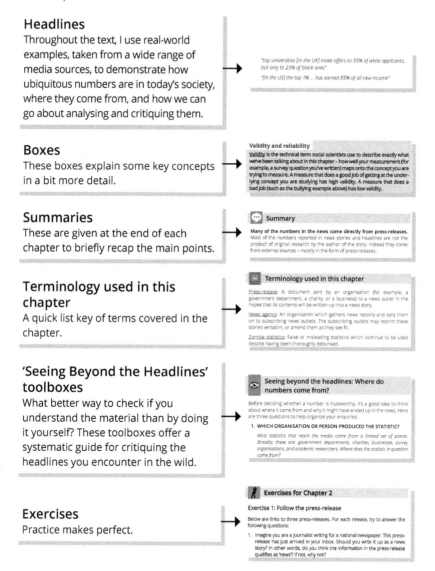

> "top universities [in the UK] make offers to 55% of white applicants, but only to 23% of black ones"
>
> "[in the US] the top 1% ... has earned 85% of all new income"

Boxes
These boxes explain some key concepts in a bit more detail.

> **Validity and reliability**
> Validity is the technical term social scientists use to describe exactly what we've been talking about in this chapter – how well your measurement (for example, a survey question you've written) maps onto the concept you are trying to measure. A measure that does a good job of getting at the underlying concept you are studying has high validity. A measure that does a bad job (such as the bullying example above) has low validity.

Summaries
These are given at the end of each chapter to briefly recap the main points.

> 💬 **Summary**
> Many of the numbers in the news come directly from press-releases. Most of the numbers reported in news stories and headlines are not the product of original research by the author of the story. Instead they come from external sources – mostly in the form of press-releases.

Terminology used in this chapter
A quick list key of terms covered in the chapter.

> **Aa Terminology used in this chapter**
> Press-release: A document sent by an organisation (for example, a government department, a charity, or a business) to a news outlet in the hopes that its contents will be written up into a news story.
> News agency: An organisation which gathers news reports and sells them on to subscribing news outlets. The subscribing outlets may reprint these stories verbatim, or amend them as they see fit.
> Zombie statistics: False or misleading statistics which continue to be used despite having been thoroughly debunked.

'Seeing Beyond the Headlines' toolboxes
What better way to check if you understand the material than by doing it yourself? These toolboxes offer a systematic guide for critiquing the headlines you encounter in the wild.

> 👁 **Seeing beyond the headlines: Where do numbers come from?**
> Before deciding whether a number is trustworthy, it's a good idea to think about where it came from and why it might have ended up in the news. Here are three questions to help organise your enquiries:
> 1. WHICH ORGANISATION OR PERSON PRODUCED THE STATISTIC?
>   Most statistics that reach the media come from a limited set of places. Broadly, these are: government departments, charities, businesses, survey organisations, and academic researchers. Where does the statistic in question come from?

Exercises
Practice makes perfect.

> 🏃 **Exercises for Chapter 2**
> Exercise 1: Follow the press-release
> Below are links to three press-releases. For each release, try to answer the following questions:
> 1. Imagine you are a journalist writing for a national newspaper. This press-release has just arrived in your inbox. Should you write it up as a news story? In other words, do you think the information in the press-release qualifies as 'news'? If not, why not?

Italic, Bold and Underline

Italics are used for rhetorical emphasis. **Bold** is used to make important factual information stand out to facilitate understanding. <u>Underlined</u> is used only for items that appear in the glossary at the end of the chapter.

GUIDE TO THE WEBSITE

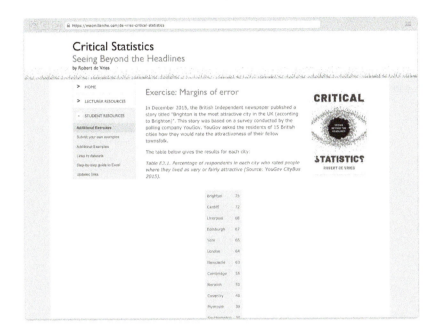

The Critical Statistics website

Accompanying this book there is a companion website, which you can find at www.macmillanihe.com/devries-critical-statistics. The resources on this website will help you get the most out of the book. They include:

More examples and exercises! In the modern media, there is a dubious statistic born every minute – meaning there were many great examples I just couldn't find space for in the book. Luckily, websites have no word limit. The *Critical Statistics* website will be home to an updated list of the media's most noteworthy numerical blunders. There will also be more exercises you can try your hand at, based on real-world data and statistics. If this inspires you to keep an eye out for misleading statistics yourself, there will also be a space for you to submit your own examples.

Materials and guidance for the exercises. Many of the exercises at the end of the chapters involve looking at real data – for example, data on gun laws in US states, on murder rates, on people's attitudes towards gay rights, and on a number of other topics. The companion website will make it easy to find and download these datasets.

Some of the exercises will also ask you to conduct some basic analyses in Microsoft Excel. For those of you whose Excel skills are a little rusty, the website will provide detailed step-by-step guides to help you.

Updated links. As I've already mentioned, this book focuses on real examples of statistical claims from the media. In many cases, I've provided links to the articles where these claims were originally made, so you can see them for yourself. However, the internet never stands still, and a link which works today might not work tomorrow. The *Critical Statistics* website will therefore maintain up-to-date links to the examples I go through in the book.

Resources for teachers. For teachers and lecturers, the companion website will provide more materials and guidance to help you make use of the book in your courses, including additional exercises and extensive sample seminar and workshop plans. These act as an ideal guide for using the book on either a traditional introductory statistics course or a course specifically dedicated to critiquing statistics in the media.

ACKNOWLEDGEMENTS

This book would not have been possible without the support of my colleagues and friends at the University of Kent: in particular Ben Baumberg Geiger, Trude Sundberg, and Tina Haux who supported me in developing the course on which this book is based; and also Heejung Chung and Jack Cunliffe, for generously giving their time and expertise.

I'd also like to thank all the friends and family who didn't run a mile when presented with a draft of a 200-page book about statistics to read: with special thanks to Geoffrey Baruch, Sam Higgs, Iain Savill, Min Allen, and to my mother Marianne for their invaluable comments and suggestions.

Thanks also to my editors at Palgrave: Lloyd Langman and Tuur Driesser, who have offered excellent support throughout the process; and to the 13 anonymous peer-reviewers whose astute critiques made a big difference to the final text. And thanks too to The Equality Trust, for generously allowing me to use their graphs extensively in Chapter 8.

Finally, and most of all, I want to say thank you to my wife Ella. Her brilliant and insightful suggestions helped me set right manifold fumbles and missteps, and her unstinting love and support kept me thinking that this was something worth doing. I really couldn't have done it without you!

1 99% OF STATISTICS ARE MADE UP

"Nearly one in five British Muslims has some sympathy with those who have fled the country to fight for IS in Syria" – The Sun, 23 November 2015

On 13 November 2015, 130 people were killed in a terrorist attack in Paris. Islamic State (IS; aka ISIS, ISIL, or Daesh depending on who you ask) claimed responsibility. Less than two weeks later, millions of *Sun* readers in Britain learned that *one in five* British Muslims sympathised with jihadis leaving the country to fight for this same organisation. According to *The Sun*, this meant that 500,000 Muslims in Britain supported people like 'Jihadi John', a British Muslim turned ISIS member who had become famous in the UK for his involvement in beheadings of Western journalists and aid workers.

This is frightening news. It's the kind of news that makes people feel differently about the country they are living in. Many non-Muslim readers of this story will nevertheless have had Muslim friends, Muslim neighbours, Muslim co-workers. Readers in big cities like London, Birmingham, and Manchester might well live near (or even in) areas where the majority of the population is Muslim. What were these readers to make of the fact that a *fifth* of these neighbours and colleagues likely sympathised with a violent, jihadist organisation like ISIS?

Predictably, there was anger. Internet commenters suggested that Muslims were hostile to Britain and British culture. Some wanted British Muslims to be deported in the interests of national security. In comments sections and forums people wrote things like 'If it means safeguarding our nation then surely mass deportations must be the answer' and 'best if they all went to a Muslim country'.[1]

People on the other side of the debate were angry too – but mostly at *The Sun* and its readers. On Twitter, they rallied around the #1in5Muslims hashtag to denounce the article as part of *The Sun*'s racist, Islamophobic agenda (and, because this is the internet, to make jokes about cats and Netflix and chill).[2] The battle lines were clear: *The Sun* is Islamophobic and intolerant, or Muslims are dangerous extremists.

Framing the debate this way, however, means losing sight of something important: whether the 'one in five' number is actually accurate.

Set against Big Talk about racism and national security, questioning the specific number in the story can seem somewhat trivial. But in this case, as in so many others, the number *is* the story. If the number were lower, say one in a hundred, there would be no story. One in a hundred is too small a number to be worth putting on the front page of Britain's biggest selling national newspaper. If the number were higher, say one in two, then it's a much *bigger* story. Half of British Muslims support terrorism? That's starting to sound like an existential crisis for the country.

If the number is the story, then our first priority should be to determine whether the number is *true*. At the bottom of all this is a real figure. There is a real number of Muslims in Britain who have some level of support for ISIS, and this number is unlikely to be zero. Once you get into populations of millions, there will be some number of people who support any crazy thing you can think of. The number of Brits who think the royal family are alien lizard-people is not zero. We can therefore legitimately ask how big this number is: how many British Muslims actually do support ISIS? *The Sun* wanted to know, so they did some research and came up with an answer: one in five.

But is this number accurate? Or is it, for want of a better word, bullshit?

On bullshit

The word bullshit has a special place in the world of fact-checking. People who lie with statistics – politicians, business leaders, snake oil salesmen of all stripes – are often quite litigious. They like to sue people who point out that they are liars. To actually prove that someone has lied is a tricky business. You have to show that they *knew* what they were saying was wrong, but that they said it anyway with the express intention of misleading people. You basically have to prove what was going on inside their mind at the time they made the statement. Unless you have an obvious smoking gun – an email in which they say 'I know our product causes 20% of people's skin to fall off, but I'm going to say it's 0.005%. lol ☺' – then you're going to struggle.

Calling something 'bullshit' is different. You're still saying the statement is false, but you're not specifically calling the person making it a liar. This makes it more difficult (though not impossible) for them to sue you.

The short answer to this question is: 'yes, it's bullshit.' The long answer is that it's a special kind of bullshit that requires some time to explain.

The first thing to note about *The Sun*'s 'one in five' statistic is that it comes from a **sample survey**. You've almost certainly filled one of these out at some point or another. Someone calls you up, or you go to a website and you answer a series of questions. 'On a scale from 1–5, how likely are you to visit Big Butt Mountain?',* that kind of thing. When I was a student, I worked for a company which conducted these sorts of surveys. I mostly called people on behalf of their local council to ask if it would be OK to collect their bins less often (in case you are interested, the answer was no. People wanted their bins collected as often as humanly possible. Every day. Every hour. They wanted binmen waiting in the shrubbery, ready to leap out at the merest hint of refuse). A lot of the statistics in the news come from surveys like this, and there are a few important things to keep in mind about them. The first is that not everyone in the country takes the survey. This is an obvious point (otherwise we'd all do nothing but take surveys all day), but it's worth remembering. *The Sun* says that one in five British Muslims sympathise with 'jihadis' in Syria, but clearly they did not call every Muslim in Britain to ask about this. Instead, they (or, more accurately, the company they hired to carry out the survey) spoke to a random (or close to random) selection of about 1,000 British Muslims. About 20% of this sample of 1,000 expressed at least some sympathy with people leaving Britain to go and fight in Syria. *The Sun* took this figure and applied it to the British Muslim population as a whole (which is around 3 million people).

It feels wrong to use the opinions of 1,000 people to make sweeping generalisations about a population of millions. However, this is a common and actually fairly well-accepted practice. If you take a random sample (see Chapter 3) of a decent number of people, their views can be a reasonably accurate representation of the views of a whole population. The same is true if you wanted to know, say, the average height of people in France. You can't go to every French person's house with a tape measure. But if you measured a thousand random French people, this would give you a reasonably good idea of how tall the average French person was. So far, *The Sun* hasn't done anything drastically wrong.**

There is, however, one important detail missing from the story which might change our interpretation of the 'one in five Muslims' number. As well as British Muslims, the survey company *The Sun* hired also conducted the same survey with non-Muslims.[3] On the headline question, 13% of *non-Muslims* were also sympathetic to people leaving to fight in Syria. This is about one in every eight people – not that different from one in five.

You might be wondering why a substantial number of non-Muslims would support people who have left the country to join a radical Islamist terrorist organisation. The answer is that, just like most Muslims,

---

* This is a real place. It's a mountain in North Carolina that is apparently quite nice for hiking. Tourist websites particularly recommend the 'Big Butt trail to Point Misery'.
** We'll return to the issue of samples in Chapter 3.

they wouldn't. Very few British people, Muslim or otherwise, support the worldview or actions of an ultra-violent jihadist organisation like ISIS.

But if that's the case, why did *The Sun's* survey find such a high level of support for British ISIS recruits? The answer to this is one of the oldest tricks in the book of misleading statistics. To show that a significant fraction of British Muslims 'support ISIS', *The Sun* asked about one thing in the survey, then pretended they'd asked about something else.

Here is the actual question *The Sun* used in their survey:

Which of the following statements is closest to your view?

1. *I have a lot of sympathy with young Muslims who leave the UK to join fighters in Syria*

2. *I have some sympathy with young Muslims who leave the UK to join fighters in Syria*

3. *I have no sympathy with young Muslims who leave the UK to join fighters in Syria*

4. *I don't know*

Twenty per cent of Muslim respondents (and 13% of non-Muslims) picked either 'some' or 'a lot' of sympathy.

It has probably occurred to many of you already, but 'sympathy with' does not mean the same thing as 'support for'. In saying that they had 'some sympathy with' young Muslims leaving the UK to fight in Syria, many people will have meant only that they felt at least a bit sorry for them. Perhaps they felt sorry for people they thought had been brainwashed into travelling to a hellish situation by stories of an 'Islamic paradise'.[4] Or maybe they felt sorry for young Muslims whose lives in the UK were so bad that they thought fighting in Syria offered better prospects. One of the interviewers who conducted the survey made exactly this point in an article for *Vice*.[5] While conducting the survey, the interviewer had spoken to a Muslim woman who had given 'thoughtful, considered answers to every question'. She thought that David Cameron 'would probably be right to bomb Syria, and that Muslims did have a responsibility to condemn terrorist attacks carried out in the name of Islam'. But she also sympathised with young British Muslims who left to go fight in Syria. She said 'They're brainwashed, I feel sorry for them'. So the interviewer ticked the box marked 'I have some sympathy for young British Muslims who go to join fighters in Syria'. This person is one of the 'one in five' Muslims *The Sun* characterised as 'supporting jihadis'.

Something else you may have noticed about the question is that the word 'ISIS' does not appear anywhere. It only mentions 'fighters in Syria'. In 2015, when the survey was carried out, ISIS were only one of many groups involved in the Syrian conflict. Not all of these groups could be characterised as radical Islamist jihadists. In fact, the UK government had been supporting several of them in their fight against Syrian dictator Bashar al-Assad.

If you go back and look at the front-page headline, you can see that *The Sun* were careful to stick to the word 'sympathy'. Perhaps they thought the mismatch with the survey question would be too obvious otherwise. But in the rest of the paper it is clear that by 'sympathy for British Muslims leaving to fight in Syria' they actually mean 'support for ISIS'. The front page is dominated by an image of a knife-wielding Jihadi John, with the caption 'Support … Brit Jihadi John who went to Syria'. Later in the paper, a heading references the survey's finding of 'backing for jihadis'. On page four, a columnist describes her shock that so many Muslims in Britain are sympathetic to the 'murderous, twisted ideology [of ISIS]'.

You may feel that we've strayed from talking about numbers. However, one of the main things to check when critiquing any statistic is whether what is reported matches up with what was actually measured (we'll cover this in more detail in Chapter 4). In the case of statistics based on surveys, this means asking whether what we are being told matches the question that was actually asked. We are being told by *The Sun* (both implicitly and explicitly) that one in five British Muslims support people joining ISIS. As we've seen, this is not what the survey question actually asked about. How a question is worded has a dramatic effect on the numbers you get back. By wording the question the way they did, *The Sun* got a high number. By wording it to more closely match the concept they wanted to measure (support for ISIS), they would have got a much lower one.

A lot of smart people spotted problems with *The Sun*'s 'one in five' figure soon after it was published. Thanks to them, the story has a somewhat happy ending. After a record number of complaints, the Independent Press Standards Organisation (IPSO) ruled against *The Sun*, who were forced to admit that the article was 'substantially misleading'.[6] They subsequently removed all record of the story from their website. This is all well and good, but most bullshit statistics are not so quickly and comprehensively refuted. This was a front-page story in a national newspaper, and Islamist extremism (and Islamophobia) is a highly emotive issue. *The Sun* consequently faced an army of sceptical people ready to dig into the nitty-gritty details behind the figure. Their efforts were aided by the fact that the problems with the statistic were so blindingly obvious. Lower profile claims, or claims with more subtle (though no less devastating) statistical flaws rarely receive the same level of attention. They slide in under the radar to become part of the public discourse on a given topic, helping people to be a little bit more wrong for years to come.

The world runs on numbers

The Sun's bullshit about British Muslims is just one drop in the ocean of statistical claims that wash over us every day. In a 2016 study, researchers at Cardiff University found that one-fifth of all British TV and radio news items included at least one statistical reference. This included three-quarters of all stories about the economy, almost 40% of stories about the environment, and around a third of all stories about the politics.[7] The media is full to the brim with numbers. And it's not just the media. Politicians use statistics to tell us there is a problem that needs solving:

> *"top universities [in the UK] make offers to 55% of white applicants, but only to 23% of black ones"*[8]
>
> *"[in the US] the top 1% … has earned 85% of all new income"*[9]

Or to persuade us to elect them or keep them in power:

> *"We created 800,000 new jobs"*[10]
>
> *"We built almost 2 million homes"*[11]

Companies use statistics to tell us that their product is better than everyone else's:

> *"Duracell batteries last up to 10 times longer"*
>
> *"Pantene conditioner makes hair up to 10 times stronger"*[12]

Doctors use them to inform us about risks to our health:

> *"People who smoke have 25 times the risk of developing lung cancer"*[13]
>
> *"150 minutes of moderate exercise per week reduces the risk of heart disease by 14%"*[14]

The list goes on and on. Our everyday lives are also not a number-free zone. Around the dinner table, or on social media, we've all used some statistic or other to make a point or to win an argument. 'Did you know that 90% of vegetarians eat meat when they're drunk?',* 'Yeah, but it's probably McDonald's and you know that like only 10% of a chicken nugget is meat.'

---

*   This comes from a real Twitter conversation sparked by a story in the *London Metro* newspaper. The story reported that 34% of vegetarians eat meat when drunk. On Twitter this was discussed variously as '37%', 'almost 40%', and '90%'.

Statistical claims crop up in almost every part of our lives, from our health, to our political views, to what we buy at the supermarket. These numbers are often important – they tell us things we really need to know. Unfortunately, when confronted with statistical claims, many of us suffer from a sort of numerical blindness. The headline says that 'the government will spend an extra £40 billion on schools', or that '80% of politicians are millionaires', but our minds slide off the specific figure and latch on to the gist instead: 'the government will spend a lot on schools', 'too many politicians are millionaires'.

In November 2015, US website *The Onion* reported that 42 million people had died in America's 'Bloodiest Black Friday Weekend On Record'.[15] Many people on social media were aghast at this news. For example, here are a just a couple of the responses that appeared under a Facebook post about the story:

> *"How stupid can you really be people you kill someone over something you don't really need you just want how pathetic are you"*

> *"This is absolutely crazy. All for gifts. So sad what monsters we have become. So much for the spirit of giving. What happened to the true meaning of Christmas????!!!"*

Noble sentiments indeed. But while composing their posts, these commenters might have profited from a moment's reflection on the actual number in the headline. The United States has a population of around 320 million people. The figure of 42 million would mean that around *one in every eight people in the country* had been killed in pursuit of cut-price TVs and *Star Wars* advent calendars. It might also have been worth examining a few previous headlines from *The Onion* (perhaps the world's most famous satirical news site), which have included such gems as 'Study Reveals: Babies Are Stupid' and 'Jurisprudence Fetishist Gets Off on A Technicality' (you might need to let that one sit a little).

I am not holding these people up to be mocked (OK, maybe I am a little …). They are simply an extreme example of our natural tendency to mentally 'skip over' the numbers in a story, and to home in instead on the core message. Does it sound important? Does it sound like a good thing or a bad thing? Doing this doesn't make you stupid – we all do it to some extent or another. But it can cause big problems, as we can see if we look at a more serious example from the world of health.

Sometimes contraception doesn't work

Contraceptive implants are small devices that can be implanted under a woman's skin (usually in the arm). Like the pill, they release hormones into the bloodstream to prevent pregnancy. They last for a few years and get removed when they run out. Rather than taking a pill every day, it's basically a thing in your arm that does the job for you automatically. In 2011 the BBC,[16] along with several other national outlets in the UK, published news that almost 600 women who'd had these implants installed had become pregnant regardless.

Just as in *The Onion*'s Black Friday story, it's easy to let our minds slip off the number in the headline and just interpret this as a Bad Thing about contraceptive implants. Lots of people are having unwanted pregnancies, so contraceptive implants must be bad (or at least worse than we thought). This is particularly troubling because implants are often described by doctors as being more effective than other forms of contraception, such as condoms and the pill.

But do these figures actually mean there is a problem? Obviously there is a problem for the individual women concerned. They thought they were protected by the implant, but they got pregnant anyway. This is a potentially life-changing event and they deserve a great deal of sympathy. But should this change *our* minds about the effectiveness of contraceptive implants? If you put the pregnancy numbers in context, the answer is: probably not. Investigating the story, the excellent Ben Goldacre (former writer of *The Guardian*'s 'Bad Science' column and all-around expert on dodgy evidence) contacted the UK's Medicines and Healthcare Regulatory Authority (MHRA) and asked how many implants had been sold up to that point.[17] The MHRA put the number at around 1.35 million. Six hundred pregnancies (the exact figure was actually 584) is a tiny fraction of this figure. Based on these numbers, Goldacre calculated the failure rate for the implants as 0.014% per year (the implants last for three years); or **1.4 pregnancies per year for every 10,000 women with implants**.* For comparison, the first-year failure rate of condoms is about 2% for perfect use. That is, in their first year of using condoms, not 1.4, but **200 out of 10,000 women** will get pregnant.[18] And that's only counting people who use condoms *consistently and perfectly*. The failure rate for the pill (again for women who never forget to take it) is 0.3%, or **30 out of 10,000**. Even when used perfectly, condoms and the pill are *much* worse at preventing pregnancy than implants are.

For there to be no opportunity for a story about women getting pregnant while having an implant they would have to work flawlessly every time. That's just not going to happen. No drug or device that humans have ever invented meets this standard. Nothing has a failure rate of zero. The '600 pregnancies' number is telling us a real story; it's just not the story the BBC are selling. Putting the number in context, the real

---

* Other studies using better data have estimated the failure rate at around 0.05% per year.

news is that 'contraceptive implants work an extremely high percentage of the time, just like we thought they did'. Of course, that's not a headline that's going to attract many clicks.

The difference between these two ways of reading the implants story could make a real difference to people's lives: pushing them away from using implants, and towards using condoms or the pill. It's only by stopping to interrogate the number that we were able to get behind the headline to what was actually going on. As a result, we're that bit better informed about the world, and that bit better equipped to make an informed decision.

If you'll excuse some slight corniness, taking off our number blinders is a bit like a superpower. Unscrupulous people, including politicians, journalists, and annoying men in bars, are counting on us not to question whatever percentage or million or billion they throw out. They are relying on our number blindness to *get things by us*. If we start actually paying attention to their statistics, we might realise just how much bullshit they are trying to get us to swallow. This is particularly important right now, in what future historians will hopefully call 'the short-lived "fake news" era of the early 21st century'.

Statistics in the fake news era

Fake news is a slippery concept. If you define 'fake news' as any article that does not accurately represent reality, then the news media has had a fake news problem for a lot longer than we've been using that phrase. The outlets that make up the 'respectable' press – the same outlets that have lately been so concerned about the rise of fake news – publish false and misleading stories all the time. This is especially true when it comes to stories about numbers. The story with which we began this chapter did not come from some niche anti-immigration blog, or from the depths of Reddit. It came from Britain's biggest national newspaper. The misleading story about contraceptive implants came from perhaps the quintessential respectable source – the BBC. You'll see much more evidence of the unreliability of the mainstream press in the next chapter (and in the rest of the book).

Politicians too – recent vocal converts to the war on fake news – have always been some of the most prolific peddlers of misleading numbers and statistics. In the run-up to the 2016 US elections, the fact-checking organisation PolitiFact published figures on public pronouncements made that year by a group of presidential candidates and former presidents.[19] Former president Bill Clinton emerged as the most honest of the bunch. But even with the decided advantage of neither being in, nor currently running for, political office, almost a quarter of his public statements were rated 'Mostly False' or worse. On the other end of the scale, 76% of Donald Trump's statements were rated as mostly false or worse, with 19% receiving PolitiFact's lowest possible rating, 'Pants on Fire'. This rating is reserved for statements that are not only false, but are so spectacularly, *heroically* false that they deserve some kind of award. Not all of these false statements were based on statistics, but many were. Putting a number on something makes it sound definitive and 'science-y', so politicians (and journalists, and everyone else) use statistics when they want to sound like they know what they're talking about.

From this perspective, we've been living in a fake news era for a very long time – perhaps as long as 'the news' has existed. However, it is true to say that something has changed in recent years. From 2015 to 2017 we saw a dramatic rise in the number of 'news' sites whose entire MO is the production of false stories. During the seemingly interminable 2016 US election cycle, sites like the *Denver Guardian* and the *Boston Tribune*,* published story after story about Hillary Clinton's failing health, or about Obama's plans to ban the pledge of allegiance, or to cut billions of dollars from veterans' care to give to Syrian refugees. These stories were not simply garbled or misleading presentations of real information (as is common in the mainstream press) – they were made up out of thin air. As Fil Menczer, a professor of information science at the University of Indiana, put it to *The Guardian* (the real one), 'There is a cottage industry of websites that just fabricate fake news designed to make one group or another group particularly riled up.'[20]

Sites like these (and there are many others) represent 'fake news' in its purest form. This is bad enough on its own. However, alongside the pure strain, another, hardier source of fake news has arisen. Mainstream media outlets have always had ideological affiliations of varying strengths. Fox News, MSNBC, the *Daily Mail, The Guardian* – we all know which side of the political aisle these organs lean towards. However, recent years have seen the emergence of outlets which take political partisanship to the next level. On the left you have organisations like *The Canary* (UK), *Occupy Democrats* (US), and *Addicting Info* (US). On the right you have equivalents like *Freedom Daily* (US), and *Right Wing News* (US).** These names might not have the brand recognition of the *New York Times* or the BBC, but they wield enormous influence on Facebook (chances are you've scrolled past one of their headlines or videos at least once today). And these days, Facebook is where people get their news.

Hyper-partisan outlets like *The Canary* and *Freedom Daily* are not pure-bred fake news – they are not in the business of cynically creating sensationalist stories from whole cloth. However, what these sites do have

---

* Fake news sites often purposefully choose titles (and purchase web domains) that make them sound like legitimate newspapers.

** Some would likely also include higher profile sites like *Breitbart* on this list.

is an overriding allegiance to one particular political team.* And when your main purpose is not to convey information, but to support a team, then you tend not to put too much effort into checking your facts. This is how you get stories like these:

> *"Bloomberg puts Trump's current net worth at $2.9 billion ... If Trump had just put his father's money in mutual fund that tracked the S&P 500** and spent his career finger-painting, he'd have $8 billion"* – Occupy Democrats Facebook post, 2 December 2015

> *"U.S. Police killed more people in just one month than the U.K.'s did in over a century"* – *Addicting Info* Facebook post, 14 April 2015

> *"OUTRAGE: Before Leaving, Obama Enacts Rules to Take $3,000 From EVERY American"* Conservative Tribune, 1 December 2016

> *"Tens of Thousands Of Scientists Declare Climate Change A Hoax"* – YourNewsWire.com, 2 September 2016

All of these stories were widely shared on Facebook. All of them are false.*** And these stories are not exceptional. In 2016, *Buzzfeed* analysed the output of the six biggest hyper-partisan Facebook pages (including *Occupy Democrats, Addicting Info*, and *Freedom Daily*) for a period of seven days. They found that between 20% and 30% of the hundreds of headlines they published over this time were either mostly or substantially false.[21]

There are plenty of liars out there. They are the people who will feed us numbers and statistics they *know* to be false because they want us to click on their website, buy their product, or support their cause. Some of these liars write headlines for fake news websites. Some write for respectable newspapers. Some of them hold high political office. However, most fake news doesn't come from people who are intentionally trying to deceive us. It comes from people who *just don't care if what they are saying is true.*

---

*   Some of this is genuine. The *Occupy Democrats* page, for example, is run by a left-wing advocacy organisation. However, some hyper-partisan sites take sides purely for the clicks. For example, the seemingly ideologically opposed sites *Liberal Society* and *Conservative 101* are both run by a single media company, American News LLC. Companies like this make their money by generating outrage-inducing partisan click-bait for both left and right.

**   A simple type of investment that makes or loses money based on the combined performance of the 500 largest companies on the stock-market.

*** The Trump investment figure conflates inheritance Trump received from his father with income from the Trump business, which the junior Trump was involved in running. The number of people killed by UK police in the last century is a very fuzzy number indeed. The $3,000 figure relates to business regulations enacted over Obama's terms and is not a sum to be paid by 'every American'. Tens of thousands of scientists believe climate change is a hoax only if you count random people with an undergraduate degree in a semi-scientific subject as 'scientists'.

They believe their policy prescription is the right one, or that their cause is righteous, or that it just doesn't matter because they get paid either way. They are the bullshitters, and they have always existed. But now they've taken over our news feeds.

Don't be part of the problem

Faced with this tide of misleading numbers, what should we do? We could be forgiven for becoming pure cynics, mistrusting any number that might cross our path – it's all lies, damned lies, and statistics. But this would mean missing out on a lot of important information: real problems in society, genuine insights into human nature, authentic scientific breakthroughs. If we disbelieve every number we read, we're going to be in the dark about a lot of things. But there is an alternative to being cynical, and that is to be *critical*. Don't believe everything you read – but don't automatically disbelieve it either. Instead take steps to try and figure out what's true and what's not.

Of course, most people already do this to some extent. It's a rare individual who trusts absolutely everything they hear without question. For example, let's say I come across a headline in my news feed which tells me that 'world wildlife populations have dropped by 50% in the last 40 years'. That sounds bad, but before I pass it on I'm going to make at least some effort to see if it's true. I take a quick look at the source: it's a BBC news article, so it seems legitimate. The statistic also resonates with my feeling that human beings are doing terrible damage to the environment. And what's more, it fits solidly within the belief structure of my political 'team'.* That's probably enough to warrant a like or a share.

This process has at least one thing going for it: it's quick and easy to apply. A few seconds of thought, a tap or a click, and I'm on to the next thing (and the next, and the next). But this quick and easy process also has quite an important downside, in that it's a *terrible* way to determine whether something is actually true. Just because a source 'feels' legitimate is no guarantee that it actually is: as we've already established, even the most legitimate sources (like the BBC) often publish false or misleading facts and figures. Whether a fact fits with your existing beliefs about how the world works is also a very bad guide as to its truthfulness.** What the quick and easy approach to factual claims amounts to is a

---

* Of course you might have the exact opposite reaction. You might consider the BBC to be part of the biased liberal media, and as such dismiss this statistic as another part of the great climate change hoax.

** In case you are wondering, the wildlife fact is not completely false. However, an investigation by the BBC's *More or Less* programme showed that it's not exactly true either (whatever else you might want to say about the BBC, they are pretty good at self-criticism).

sure-fire recipe for believing (and spreading) a lot of comfortable facts that aren't true, while missing a lot of surprising (and sometimes difficult) things that *are*.

The alternative is to take the time to delve into the details behind the claims we hear, and to determine for ourselves what they mean and don't mean. This is, admittedly, a harder path to walk. But it's worth it. It *matters* whether the things we read are true or false. It matters whether 50% of the world's wildlife has disappeared or not. It matters if the richest 1% of the world's population earns 85% of all the income. It matters if the government have built 2 million homes or if they've actually built a lot less. Knowing what's real and what isn't protects us – from duff products, from dodgy health advice, from mendacious politicians – but it also protects everyone else. The decisions we make – about how to vote in an election or a referendum, about which charities and causes to support, about which products to buy – have consequences. If we want our actions to do more good in the world than harm, we have to start from a position of understanding how the world actually works. A good first step is therefore to abdicate our role in propping up the bullshit information economy.

If you're someone who is not particularly comfortable with numbers and statistics, you may be thinking that you don't have the skills or the expertise to take this on. But piercing the veil of numerical nonsense that surrounds us doesn't need to involve equations and complex maths. A few tricks and some simple concepts are all you really need to decipher the vast majority of statistical claims you'll encounter. These tricks and concepts are what this book is about.

These techniques are particularly important for students in the social sciences. Students taking courses in psychology, anthropology, sociology, criminology, politics, social work, and so on, need to get to grips with quantitative evidence (see the box below for more on this). These students are the primary intended audience of this book (hence the exercises at the end of each chapter). However, numbers and statistics are such a big part of our everyday lives that statistical skills are increasingly essential not just for students, but for all of us. In 1903, H.G. Wells predicted that 'statistical thinking will one day be as necessary for efficient citizenship as the ability to read and write'.* With so much of the information we receive – about politics, about the economy, about the environment; about everything – coming in the form of statistics, it's safe to say that day has arrived.

---

*   Actually Wells didn't really say this. He said something very similar, but a lot wordier – and hence harder to quote. In the 1950s the president of the American Statistical Society shortened it to this pithy one-liner and this is the version that has stuck around. This happens a lot. Gandhi never said 'Be the change you wish to see in the world'. Mary Antoinette never said 'Let them eat cake'. It's not only statistical bullshit you have to watch out for.

Statistics for social science students

Numbers and your degree

Social scientists are interested in a lot of different things: What is personality and why do people end up with the personalities they have? Why do people become terrorists? Why do women earn less than men? Should we give more money to unemployed people, or less?

There are two broad approaches researchers take to try to answer questions like these. One approach is based on collecting **qualitative** data. Qualitative research might involve spending long periods embedded within a specific community, like hunter gatherers in the Amazon, or sex workers in New York City (this is called ethnography). Or it might involve conducting a series of in-depth interviews with a particular group of people, like athletics coaches or survivors of terrorism (these are called qualitative interview studies). The purpose of this kind of work is not to produce statistics (20% of terrorism survivors think X; the average income of sex workers is Y). Instead it is to get at the subtle and complex nature and meaning of people's experiences.

The purpose of **quantitative** research on the other hand *is* to produce statistics. This may strike you as a little reductive – turning people into numbers. But the truth is that we need numbers to answer some of the most important questions in social science. If you want to understand why women tend to earn less than men, you'll need statistics on how much men and women earn in different types of jobs (we'll come back to this question in Chapter 10). If you want to know whether the death penalty really dissuades people from committing crimes, you'll need to compare crime statistics in different places and at different times. If you want to know whether politicians are really in the pockets of their rich donors, then statistics on donations and voting patterns are a great place to start.

At bottom, a social science degree is about understanding what we know about how people and societies operate. This painstakingly accumulated knowledge is written in books, reports, and academic papers, and a good part of it is based on numbers. If you read this research without understanding the numbers, you're only getting half the story (or even less). That's why almost every social science degree – whether it's in psychology, sociology, criminology, politics, or any other subject – requires students to take at least one course in statistics. Traditionally, these courses have been quite dry and technical – dwelling excessively on the abstract mathematics behind the numbers. This book takes a different approach – focusing on real-world stories of statistics gone wrong, and using these stories to illustrate the fundamental statistical principles you really need to know.

Numbers and your career

Many of us, as teenagers sitting staring at equations in maths class, asked ourselves 'What's the point of this? When are we going to use this in real life?' Maths teachers, by ancient tradition, are required to tell us that of course it is all useful. We need quadratic equations to work out profit margins, or the velocity of a thrown object! We can use differentiation to work out the maximum area you can fence off with a given length of fence!

The trouble is, as we get older, most of us notice that these predictions of practical usefulness have not really come true. We are not out there with a pen and paper using differential equations to work out how big a field of wheat we can plant. And if for some reason we do need a difficult equation solving, a computer can do it for us. There are good reasons to learn advanced, abstract maths, but everyday usefulness is not one of them.

But just because abstract maths is practically useless in most people's lives does not mean that all maths is. Basic numeracy is obviously important in all kinds of situations. If you want to work out anything involving time, distance, or money, you need to be able to add up. Splitting a restaurant bill is much less painful if someone in your group has a good mathematical head on their shoulders. Beyond basic numeracy, I hope this chapter has shown that an understanding of statistics is also important if you want to know what's really going on in the world (and avoid falling for people's BS). But the importance of numbers and statistics extends beyond everyday life to getting (and keeping) a job after university.

Almost all jobs require some understanding of numerical and statistical information: even jobs you wouldn't expect. Maybe you want to work for a charity – where you'll be travelling to exotic locations and helping the world's less fortunate. These things might be part of your job, for sure. But you also need to understand how money is raised and spent, how to interpret research relevant to your area, and how to conduct new research of your own to help people understand your cause (have a look at the 'research' sections on the websites of a few famous charities).

Or maybe you want to be a journalist. We've already talked about how much of the news is based on numbers, and if you want to write about them competently then you'll need to understand them (a lot of current journalists aren't great at this part of their jobs, but this is becoming less and less acceptable). Or maybe instead of writing the news you want to make it, with a high-profile career in business or politics. Again, a good understanding of statistical information is crucial.

Employers in all sorts of fields, from publishing to PR to medicine to marketing (and all points in between), are crying out for graduates with numerical and statistical skills. Survey after survey has shown that companies see quantitative skills as among the most important things graduates need to have to be employable.[22] Put simply, in every field you can imagine, it is a distinct advantage to be able to look at a bunch of numbers in a report or a presentation and actually understand what they mean. If you go into an interview able to prove you know this stuff, you're going to get picked over someone who doesn't. It's as simple as that.

So statistics are important in your everyday life, for your degree, and for your career prospects. This might be starting to sound like an 'eat your vegetables' type of a deal. Learn statistics or Bad Things Will Happen. But carry on through the rest of this book and I think you'll see that this is not really the case. It's deeply satisfying to finally see the real world through the hail of statistical bullshit pelting down on you every day. And proving somebody wrong through your superior knowledge of numbers is just plain good fun. Honestly, even if understanding statistics was irrelevant to your degree and did nothing for your career, I'd learn it anyway just for that.

www.macmillanihe.com/devries-critical-statistics

Go to the book's companion website for further examples, data, links, and other useful resources.

ONLINE RESOURCES AVAILABLE

2 WHERE DO NUMBERS COME FROM?

There is a powerful force abroad in the world. It affects people's nervous systems, changing the structure of their brains – altering how they think and feel. This happens to millions of people every day, but very few will notice anything is wrong

No, it's not Wi-Fi, or mobile phone radiation, or chemtrails, or something in the water. It's actually a document. A couple of pages of text sent and received by thousands of organisations every day. This document is called a <u>press-release</u>, and it is one of the invisible forces that shape how the world works. Through press-releases corporations, governments, and pressure groups can inject ideas into the media, and through the media, directly into people's brains.*

Understanding the power of press-releases means overturning some commonly held assumptions about how journalism works in practice. In the absence of any direct personal experience of a job, our overriding impression of it tends to come from movies and TV – and journalism is no different. TV and movie journalists are pretty active. They run around a lot, shouting at people, chasing leads, meeting with shady sources in dive bars and parking lots. This type of journalism does exist in the real world. There are real-life reporters who regularly put their lives on the line to cover conflicts and natural disasters. There are others who risk the wrath of rich, powerful men to courageously report on alleged sexual abuses, like those of Harvey Weinstein. Less dramatically, there are also journalists doggedly following paper trails to discover how politicians are influenced by lobbyists,[1] or how African American families are unfairly targeted by debt collection agencies.[2]

However, these types of stories represent a tiny fraction of what ends up in the papers or on the TV news. For the modern reporter, a typical day will not involve pounding the pavement (or even making phone calls) in search of a story. Instead, it will involve sitting at a computer, waiting to be given something to write up.

---

* Any idea will change the physical structure of your brain – this is how brains (and therefore 'you') register experience. So if you find out today that all of the planets in the solar system could fit between the Earth and the moon (this is actually true), your brain is necessarily different than it was before you knew that. This is why you shouldn't take stories like 'The Internet Is Changing Children's Brains!' very seriously. The internet *is* changing children's brains. But so are books, cars, funfairs, and everything else in the world.

Take the following headline from American conservative news site *The Daily Caller*:

"Synthetic Opioid Deaths Surge 72 Percent, Ravage States Across US" – *The Daily Caller*, 18 December 2016

The article that follows calls attention to a dramatic increase in the prevalence of synthetic opioid abuse in the USA (synthetic opioids include heroin, but also prescription painkillers like fentanyl). In the movies the reporter would be an active participant in seeking out this story. In the trailer we see Steve (played by a dishevelled Mark Ruffalo) digging through hospital records and government files, shouting at cowardly bureaucrats who want to hide the scale of the problem from the public.

In reality, a government agency (the Centers for Disease Control, or CDC for short) simply sent out a press-release.[3] Steve got an email with all the details, added a few pieces of information for context, and cobbled it together into a story. The same CDC press-release yielded almost identical stories in numerous national media outlets, including CNN, CBS, and Fox, and in local papers across the country.

This, in a nutshell, is the answer to the question posed by this chapter's title. A large proportion of the numerical information you see in the news (and, in fact, a large proportion of the *news* you see in the news) will have originated from a press-release. An organisation decides that they want the public to know some piece of information, so they send out a press-release. This release reaches journalists around the country (or around the world) either directly – an email dropping into their inbox – or indirectly through news agencies (see the box below). The reporter then writes up this story into a news article, or a TV or radio news item. In this scenario the reporter is not actively seeking out information to convey to the public. Instead they are simply conveying, more or less faithfully, the messages they receive from various organisations' PR departments; whether those organisations are governments, NGOs, or businesses.*

This is not necessarily a bad thing. Organisations need a way to get information out to the public. Getting in touch with media outlets through press-releases is a sensible way to do that. In the opioids example, it makes sense that the US government would want to warn people about a growing public health problem. It is also completely reasonable

---

* Of course, press-releases are not the *only* source of numbers in the news. Journalists do occasionally instigate their own stories – a political journalist might keep a purposeful eye on a president's business affairs, an entertainment reporter might dig out unflattering figures about a movie that flopped. Newspapers also sometimes commission or conduct their own research (a lot of which – as we saw in Chapter 1 – is quite bad). However, these are not the source of the majority of quantitative stories.

The wires

People expect a lot from a national newspaper. They want all the big national stories of the day – political scandals, changes in the economy, sporting events, consumer affairs – but also news from around the world. It would be (and always has been) impossible for any newspaper to have enough reporters on their payroll to collect all this news first-hand. Stringers and one-off freelancers can make up some of the shortfall, but for the rest papers rely on news agencies.

News agencies (also called news wires, or wire services) are organisations which gather news reports and then sell them on to media outlets. These outlets then reprint these stories on their own pages; sometimes after their own reporters have made changes and added content, but often simply word for word. Some newspapers will add a note to the article indicating that it is news agency copy, but many will not. In fact, it is relatively common practice for papers to simply add the name of one of their own reporters to the piece, as if they wrote it themselves (though news agencies are less comfortable with this practice than they used to be).

A reasonable fraction of all the stories you see when you pick up a newspaper or visit a news website will be 'wire stories'. In other words, they will have been originally written by a reporter for one of the big news agencies (Reuters, the Associated Press, Agence France-Presse) and then simply reprinted. You can see this for yourself if you buy multiple newspapers on the same day: you will find that quite a few of the stories read very similarly.

This is not necessarily a problem. You may feel mildly deceived by the fact that the *New York Times* article you are reading was not written by a *Times* journalist (and that an almost exact copy of the same article appears in the *Washington Post*, the *Toronto Star*, the *Daily Telegraph*, and the *Sydney Morning Herald*). However, without the news agencies, no single newspaper would be able to cover all the things you, as a news consumer, want to read about. The problem arises when the news wires function as an on-ramp by which PR bullshit makes it onto the world news highway. The *Times* may feel at least a little unsure about reprinting a press-release from some organisation with an obvious axe to grind, but if the same press-release appears in the form of a story from the *Associated Press*, then it suddenly feels a lot more like something worth printing. To mix metaphors for a second, you can think of the news like your office's coffee supply. If you want to poison your colleagues, you can either sneak around slipping arsenic into everyone's mugs individually, or you can tip a bunch of it into the coffee machine.

that news organisations would be happy to relay that information to their readers: America's continuing opioid epidemic is certainly a news-worthy story. However, this relatively benign example is only the tip of the iceberg. Beneath is a vast, dark mass of PR bullshit, steadily seeping into the public discourse disguised as real information.

Making the news

I'd like you to join me in a brief thought experiment. I want you to imagine that you are the CEO of a British travel company. It's coming up to the summer holiday season and you want people to think of your company when they start booking their trips. One obvious way to achieve this would be to take out an advert – let's say a full-page spread in a national newspaper. A single full-page ad in the *Daily Mail* (Britain's second biggest selling newspaper) might cost £60,000. This is a pittance for a decent size company, but an ad in one newspaper on one day is probably not going to do much good. You're going to need the same ad in lots of newspapers for a reasonable length of time. When you add it all up (and include online editions), you're starting to talk real money. And it's very possible that this ad will not do much good. In our increasingly ad-soaked world, people are getting better and better at filtering out obvious marketing messages.

So how else can you get your brand into the minds of potential customers? The answer the public relations (PR) industry has come up with is to *get the media to treat your advert as if it is news*. If you can get newspapers and websites to write about your brand in a news story, then not only can you get into many different outlets for free, you can also get around the selective blindness many people have developed when it comes to adverts. It's a win-win!

The trick here is to manufacture something that looks sufficiently 'news-like'. You can't just write to the *Times*, or the *Mail* and say 'Please write a news story about how great our brand is'. They'll quite rightly tell you to take a hike or buy an ad. So you're going to have to put in at least a bit of effort to create some news. By far the easiest way to do this is to conduct a survey. Ask your customers (or your employees, or some random people on the internet) some questions like 'What's your favourite part of a holiday?', or 'What do you always forget to pack?'. Add up the answers, and hey presto: you can put out the 'news' that '60% of Brits think the best part of a holiday is coming home', or that '1 in 3 British people have forgotten to take underwear on holiday'. Of course, neither of these 'facts' is actually likely to be true – your customers or employees probably aren't representative of the British public as a whole (we'll discuss this problem in more detail in the next chapter). But if you bundle them up into a press-release there's a good chance the papers will run it as a news story. Millions of people will read a fun story about holiday trivia, which incidentally contains a prominent mention of your brand.

In case you think this picture is exaggerated or simplified, here are the opening sentences of a genuine press-release issued by travel booking website lastminute.com in August 2016:[4]

Naked Ambition: Why Nudist Holidays are Now on the Cards for Half of Brits

35 per cent of men, 17 per cent of women would bare it all on beach

More than a third of nudists keep it secret from friends, family and colleagues

Online searches for nudist beaches in Europe up 52 per cent since January

OVER half (59 per cent) of Brits would now consider going on a nudist holiday, sunbathing in the buff or visiting a nudist beach, a survey from lastminute.com reveals.

The release goes on to discuss people's reasons for stripping off (the most popular is getting an all-over tan), includes an approving quote from 'Andrew Welch of British Naturism, the UK's organisation for Naturists', and ends with a list of 'lastminute.com's top 10 nudist beaches' (topped, perhaps surprisingly, by Holkham beach in Norfolk).

For comparison, here is the beginning of a news article in the *Daily Mail's* online edition:[5]

Naked Ambition! More than HALF of Brits would go nude on holiday ... and men are twice as willing

By ANNABEL FENWICK ELLIOTT FOR MAILONLINE

PUBLISHED 17:32, 3 August 2016 | UPDATED: 10:36, 4 August 2016

- **35 per cent of men and 17 per cent of women would bare it all on beach**
- **More than a third of nudists keep it secret from friends and colleagues**
- **Online searches for nudist beaches in Europe up 52 per cent since Januarys**

More than half of Brits would now consider taking their clothes off for a summer holiday, a new survey reveals.

The story then goes on to discuss people's reasons for stripping off, and includes a helpful quote from one Andrew Welch, of British Naturism. A sidebar also gives the top 10 nudist beaches in the world, with Holkham beach in Norfolk as the surprising top pick.

If it seems like Annabel Fenwick Elliott has simply copy-pasted the press-release and moved a few words around, then you'd be exactly right (if you're wondering where the reference to lastminute.com has disappeared to, it's been moved down to paragraph four, which reads: 'More than a third of British men polled in the Lastminute.com survey say they would consider sunbathing naked'). And the *Daily Mail* were not alone. Identical stories also appeared online in *The Sun*,[6] the *Express*,[7] the BT News website,[8] and a number of other outlets.

This is a clear PR win for lastminute.com. They used a cheap, unscientific survey (we'll get into what makes a survey 'scientific' in the next chapter) to churn out some numbers. Then they used these meaningless numbers to bait the media (including the *Mail Online*, the world's most visited English language news site) into talking about their brand – not in a straightforward advert, but in articles which purported to be news.

This is not an isolated incident – it happens *constantly*. Here is the *Evening Standard* treating some ridiculous numbers from an HSBC press-release (which helpfully links the HSBC brand to the idea of saving for a deposit on a house) as if they are news.

> "Children 'should save pocket money and gifts from birth' to afford a house ... Experts have suggested parents are not making the most of lucrative pocket money and childhood gifts in order to provide for their kids' future ... The figures, published by HSBC, suggests (sic) the average child receives **£131,832.94** in the first 25 years of their live through pocket money, tooth fairy donations, gifts, and money for odd jobs and part-time work" – The Evening Standard, 24 February 2017 (my emphasis)

Here is online women's magazine *Bustle* treating a press-release from Reebok as if it is news:

> "Here's how much time you spend having sex in your lifetime ... According to a new global survey by Reebok and PR consultant firm Censuswide, people actually spend a lot less time having sex than you might think – we spend 0.45 percent of our lifetimes having sex" – Bustle.com, 17 May 2016

Here is the *International Business Times* treating a press-release from a company that makes teeth whitening products as if it is news:

> "Millenials (sic) selfies: Young adults will take more than 25,000 pictures of themselves during their lifetimes: report ... a recent survey

from Luster Premium White ... calculated that the average millennial could take up to about 25,700 selfies in his or her lifetime." – Interna-tional Business Times, 22 September 2015

And finally (though I could fill a whole book with these) here is Britain's *Daily Telegraph* treating a PR survey from the UKTV Gold television channel as if it is news.

"A fifth of British teenagers believe Sir Winston Churchill was a fictional character, while many think Sherlock Holmes, King Arthur, and Eleanor Rigby were real ... " – The Telegraph, 4 February 2008

And this last example has a sting in the tail. Here is Michael Gove, then UK Secretary of State for Education, justifying his plans to overhaul the national history curriculum:

"Survey after survey has revealed disturbing historical ignorance, with one teenager in five believing Winston Churchill was a fictional character while 58 per cent think Sherlock Holmes was real" – Mail on Sunday, 23 March 2013

Just to be clear, what has happened here is that:

1) As part of a marketing exercise for some historical TV shows, a television channel has conducted a meaningless survey.

2) A British national newspaper has written about the numbers from this survey as if they are real news.

3) The British Secretary of State for Education has used these numbers as a justification for a major change in national education policy.

This is why we need to be alert to where numbers come from. Not all numbers are created equal. Some numbers tell us useful things about how the world works, but many are meaningless or just plain wrong. On the evidence of the examples we've just seen, it appears that we can trust neither journalists nor politicians to tell the difference.

#nofilter

Why do newspapers (and other outlets) publish PR junk? As we'll see in future chapters, the truthfulness of a number depends entirely on how it was produced. Good, robust methods produce useful, accurate numbers. Weak, lazy methods produce numbers that are at best meaningless, and at worst, harmfully misleading. As I mentioned in the previous chapter, it's often quite easy to detect rubbish numbers. And the PR numbers from the headlines you just saw are clear examples of this – either laughably false on their face (like HSBC's pocket money stat) or obviously unsupported by the data (lastminute.com's customers clearly do not represent all British people). So how did these figures slip through the net to end up as published news stories? How did they get past reporters' bullshit detection filter?

Put simply, the answer is that there is no net. There is no filter.

In his groundbreaking 2008 book, *Flat Earth News*,[9] Nick Davies gives one of the most famous critiques of the failings of modern journalism. He describes a news industry in 'wholesale retreat from truth-telling'. An industry which, in its desperation to generate profitable content, has abandoned almost all efforts to distinguish true, useful information from self-serving bunkum. Where once there might have been some resistance against false and misleading facts and statistics, now they can simply waltz through the 'unguarded gates' of the media and into the public square. All one need do is send out a press-release. If it seems like it will attract some clicks, or fill some space in the paper, then the media will lap it up. PR reps need not worry about whether their 'facts' will hold up to scrutiny – because there won't be any.

Davies identifies one of the main drivers of this decline in journalistic standards as the increasing volume of content modern news outlets are required to produce. Have you ever bought a newspaper and wondered at how cheap it is? A broadsheet newspaper (especially the weekend edition) is almost as long as this book, but it costs less than a coffee. And papers have been getting longer. Davies cites a report by academics at Cardiff University, which found that, on average, the number of pages of editorial content in British newspapers had *tripled* between the 1980s and the 2000s, while staff levels had stayed roughly the same.[10] This means that a newspaper journalist in 2005 was producing three times as much material as they would have been in 1985. And this is without even considering additional content for websites and blogs.

This is not just a British phenomenon. In the USA, the *Washington Post* website now publishes an average of 1,200 stories, graphics, and videos *a day*.[11] The output of the *New York Times* site rose by more than 35% between 2010 and 2016.[12] American news outlets are producing more and more content with fewer and fewer journalists. It is not unrealistic for a modern reporter to be producing between 5 and 10 stories every single day.

The news media are therefore absolutely desperate for stories to push into their ever-hungry content pipelines. Scraping material from press-releases is a quick, cheap solution to this problem. Especially if that material can be made to fit an existing news agenda, or includes sexy click-bait words or the name of a celebrity (or preferably both). Think about it from the perspective of a harried *Daily Mail* reporter. It's 4pm and you've got six more stories to write before you can go home. The lastminute.com release plops into your inbox. It's a fun story about holidays with some solid gold click-bait language (about 10 different synonyms for the word 'naked'). It's already written for you (with quotes and everything) – all you need to do is make a few tweaks and put it straight up. You'd be stupid *not* to do it.

There's a word for this, coined by BBC journalist Waseem Zakir: 'churnalism'. Original journalism requires the reporter to make a substantive contribution to a story (seeking it out, talking to sources, checking its veracity). Churnalism simply involves recycling (often with very little modification) existing content, either from press-releases, or from news agency copy (which might itself have originally come from a press-release). As Davies describes in *Flat Earth News*, this practice represents a much larger proportion of the news than most people think. He describes the modern journalist as less like an independent professional, and more like a factory worker – content comes in, you copy and paste it, tweak it a bit, then put it back on the line for release.

A subsequent study by the academics behind the Cardiff report backs this up.[13] They examined the output of British broadsheet newspapers (plus the *Daily Mail*) for two weeks in 2006. They found that around half of all articles derived wholly or mostly from stories originally published by news agencies (mostly the Press Association), and one in five derived mainly or wholly from PR material. *Less than half* of all of the stories they examined showed no evidence of PR influence. This study focused exclusively on print articles in Britain's most prestigious newspapers. The figures for online stories and for less selective outlets are likely to be much higher (this is without even considering online 'content-farms', which consist almost solely of recycled content). And again, this is not just a British problem. Researchers in the USA,[14] Australia,[15] and elsewhere have similarly demonstrated the enormous influence of recycled PR in their national and local newspapers. The scale of this problem is almost invisible to news consumers – the people at home reading a newspaper, browsing the web, or watching the news on TV – because news organisations are not transparent about where these stories come from. Newspapers are understandably not keen to say 'we copied and pasted this story from a press-release HSBC sent us'. Instead, recycled material is attributed to an un-named 'staff reporter', or even (as was the case for the lastminute.com story) a named writer. If you were to do this as a student, it would be called plagiarism and you would suffer serious consequences. In modern media organisations it's simply called 'doing your job'.

The results are as clear as they are unfortunate. If you read a story online or in a newspaper that makes a quantitative or factual claim, there is a good chance this claim started life as part of some organisation's PR strategy – a government department wanting to spin some good or bad news, a think-tank seeking to promote their agenda, or just a private business trying to sell you something. The problem is not that these organisations have a way of getting messages out to the public. The problem is that, as consumers, we have a reasonable expectation that the media will do some basic journalistic work on these messages – that they will check to make sure that the information contained in them is actually *true*. As Davies says in the first chapter of *Flat Earth News*:

> "Journalism without checking is like a human body without an immune system. If the primary purpose of journalism is to tell the truth, then it follows that the primary function of journalists must be to check and to reject whatever is not true"

As he (and others) have shown, this is no longer a function that journalists can be relied upon to perform. This is particularly the case for statistical claims and the results of scientific research, as is aptly demonstrated by a 'health' story which did the rounds of the global media in early 2015.

A sweeter way to shed the pounds

"Excellent News: Chocolate Can Help You Lose Weight" – Huffington Post, 31 March 2015

"Chocolate accelerates weight loss: Research claims it lowers cholesterol and aids sleep" – The Daily Express, 30 March 2015

"Those who eat chocolate stay slim!" – Bild, 30 March 2015

"Need a 'sweeter' way to lose weight? Eat chocolates!" – The Times of India, 30 March 2016

In late March 2015 headlines like this appeared in newspapers and magazines around the world. The stories were based on a study carried out by Dr John Bohannon of the German Institute for Diet and Health. The study took 16 people (5 men and 11 women) and split them up into three groups. The first group followed a low-carb diet. The second followed the same low-carb diet with the addition of a daily bar of dark chocolate. The third group made no dietary changes. After 21 days, the 'low-carb plus chocolate' group had lost weight 10% faster than the 'low-carb only' group.

This is an absolutely terrible study for two reasons – one obvious and one not so obvious. Starting with the obvious, 16 people is far too few to draw any kind of generalisable conclusion about the effect of diet on health. Split into three groups, this is fewer than six people per group! You could probably do a bigger study than that this afternoon if you wanted to.

The second reason this study was so bad is that the researchers compared so many different things between the groups that, by chance alone, they were bound to find something that was different. If you compare 20 things between three groups of five or so people, you are bound to find some differences. And this is exactly what the researchers did, they compared a lot of different measures of 'weight-loss' and then picked the one the chocolate eaters did better on.

The reason this study was so badly designed is not because the researchers were incompetent – it's because it was a deliberate hoax. The German Institute of Diet and Health does not really exist (beyond a cheap-looking web page and an email address), and Dr John Bohannon, while genuinely a 'Dr' (he has a PhD in molecular biology), is not a medical researcher. He's not a con-artist either. He's actually a journalist, and he tricked the global news media into running this story not because he has a chocolate business to promote – but just to see if he could. His press-release explaining the study was a sort of test for journalists.[16] Would they check to see if this too-good-to-be-true story about chocolate helping you lose weight was genuine (for example, by calling him up or checking with other scientists)? Would they even read the details of the study and see that it was obviously rubbish? Or would they do none of these things, and simply convey this nonsense story straight to their readers?

You already know the answer. Following the exact pattern we've already seen, media outlets around the world received this press-release – describing an obviously crap study from a fake German 'institute' – and just put it straight out. Many simply copied and pasted the text straight from the press-release Bohannon wrote.

Even if we don't think about it, most of us place at least a little bit of faith in what we see in the news. Even the most cynical of us would probably place a little bit more stock in a claim we read in the newspaper, or on a 'real' website (like BBC News or the Mail Online), than we would if we heard the same claim from some random guy on the bus, or on Twitter. This faith rests on the implicit idea that journalists are doing at least *some* work to check the truth of the stories they print. Unfortunately, the evidence suggests that large parts of the news media just do not have the time, the incentive – or, when it comes to science and statistics, perhaps the basic training and know-how – to perform this fundamental task.

Where's the harm?

"Nearly 90,000 Christians were killed for their faith in 2016, equivalent to one every six minutes, according to a new study ... " – International Business Times, 30 December 2016

In January 2017 this shocking statistic appeared in a story on the *International Business Times'* website. This same statistic subsequently appeared in many other outlets around the world, including *Russia Today*,[17] *Newsweek*,[18] *Breitbart*,[19] *MSN.com*[20] (Microsoft's news page and the default homepage for all Microsoft web-browsers), *Yahoo News*,[21] and *Fox News* television broadcasts.[22] The story was also covered by many Christian-focused news sites such as *One News Now*,[23] and *The Christian Post*.[24]

This is not some frivolous factoid about naked holidays, or a silly fake story about chocolate and weight loss. Christians being targeted and killed in these numbers is real news – news that might have a substantial effect on how people see the world. This is particularly true for a subset of American Christians who are fearful of becoming a persecuted minority in their historically Christian country (the headline for the *Newsweek* story was 'Christian's were 2016's Most Persecuted Religious Group: Study'). The statistic has been cited in this context by US politicians (including former Republican presidential candidate Ted Cruz),[25] and continues to crop up in debates around, for example, President Trump's policies on Muslim immigration.

Given the sensitivity of the issue, did journalists at *Newsweek* and the other outlets subject this shocking claim to a reasonable level of journalistic scrutiny? The fact that you are reading about this story here should give you a hint as to the answer.

The story is based on research by the Center for the Study of Global Christianity (CSGC), a research centre attached to Gordon-Conwell Theological Seminary (a religious college in the USA). Each year, the centre produces a report on the status of global Christianity, providing various facts and figures about Christians around the world. One of the figures included in the report is the number of Christians who have been martyred (i.e. killed for their Christian faith) that year. In the 2016 report (published in January 2017) this figure was given as 90,000.[26] This is the statistic the media reported. However, there are fundamental problems with this number that almost all of the media coverage overlooked.

First, the '90,000' number (corresponding to one Christian killed every six minutes in 2016) was not calculated for 2016 specifically. Instead, the researchers estimated the number of Christians killed for their faith in the 10 years from 2006 to 2015 (around 900,000) and then divided the number by 10. Not a fatal problem perhaps, but still a key detail that was missing from almost all the writeups of this story – which treated the number as if it specifically related to Christians killed in 2016 (a year which was not actually included in the calculation).

A much more serious problem comes from the way in which the authors of the study defined martyrdom. Many readers, I imagine, would assume that this would include only Christians who were killed *because they were Christian*; in other words, people who were specifically targeted due to their Christian faith. However, this is not the definition the researchers used. They counted a Christian as having been killed for their faith if they died prematurely while 'acting out their faith'.* Whether someone had died 'while acting out their faith' was also defined extremely broadly. For example, if an American Christian drowned while trying to save a child from a river, they could plausibly be considered to have been motivated by their Christian faith, and would therefore count towards the 90,000 figure. This incredibly broad definition of martyrdom is particularly problematic given that at least 70% of the 90,000 deaths counted in the report occurred in civil wars in Africa (particularly in the Democratic Republic of Congo). These are conflicts in which most of the combatants will have been Christian. In other words, a large fraction of the 90,000 Christians 'killed for their faith in 2016' will have been killed by other Christians during a civil war. The researchers justify their inclusion of these deaths by assuming that many Christians in these conflicts will have refused to fight due to their Christian beliefs and will have died for this reason. This is a truly heroic assumption which renders the '90,000 martyrs' figure basically meaningless. If this fatal problem with the number was mentioned at all in the media coverage, it was only as a vague reference to the study using a 'broader definition' of what constituted martyrdom, and a note that many of the deaths had occurred in Africa.

Although it does not start with a press-release, the journey of this statistic – from a rough, poorly explained, deeply problematic estimate produced by an American seminary, into the global media (and the mouths of US policymakers) – is dispiritingly familiar. It began with an interview on Vatican Radio on 26 December 2016 with Professor Massimo Introvigne, an Italian religious scholar. Professor Introvigne described a forthcoming CSGC report which would reveal that 'about 90,000 Christians had been killed for their faith, one death every six minutes' and that 'of these, 70% … were killed in tribal conflicts in Africa … The other 30% … derives from terrorist attacks, the destruction of Christian villages, and governmental persecution, as in the case of North Korea.'[27] He also said that 'Without wishing to forget or belittle the suffering of members of other religions' the report showed that 'Christians are the most persecuted religious group in the world.'

It is these comments which form the basis of the *International Business Times* story I quoted above. Published on 30 December, this appears to be the first story covering these figures. Headed 'Religious war? A

---

* This quote comes from an interview with one of the study authors conducted by the BBC radio programme *More or Less* (More or Less: World Service edition, 13 January 2017).

Christian was killed for their faith every six minutes in 2016', the story begins by repeating the claim that 90,000 Christians were killed for their faith in 2016. The rest of the story simply repeats Professor Introvigne's statements from the Vatican Radio interview, with a couple of additional facts added for flavour: a note about Islamist terrorism in Africa, and about the imprisonment of a Canadian pastor by the North Korean government. The only comments about the study's methodology are directly lifted from Professor Introvigne's statements: including the fact that the study used 'a broader definition of what constitutes a person being killed for their faith' and that the number of Christians killed in Africa was likely due to them 'refusing to take up weapons for reasons of conscience'. At this point the CSGC report itself had not yet been published, so the reporter could not consult it.* Nevertheless, there was apparently no attempt to determine how the core 90,000 figure had been arrived at (for example, by contacting the report's authors or even Professor Introvigne), and therefore what it actually meant in terms of Christian persecution.

From the original *International Business Times* report, the story spread through the global media – with almost all outlets sticking to the same discussion points (90,000 Christians killed for their faith, one every six minutes, Christians as the most persecuted group). Some reporters did add significant new material to the story. However, often (as was the case with *Breitbart*'s coverage) this was to place an increased emphasis on the role of Islamic fundamentalism. None of the news coverage I found made any real attempt to engage with the methods behind the 90,000 number, or to convey what the methods might mean for the interpretation of this figure. As happens on a daily basis, a statistical claim by an organisation – a claim which basic checks would have shown to be deeply problematic – sailed smoothly through the unguarded gates of the global media and into the public discourse. The only outlet to have interrogated this statistic in any depth was the BBC radio programme *More or Less* – a programme dedicated to examining statistical claims in the media. In fact, the *More or Less* team had covered the media falling for a very similar statistic produced by the same researchers two years previously (a number plagued by exactly the same problems).[28] However, the fact that the BBC had already thoroughly debunked the methodology behind the figure in 2014 did not stop reporters falling for it all over again in 2016.

Journalists might argue that they did nothing wrong here. A high-profile religious scholar made a claim based on a report by a respected American theological college, and they reported that claim accurately (for the most part). In other words, somebody said something and they

---

* Even when the report was published it contained very few details about the methods behind the figures.

reported what he said. But as the journalism scholars Stephen Cushion, Justin Lewis, and Robert Callaghan argue, the proper function of journalism must go beyond this, especially when it comes to numbers: 'Since most people do not read raw data-sets, journalism has a key role to play in the discovery, translation and interpretation of statistics.'[29] As we will see in the rest of the book, numbers mean very different things depending on how they were worked out. Part of a reporter's job when dealing with statistics must be to make a reasonable effort to ensure that a number is accurate and really means what it seems to mean. Unfortunately this is not how the modern media works. For example, in 2015 Cushion and his colleagues looked at a sample of 237 news stories in the British media which were based around a statistical claim, and found that *only* 10 included any attempt to meaningfully explain or question the figure.

The consequence of all this is that misleading facts and statistics flow easily through the media without challenge, polluting public debate about issues both trivial and vital, and contributing to the uncoupling of public discourse from anything resembling the real world. In *Flat Earth News* Nick Davies describes this as a bigger threat to public understanding than anything posed by the perennial bugbears of political bias or corporate interference. Roy Greenslade, former editor of the British *Daily Mirror* and now Professor of Journalism at London City University, describes the lack of a media 'filter' as nothing less than 'an assault on democracy'.[30] Professor of Political Communication Robert McChesney describes the state of journalism in the USA as 'a crisis of the greatest possible magnitude'.[31] He argues that the news media's failure to properly distinguish truth from falsehood denies the public the information they need to effectively participate in politics, and as such is an existential threat to democracy itself. If you can't rely on the news media to tell you what's really going on, then how can you decide who to vote for, or what causes to support?

Fortunately, faced with the dilemma of either trusting journalists to give you the right information, or being cast adrift in a world of uncertainty – neither of which is a particularly appealing option – there is a solution. The solution is to take on for yourself the fact-checking role the media has abdicated. If the journalists don't have the time or the inclination to check whether the numbers they print are accurate, then you need to do it yourself. It has never been easier to find the original source of a number – the press-release or the original report – and to read exactly how it was worked out.* The rest of this book will give you the tools to understand these details, and to judge for yourself whether a number really means what it seems to mean.

---

*   If these sources don't explain the methods clearly then it's usually safe to assume that the number is not worth your time.

A lie can run around the world before the truth can get its boots on

Up to now we have focused on how misleading statistics can get into the news in the first place (the answer being far too easily). But these figures don't just appear in a wave of media coverage and then disappear without trace. They hang around, waiting for someone to pick them up and use them – in an op-ed, a political speech, a documentary, or just an argument. Some misleading statistics hang around long enough that they take on the role of accepted facts:

- In the UK there is a CCTV camera for every 14 people

- We only use 10% of our brain

- We swallow an average of 8 spiders a year while sleeping

- In a city you are never more than 6 feet from a rat

Not one of these 'facts' has any real evidence to back it up, but this does not stop them being repeated in newspaper articles, TV shows, and movies on a daily basis. They are 'zombie' statistics – no matter how many times they are debunked, they rise again to infect a new crop of minds. In particular, the British CCTV statistic, despite having been demonstrated to be nonsense more than a decade ago, still regularly rears its head in debates about privacy and civil liberties.

This happens for basically the same reason that nonsense numbers enter the media in the first place: the people using them don't care enough to check if they are true. Put yourself in the position of a speech-writer for a US politician. Your candidate wants to say something about Christian persecution, and you know the point will have more force if you can provide some numbers as evidence. A quick Google search gives you the *Newsweek* article and the 90,000 (one killed every six minutes) figure. *Newsweek* is not some random blog – it's a well-known news magazine sold on news stands across America – and they're writing about what sounds like a piece of academic research. That seems solid enough, so it goes in the speech.

This precise thought process will land the statistic in any number of newspaper opinion pieces, television debates, and comment thread squabbles. And the process is self-reinforcing. The more often a number is cited, the easier it becomes for other people to find it and use it. And the more people who use it, the more reliable it seems to be and the 'safer' it feels to use: if so many other people have said it, then it must be true (or at least close to true).

PolitiFact's Jon Greenberg has documented this process in action. He took an interest in an often-used statistic about gender inequality and poverty: that 70% of the world's poorest people are women.[32] This statistic has been used by a variety of political figures and campaign organisations over the years. And you can see why it is a useful piece of evidence. The fact that the majority of people in poverty are women makes a powerful statement about gender inequality on a global level. Or at least it would do if it were true.

Greenberg traces the origin of the statistic to a 1995 report by the United Nations Development Programme (UNDP). Even if the statistic were true, it would now therefore be more than 20 years old – making more recent uses of it (such as by 2016 US presidential candidate Carly Fiorina) questionable. However, in addition to being out of date, it is also very unlikely to be true. The number was given in the foreword to the 1995 UNDP Human Development Report, but was not supported by any of the figures contained in the report itself. When Greenberg questioned Robert Johnston, the former chief of statistical services at the UN Statistical Division, Johnston concluded that the number must have been a mistake: whoever wrote the foreword to the report simply made an erroneous extrapolation from a jumble of previous reports.

Despite the fact that the real meat of the UN's Human Development Reports is in the main body of the text – in the statistical tables and in-depth descriptions of methodology – the foreword is all that many people will read. So it was that Hillary Clinton, then First Lady, used the 70% statistic in a speech at the 1995 World Conference on Women in Beijing. Shortly afterwards, the president of the World Bank, James Wolfensohn, also used it in a high-profile speech. The statistic took off from there, and has since been used by any number of journalists, political figures, and campaign groups to make a point about global gender inequality. Subsequent World Bank research has suggested that extreme poverty is actually likely to be equally divided by gender, but this has not dented the popularity of the 70% statistic. When speechwriters, opinion journalists, and campaigners are looking for something to say about global gender inequality, they are much more likely to stumble across the 70% number than they are to dig for an obscure World Bank research paper.

It would be hypocritical to judge the users of this statistic too harshly. The truth is that we've probably all done something like this, either at work, at school, or at university. We know the point we want to make, so we Google around for some numerical evidence to back it up. Then we use the first relevant, reliable-looking stat we come across. Really digging and figuring out if this statistic is accurate takes time and effort: probably a lot more than we're willing to invest for a single sentence.

There's one scenario in which this lazy approach might work. We know that as well as good numbers – statistics that tell us something true and useful about the real world – there are bad numbers. In an ideal world we would be able to come up with a list of sources that could be relied upon to only publish the good numbers, while ignoring the bad. Publication in these outlets would serve as a badge of quality, reassuring us that a statistic is at least somewhat accurate. In this world we would not need to investigate statistics ourselves. We could simply trust that if a number was printed in, say, the *New York Times*, then it was probably true. Unfortunately, as this chapter has shown, this is not the world we live in. The fact that a statistic has been published in a 'reputable' source is no guarantee that it is anywhere close to true. We are like bar staff serving drinks to all comers, trusting that the bouncer will have checked IDs at the door – when the truth is that the bouncer has been asleep for a long time. The news media are letting any statistic walk through the door to your brain with barely a glance. In this world we all have to be our own bouncers.

 ## Summary

Many of the numbers in the news come directly from press-releases. Most of the numbers reported in news stories and headlines are not the product of original research by the author of the story. Instead they come from external sources – mostly in the form of press-releases.

Press-releases are part of an organisation's PR strategy. Statistical claims are sent to the press because the organisation sending them wants them to appear in the news. For example, this may be an environmental campaign group who want to draw attention to the latest figures on species loss; or it may simply be a business who have a product to sell. Whether an organisation wants a particular number in the news has no necessary relationship with said number's validity or truthfulness.

The news media does not effectively filter out misleading statistical claims. The news media often publishes stories based on statistical claims without conducting the necessary checks to determine whether these claims are true or false. This is true of well-known, 'reputable' newspapers and broadcasters, as well as less well-regarded outlets.

 ## Terminology used in this chapter

Press-release: A document sent by an organisation (for example, a government department, a charity, or a business) to a news outlet in the hopes that its contents will be written up into a news story.

News agency: An organisation which gathers news reports and sells them on to subscribing news outlets. The subscribing outlets may reprint these stories verbatim, or amend them as they see fit.

Zombie statistics: False or misleading statistics which continue to be used despite having been thoroughly debunked.

Seeing beyond the headlines

Before deciding whether a number is trustworthy, it's a good idea to think about where it came from and why it might have ended up in the news. Here are three questions to help organise your enquiries:

1. WHICH ORGANISATION OR PERSON PRODUCED THE STATISTIC?

Most statistics that reach the media come from a limited set of places. Broadly, these are: government departments, charities, businesses, survey organisations, and academic researchers. Where does the statistic in question come from?

2. IS THE ORGANISATION/PERSON LIKELY TO HAVE AN AGENDA?

Different organisations have different agendas. For example, government departments want you to think they are doing a good job; charities want to make a problem seem important; and businesses want to sell products. Academic researchers are theoretically unbiased, but they may have a personal political agenda, or just a dearly held theory.

Just because an organisation has an agenda doesn't mean the statistics they disseminate are false. However, statistics that appear to support a particular agenda should be treated with an extra degree of scepticism.

3. DOES THE JOURNALIST CHALLENGE THE STATISTIC?

Does the article (or video, or podcast, or radio news item) make any attempt to interrogate the statistic, for example by questioning (or even explaining) the methodology behind it? Or has the statistic merely been reproduced without any apparent checks?

To help illustrate how these questions help with spotting suspicious statistics, I've laid them out below in the form of a table (with one of the examples we've gone through in the chapter filled in):

CLAIM	ORGANISATION BEHIND THE STATISTIC	LIKELY AGENDA?	STATISTIC CHALLENGED?	VERDICT
1/5th of British teenagers think Winston Churchill was a fictional character	UKTV Gold (television channel)	Promoting their historical TV shows	No. No discussion of methodology behind the survey	Suspicious statistic. Unlikely to be reliable. Further investigation required.

CLAIM	ORGANISATION BEHIND THE STATISTIC	LIKELY AGENDA?	STATISTIC CHALLENGED?	VERDICT

 Exercises for Chapter 2

Exercise 1: Follow the press-release

Below are links to three press-releases. For each release, try to answer the following questions:

1. Imagine you are a journalist writing for a national newspaper. This press-release has just arrived in your inbox. Should you write it up as a news story? In other words, do you think the information in the press-release qualifies as 'news'? If not, why not?

2. Why might the company sending the press-release want this story to appear in the news media?

3. Have these press-releases actually been covered in the media? If so:

   a. Which outlets have covered them?

   b. How much has the journalist changed from the original press-release? Has any new information been added?

   c. Who is given as the author of the news story?

The press-releases:

Press-release #1: Three quarters of Brits admit lying to their partner

Link: *http://www.virginmedia.com/corporate/media-centre/press-releases/virgin-tv-poll-reveals-three-quarters-of-brits-admit-to-lying-to-their-partner.html*

Press-release #2: American workers need to get more sleep

Link: *https://www.prnewswire.com/news-releases/two-thirds-of-american-workers-would-be-better-employees-if-they-got-more-sleep-according-to-glassdoor-survey-300542688.html*

Press-release #3: Smartphones causing back pain

Link: *http://newsroom.simplyhealth.co.uk/iposture-generation-facing-a-lifetime-of-back-pain/*

Exercise 2: Zombie statistics

In the chapter I listed four 'zombie statistics'. These are statistics which are often repeated despite having little or no evidence to back them up. Here are the four statistics again:

- In the UK there is a CCTV camera for every 14 people
- We only use 10% of our brain
- We swallow an average of 8 spiders a year while sleeping
- In a city you are never more than 6 feet from a rat

Can you work out where these statistics came from? Are they just made up? Or do they come from a misunderstanding of a real study?

---

www.macmillanihe.com/devries-critical-statistics

 ONLINE RESOURCES AVAILABLE

Go to the book's companion website for further examples, data, links, and other useful resources.

SAMPLES, SAMPLES EVERYWHERE ...

"25% of Americans Don't Know the Earth Orbits the Sun" – Jezebel
.com, 15 February 2014

"15% of British Men ... Would Have Sex with a Robot" – The Sun,
2 September 2015

In the thousands of pages of fact and opinion churned out by the media every day, headlines like this are ten a penny. You can't swing a cat (GIF) on the internet without hitting some fact about 20% of dog owners or 60% of conservatives or 1 in 10 millennials.

But how do the headline writers *know* these things? How do they know that a quarter of Americans are living with a model of the solar system that is 500 years out date? How do they know that 15% of British men saw *Ex Machina* and took away *entirely the wrong message*? We covered some of the answer to this question in Chapter 1, but here we're going to delve a bit deeper.

Let's say that, for some no doubt excellent reason, I really wanted to know what proportion of British men would sleep with an artificially intelligent robot. The only way to find this out definitively would be to speak to every single man in the country – all 25 million of them. This is ... impractical to say the least. I'm not going to sidle up to every man in Britain and ask them if they wish Amazon's Alexa was more than just a disembodied voice. Aside from being unlikely to end well, it would simply take too long.

What *Sky News* (the people behind the robot number) did instead was to speak to 500 men and use their answers as an indication of what all British men would say.[1] 75 (15%) of the men *Sky* spoke to indicated that 'if the technology was sufficiently advanced' they would be willing to sleep with a robot.* *The Sun* took this 15% and generalised it to the entire male population of Britain.

As I mentioned in Chapter 1, this idea – taking the answers of a small number of people as indicative of what the whole population

---

* In fact, the actual question was 'To what extent, if at all, do you agree or disagree that if the technology was sufficiently advanced, it would be possible to have a fulfilling sexual relationship with an artificially intelligent robot?' This is not exactly the same as asking 'Would you personally have sex with a robot?' Just as with the 'one in five Muslims' story in Chapter 1, *The Sun* have twisted the statistics to make a better story.

think – strikes a lot of people as just obviously wrong. How can you say something about 25 million men after having talked to just 500 of them? *Sky News* didn't ask me if *I* would have sex with a robot; and (even if you're a British man) they probably didn't ask you either. It's tempting to draw the line there: if you haven't spoken to everyone in the group you're interested in, you shouldn't make sweeping generalisations about what all of them think.

This sounds fair, but it leaves us with a pretty big problem. We (governments, charities, researchers, companies, and society in general) need information we can only get by asking people direct questions. OK, maybe it's not *essential* for us to know how many people would have sex with a robot, but there are plenty of other things we *do* need to know. Things like what proportion of students are happy with their degrees, or what percentage of women have experienced sex discrimination, or how many older people are struggling to heat their homes – the list goes on and on.

Given that it's basically impossible to speak to every member of a large population (like all students, or all women, or all older people), we are left with only one option: we have to speak to a small selection of people (a <u>sample</u> of say 500, or 1,000 or 10,000) and hope that what they say tells us something useful about the population as a whole. Researchers do this all the time. In fact, most of the facts and figures you will ever see will not be precise, definitive answers from a whole population – they will be <u>estimates</u> (educated guesses) based on small samples. This is true even for statistics that sound very concrete and official.

It's samples all the way down …

Below is a list of real statistics, some of which are rock-solid, precise figures, and some of which are estimates (guesses) based on small samples of people. Which do you think is which?

1. One in five Australians don't believe in climate change. *Source*: Research by academics at the University of Tasmania, Australia.[2]

2. There are 1.4 million unemployed people in the UK, and 771,000 job vacancies. That's 1.8 unemployed people for every vacancy. *Source*: UK Office for National Statistics (2017).

3. In 2013/14, 28% of people convicted of homicide in Canada were not given prison sentences. *Source*: Statistics Canada.[3]

4. 8.9 million people in the USA watched the Season 6 finale of *Game of Thrones*. *Source*: Nielsen Television Ratings (as reported in the *New York Times*).[4]

A lot of Australians don't believe in climate change

An easy one to start us off. The source is reputable – the statistic was produced by real scientists and published in a peer-reviewed scientific journal – but we also know that the researchers can't have interviewed every single Aussie alive. This means the statistic *must* be an estimate from a sample – and indeed it is. The researchers spoke to 1,946 randomly selected Australians, 331 of whom (17%, close to one in five) were sceptical of climate change. This is not definitive proof that one in five of *all* Australians feel this way – but it's not bullshit either. Two thousand is a good number of people to speak to, and the survey was well conducted (I'll talk more about what this means in the next section). 17% (plus or minus a few percentage points) is therefore a reasonable estimate of the real percentage of Australians who are climate sceptics. This is useful information. Before the survey, we didn't know what Australians thought about the environment. Now we have at least some idea. Without infinite time and money, this is about the best we are going to manage.

1.9 unemployed people for every vacancy

In every country in the world, people argue about whether unemployed people could find a job if they wanted one, or if there are just not enough jobs to go around. This argument has been going on forever, and will likely only end when the earth is reduced to a scorching nuclear wasteland. (The argument will then resume when two of the last three survivors meet to complain that Jeff isn't pulling his weight in the irradiated squirrel-catching department.)

In the meantime, a crucial piece of information in the unemployment debate is the number of unemployed people per vacancy in the economy. In the UK, we can see that the jobs numbers come from the UK Office for National Statistics (ONS). As a source, this is about as reputable as it gets. But, again, by itself this doesn't tell us anything about whether the numbers (1.4 million unemployed people, 771,000 vacancies) are concrete figures or estimates. With nothing else to go on, our only real option for figuring this out is to ask ourselves how the ONS would go about calculating these numbers.

When I discuss these examples with my students, many of them assume that the government 'just knows' stuff like this. But governments 'just know' a lot less than people think. The exact number of people who are unemployed at any given time is one of these things they don't know. As is the exact number of businesses who are currently hiring, and how many jobs they are advertising.

It makes sense if you think about it. The only way the government would know exactly how many people were unemployed at any one time would be if you had to submit a form every single time you got a job, or lost one and became unemployed. Something like this happens if you are claiming out-of-work welfare benefits – but not all unemployed people claim these benefits. It's a similar situation with the number of vacant jobs. The only way for the government to know this figure exactly would be if businesses were required to register every single vacancy with some government agency.

Since neither of these things is true, the only way for the government to find out how many people are unemployed, or how many vacancies are being advertised, is to ask people and businesses these questions directly. This brings us back to the same problem we had earlier: there are far too many people and far too many businesses for it to be practical for the government to talk to every single one of them.

The solution to this problem is the same as for the robot sex and climate change questions. Instead of talking to every person and business, the British government instead talk to a sample and use their answers to estimate what's going on more generally. To find out how many people are unemployed, they use something called the Labour Force Survey (LFS). This survey gets sent out to around 100,000 working-age people around the UK every quarter. Let's say 10% of those people respond to the survey saying that they are unemployed. The working-age population of Britain is about 40 million people. 10 per cent of 40 million is 4 million. We can therefore estimate that there are around 4 million unemployed people in the country. You can see that despite sounding very official and concrete when you see it in the news, this number is still a sort of guess (albeit a highly educated one).

The same principle applies to the job vacancies number. Every month the UK government send out a survey to a sample of 6,000 businesses. This is the unimaginatively titled Vacancy Survey, and it asks employers how many jobs they are currently advertising. All the numbers are added up, and the total is extrapolated to all the businesses in the country.

Canadians, despite being Canadian, still sometimes kill each other

Do we know for a rock-solid fact that 28% of convicted murderers in Canada do not get a prison sentence? Or is this an estimate from a sample? You might be getting a sense of a pattern emerging, but actually this time it's the former. Unlike people's employment status, details of criminal trials are always recorded. Every time someone is tried and sentenced for murder (or any other crime), it gets written down somewhere. The Canadian government know exactly how many people were convicted of homicide in 2013/14 (137) and exactly how many of them received custodial sentences (98 – i.e. 72%). They do not have to send researchers to hang around outside courthouses asking random defendants what sentence they got.

Swords and dragons: not just for geeks any more

Are we guesstimating that 8.9 million Americans tuned in to watch what happened to a room full of people Cersei Lannister was displeased with? Or do we know that figure precisely?

This is another one that might be surprising. I must admit that I was surprised the first time I looked into it. In the back of my mind I'd sort of assumed that the television companies knew exactly how many people watched a particular programme when it was broadcast. My TV is connected up to a cable after all, so maybe it's sending some kind of signal back about which channel I'm tuned in to?

I think this assumption is partly due to the specificity of the numbers. When the newspapers say 8.9 million people watched *Game of Thrones*, or that 31 million watched the Rio Olympics, or that 600 million watched Neil Armstrong land on the moon, it doesn't sound like they are making an educated guess. It sounds very definite and specific. But the last of those examples should give you pause. Some televisions these days may have the technology to send back data on what you are watching, but not all of them do – and televisions in 1969 certainly did not. For the most part, televisions are dumb boxes that receive a signal and display an image. Neither the TV companies nor the government, nor any other mysterious organisation, have any idea what we are watching at any given time.*

In the USA, most ratings statistics are produced by a company called Nielsen. The way they work out how many people watched a specific programme is by using a box called a 'TV meter'. They send these boxes to a selected sample of families to plug into their TVs. These meters allow the TV to do what it wouldn't be able to do normally – beam information back to Nielsen about what the household is watching.

Nielsen only send these boxes to around 20,000 households (so-called 'Nielsen families'). What these 20,000 families are watching determines a show's ratings. For example, let's say 5% of the Nielsen sample watched the Season 6 finale of AMC's bizarrely boring zombie epic *The Walking Dead*. Nielsen estimate that this means 5% of *all American TV owners* (which is basically all Americans) watched it. This would be about 12 million people. This is how most TV ratings numbers are calculated (and not just in America).

---

* In Britain, all televisions can receive a signal to watch a few standard television channels (including the BBC). However, people are still supposed to pay an annual licence fee to watch these channels. To put people off watching TV without paying for a licence, the BBC used to advertise the existence of 'detector vans'. These vans would supposedly park outside your house and, through some mysterious means involving the pattern of light coming through your window (seriously), determine if you were watching a BBC broadcast. They would not have had to go through all this palaver if your TV sent a signal back about what channel you were watching.

Samples *almost* all the way down …

So most statistics are not concrete, precise counts: they are estimates (educated guesses) from small samples of people. This is true no matter where they come from or how specific or official they seem. A lot of very important government numbers – including things like carbon emissions, employment rates, and economic growth (GDP) – have their roots in sample-based estimates.

It's perhaps easier to get a handle on this if we consider the rare instances where this is *not* the case: where we do have solid information for every member of the population we are interested in. For the first example we can go back to TV. Regular televisions might not be sending a signal back about what you are watching, but internet services like Netflix or YouTube or the BBC iPlayer *absolutely* are. Every time one of Adam Sandler's three remaining fans watches *The Do-Over*, Netflix knows. Every time even they get bored and switch over to *Orange Is the New Black*, Netflix knows (and by 'knows' I mean this information gets recorded in Netflix's databases). This means that if Netflix said *Making a Murderer* had been watched 10 million times, this would not be an estimate, it would be the exact number of times it had been watched on the service.*

The same thing is true of most online services. Every time you send an email, search Google, or visit a website, information about that interaction is stored in a database somewhere. If you wanted to know how many people asked Google 'how to put on pants' in 2016, Google can give you the exact answer (840 as of around September that year). They don't have to take a sample of computer users and ask them if they are having some problems they'd like to talk about.

The data we produce when we use online services is a subset of what you might call 'automatically collected data'. Doing a survey – going out and asking people questions – is *purposefully* collected data because you are collecting it … on purpose. Automatically collected data is the opposite. It's data that's generated automatically whenever a particular thing happens. The Canadian homicide statistic we looked at is an example of this. Someone goes on trial and the information about this trial gets written down and stored in a database somewhere. No researcher has to go and purposefully collect that data: it's automatically recorded as a matter of course. The same is often (though not always) true of 'official' things like school exam results, hospital admissions, and people's tax payments.

---

*   Netflix don't actually release their viewer numbers publicly, so I can't point to a real example. This may be because they want old-school broadcast TV execs to be scared of the number of customers they *might* be losing to Netflix. Hard statistics on Netflix's viewership would go some way to alleviating this fear.

After automatically collected data, the second exception to the 'most statistics come from samples' rule is the national <u>census</u>. There are a few topics that most governments have decided are too important to trust to sample-based estimates. These are mostly to do with counting populations in different areas in order to allocate services and political representation (for example, deciding how many congresspeople each state in America should have). To get this data the government do what no other organisation could really do – they actually contact every single household in the country. This is the national census: the only survey that absolutely everyone in the country has to fill out. A national census is so enormously expensive and time-consuming that most countries only do one every 10 years or so (and some countries are thinking about phasing it out entirely). Because everyone has to fill it out, a national census also tends not to include many questions. For example, the US census basically just asks 'Who lives there? How old are they, and what is their gender and ethnicity?'

The final exception to the rule – the final case in which you don't really need to do a sample survey – is when the group of people you are interested in (this is called your <u>population of interest</u>) is very small. If you're interested in all British Muslims, or all American dog owners, or all Australian students then yes, you have to use a sample. But if you're only interested in, say, Fortune 500 CEOs or members of your 200-person college class, then you can probably interview all of them. No sample needed.

You can see from these exceptions why most statistics come from samples. There's a limit to how much information you can extract from the national census and from automatically collected data. If you want to know about people's average tax payments, or the number of single-parent households there are in Delaware, then these are your go-to sources. But if you want to know something a bit more exciting, then you're going to have to do a sample survey. Some sample surveys provide us with interesting, useful information. Others are a complete waste of time and generate only meaningless bullshit. The rest of this chapter is dedicated to explaining how to tell the difference.

Size matters

The first, most obvious step in checking whether a sample is good or bad is to look at its size. For example, in 2015, researchers in Switzerland published the results of a study they had conducted into women's opinions on the subject of penises. Their findings prompted headlines around the world:

"Penis Size Doesn't Matter to Women, But its Appearance Certainly Does, New Study Finds" – Bustle.com, 21 July 2015

"Is YOUR penis 'good looking'? Medical study reveals what women really rate as important (and it's NOT length)" – Daily Mail, 22 July 2015

"What makes a beautiful Penis? No! Size doesn't really matter" – India.com, 24 July 2015

'Science proves that women don't care about penis size' certainly seems like a newsworthy story. So how many women did the Swiss researchers survey to find this out? The headlines seem to suggest that the results relate to all women everywhere, so surely this must have been a large-scale international effort, probably involving many thousands of participants?

In fact, the researchers spoke to a grand total of … 105 women, mostly recruited from in and around the Swiss city of Zurich. I hope it goes without saying that the opinions of these 105 specific women are unlikely to tell us anything particularly meaningful about the preferences of the world's female population in general. And in fact they were not supposed to. The Swiss scientists were actually studying a specific type of plastic surgery intended to help men with a birth defect called hypospadias. They were interested in women's aesthetic responses to the penises of men who had undergone this surgery. As part of this research, they also asked the women in the study some more general questions about what made a penis attractive or unattractive. It was these findings which were seized on by the global media.

Stories like this, which draw sweeping conclusions from tiny studies, are thankfully much rarer than they used to be. Journalists have largely caught on to the idea that surveys of 50 or 100 people don't tell us much about what's going on with the general public. However, once in a while, a headline is just too good to pass up.

Brexit errors

So if a sample of 105 people is too small to tell us anything useful about the entire female population, the natural question to ask is 'how big a sample do we actually need?' To address this question, we'll look at another headline based on a survey:

"EU Referendum: British public wrong about nearly everything, survey shows" – The Independent, 10 June 2016

In 2016, Britain held a referendum to determine whether it should leave the European Union (EU). Those of you who live in the UK (and probably quite a few of you who don't) know that the referendum campaign was not exactly a calm and reasoned exchange of views. In the run-up to the vote, there was a lot of concern (mostly on the Remain side) that people didn't really know enough about the EU to make an informed decision. Tapping into this debate, the polling company Ipsos MORI conducted a survey testing the British public on their knowledge of some EU facts. The results were less than encouraging:[5]

- Despite the fact that a lack of control over EU decisions was one of the flashpoints of the Brexit debate, 40%(!) of the Ipsos sample did not know that UK citizens got to elect Members of the European parliament.

- On average, the sample believed that immigrants from the EU made up 15% of the total UK population. This was three times higher than the real figure of 5%.

- 25% of the sample believed the myth that the EU had banned bananas that were 'too bendy' from being imported into the UK (non-Brits will have to take my word for it that this was a bigger deal than it sounds, with many pro-Brexit politicians using this fictional ban as a symbol of excessive European meddling in British affairs).

The first thing we need to do when examining any claim based on a survey is to establish who the <u>population of interest</u> is. This is the group of people the claim is trying to say something about. In this case, identifying the population of interest is pretty straightforward. Ipsos MORI are trying to use their sample to say something about the entire British public (we can probably safely assume that this is restricted to the adult population).*

Our next step is to take a closer look at the sample. The first thing we can see is that it was made up of about 1,000 people – that's a lot more than the 105 women in the penis example. However, there are around 48 million adults living in Britain. This means only about 0.002% of the British population filled in Ipsos' survey. It feels like such a tiny fraction of the population can't be enough to come to any kind of conclusion about what 'the British public' do or don't know about the EU. But actually, a sample size of around 1,000 *is* enough (just about) to start making reasonably accurate estimates as to what's going on in a whole population – even if that population is made up of

---

* The only confusion that might arise is from the UK's slightly odd status as a nation made up of several different countries. The full name for the UK is 'The United Kingdom of Great Britain and Northern Ireland'. Great Britain refers to the combination of England, Wales, and Scotland. The UK is these countries plus Northern Ireland (and a few other small islands). The confusion comes about because people sometimes use 'Britain' to refer just to Great Britain and sometimes to refer to the whole UK. This can actually be quite important because people in Northern Ireland might think very differently to the rest of the nation about some issues. However, for the sake of keeping things simple I'm going to stick to Britain being England + Scotland + Wales.

millions of people. This is due to a statistical concept called the margin of error.

The first step to understanding the margin of error is to remember that a number from a sample survey is a kind of educated guess (an estimate) as to what's really going on in the whole population. For example, 25% of the 1,000 people who filled in the Brexit survey believed that the EU had banned bendy bananas. This is an *estimate* of the real number – the real proportion of the whole British population that believe the bendy banana myth. Because it's only an estimate, it's unlikely to be dead-on correct – the real number might be a bit higher or a bit lower. The margin of error is an attempt to specify how wrong we think our estimate might be. The size of the margin of error is determined by the size of the sample: the bigger the sample, the more accurate the estimate is likely to be, and therefore the smaller the margin of error.

Numbers from sample surveys are often presented in the media as if they are concrete, precise figures. But it's actually better to think of them as more like a fuzzy range of possible numbers. The margin of error tells you how wide this fuzzy range is likely to be.

22%   25%   28%

In this case, the sample consists of 1,000 people. Because we're dealing with a percentage, this means that the margin of error is around 3 percentage points either side of the estimate. (I've skipped over a lot of the detail here about how margins of error actually work. It's a bit tricky to explain and requires at least one equation. If you're up for that then you can read a fuller explanation in the box "margins of error".) This means Ipsos can't say definitively that 25% of British people are bendy banana truthers, but they *can* be confident that somewhere between 22% and 28% are (a 3 percentage point margin of error either side). This range (22%–28%) is called the 95% confidence interval. Roughly, this is the range within which we can be 95% confident that the real number actually lies.

Pinning down a number for the whole British population to within a 6 percentage point range is pretty damn good. The survey may not have given us a perfect, precise figure, but it's given us some genuinely useful information. This is why most polling companies aim for samples of around 1,000 people. If they only interviewed 100 people, their guesses would be much more uncertain – the margin of error would be around 10 percentage points. In the case of the banana statistic this means they'd only be able to put the number somewhere between 15% and 35%. This is not nearly as useful. If on the other hand they'd interviewed

Percentage points

In a few places here I talk about the margin of error in terms of 'percentage points' rather than just percentages. These terms may seem interchangeable but they are actually different in quite an important way.

One way to express the difference between two numbers is in terms of a percentage difference. Let's say I can run 100m in 13 seconds (this is entirely hypothetical since the last time I ran anywhere was when I was late for a bus sometime in the late nineties) but my friend can run it in 11. One way to express that difference is that my time is 2 seconds longer than my friend's. This is the **absolute** difference between our two times.

Another way to express the differences is to say that my time is 18% longer than my friend's time. This is the difference (2 seconds) expressed as a percentage of my friend's time (11 seconds). This is the difference between our times expressed **relative** to my friend's time.

Let's keep the same numbers but change the context to scores on an exam. I score 13% on the exam and my friend scores 11% (not a good day for either of us). Your natural inclination might be to say that I scored 2% higher in the test, but that's not actually correct. 13 is still 18% higher than 11. To express this difference in absolute terms you would say that I scored 2 **percentage points** higher. The 'percentage point' terminology allows you to talk about differences between percentages without getting confused about whether you're talking about absolute or relative differences.

10,000 people, then their estimates would be *more* accurate – only a 1 percentage point margin of error either side of the estimate. But interviewing an extra 9,000 people costs a lot of money. And, depending on the survey, it might not be worth the extra cash for the sake of a modest reduction in the margin of error. If you start looking out for the sample sizes of most surveys reported in the news, you'll see that they're almost all in the 1,000 to 2,000 person range.

By interviewing 1,000 people Ipsos can say, with a reasonable degree of confidence, that the real percentage of the British population who believe the EU has banned bendy bananas is somewhere between 22% and 28%. They can also pin down some other, potentially more useful numbers too, such as the proportion of who don't know that they can elect Members of the European Parliament. There might be something else wrong with the survey (for example with the way the questions were worded), but we'll deal with those issues in future chapters.

Margins of error: the maths bit

Let's say we are interested in finding out what percentage of Americans think abortion should be legal. We survey a sample of 1,000 randomly selected US residents, and find that about 480 (48%) of them think it should be legal (i.e. they are pro-choice).

Now let's say we interviewed another random sample of 1,000 people. It's likely that we would get a different number: maybe 30% or 60%, or even 70% pro-choice.

If we kept doing surveys, we'd end up with a lot of different numbers. Each number is an estimate (a guess) as to what the real number is in the population (the actual percentage of *all* Americans who are pro-choice). However, these estimates would not be completely random – they would have a pattern. Specifically, we would get more numbers closer to the real number than we would numbers that were far away from it.

Say the real proportion of Americans who believe in legal abortion is 50%. If we carried out 100 different surveys, each containing a sample of 1,000 random Americans, a few of those surveys would probably give us very high or very low figures for the proportion pro-choice. When drawing a random selection of 1,000 people out of the 'bucket' of all Americans, there's always a chance we might end up with a disproportionate number of pro-choice or a disproportionate number of pro-life people. However, if we do a lot of these draws there will be fewer of these 'weird' samples than there will be of 'normal' samples (samples where the number is closer to what it really is in the whole population).

It might be easier to get to grips with this if we take a step back and think about it in the abstract. Imagine you have a sack of coloured balls. The sack is the USA and each ball is a person. Green balls are pro-choice; red balls are pro-life. Half the balls in the sack are green and half are red. If you dip into the sack and draw out 1,000 random balls, you might end up, by chance, with 90% red balls or 90% green balls. However, if the bag is really well shaken up, this won't happen very often – you'll more often get something closer to 50/50. In other words, if there really are 50% green balls in the bag, you're much more likely to get a sample of close to 50% green balls than you are to get a 'weird' sample of 10% green balls or 90% green balls.

From this fact – that in a set of hypothetical random samples, the numbers you get back will cluster around the right answer – statisticians in the 1930s realised that, starting from a **single estimate from a single survey**, you can work out the range within which the real number in the population is likely to fall.* This range is called the 95% confidence interval and the equation to work it out for a percentage is, roughly, your estimate plus or minus $\frac{1}{\sqrt{N}} \times 100$ (where N is the number of people in your sample).

Let's say we'd sampled 50 Americans instead of a 1,000 in our survey and got the same result: 48% of the sample said they agreed with a woman's right to choose. We can use the equation to work out how big the confidence interval around this 48% should be:

- We start by working out the square root of N. Our N is 50, so the square root is a little over 7.
- Now we divide 1 by the result: 1 divided by 7 is 0.14.
- Now we multiply this by 100, which gives us a final answer of 14.

This means the margin of error is 14 percentage points. Place that either side of our original estimate of 48% and we get a 95% confidence interval of 34% to 62%. This is the range within which we are 95% confident that the real number lies.

Fourteen percentage points either side makes for a pretty big window. By speaking to 50 people we've only managed to establish that the real proportion of Americans who are pro-choice is likely somewhere between 34% and 62%. Better than a completely uneducated guess – but not by much. However, by increasing our sample size we can shrink down the margin of error. This is clear if you look at the equation: the bigger the N, the bigger the number you are dividing 1 by, and therefore the smaller the number you end up with. Increase the sample size to 100 and the margin of error shrinks to about 10 percentage points. Increase it to 1,000 and it shrinks to 3 percentage points. Three percentage points is not bad. By sampling 1,000 people we've identified the likely proportion of Americans who are pro-choice to within a 6 percentage point range. Most people would call this 'reasonably accurate'.

So 1,000 people is OK for America, but what about a bigger country like China (population 1.36 billion)? We can go back to the equation for the margin of error and see what size sample we would need to get a reasonable estimate for the whole Chinese population:

$$\frac{1}{\sqrt{N}} \times 100$$

And from this we can see that ... it doesn't matter. There is nowhere in the equation to plug in the size of the Chinese population. The margin of error for a sample of 1,000 (or 100, or 50, or whatever) is the same for a population of 1.36 billion as it is for a population of 320 million (or 60 million or 4 million). As strange as it might seem, a sample that is big enough for America is big enough for China (and for any other size population).

---

* This is actually not quite correct. The 95% confidence interval actually means that in 95% of random samples, the interval you calculate will include the true value for the population. However, this is much harder to wrap your head around, and even this definition is not unproblematic. If you just think of confidence intervals as basically a rough guess at the precision of your estimate, you won't go far wrong.

Low fidelity

In which European country do you think it's most common for people to cheat on their partners? In which do you think it's least common? I'm sure you'll have your own ideas, but according to research conducted by the French polling company IFOP (*Institut français d'opinion publique*),[6] the league table is as follows:

- Tied for first place are Italy and France, where 55% of men have cheated, along with 32% and 34% of women, respectively.

- Second is Belgium, where 51% of men and 29% of women have been unfaithful.

- Third is Spain (50% of men, 28% of women).

- Fourth is Germany (46% of men, 43% of women).

- And in last place is Britain, a model of fidelity and restraint, where only 42% of men and 29% of women have cheated on a romantic partner.

This research (which was conducted in collaboration with Gleeden, a 'dating' website for people seeking extramarital encounters) received a lot of attention from the global media. Here is a flavour of some of the coverage:

> *"Quelle surprise: French men 'least faithful' in Europe – but good news if your other half is British"* – Daily Mirror, 28 February 2014

> *"Survey Reveals Which European Country Cheats Most"* – Huffington Post, 3 March 2014

> *"French and Italians are the least faithful of Europeans"* – Slate (France), 1 March 2014

So, does the underlying research justify all this coverage? A glance at IFOP's website shows that 4,879 people (all of whom were over 18) took part in the survey. I've already said that 1,000 people can give us a reasonable idea of what's going on in a population of any size, so almost 5,000 seems like more than enough. But, there's a catch. In this story, it's not the overall sample size that's important. IFOP are not estimating a single overall number here – they are estimating the proportion of men and women who cheat in each of the six countries separately. That's **twelve different populations and twelve different estimates**. It is the size of the sample within each of these populations that matters, not the total number of people who filled in the survey.

On their website, IFOP give the sample size for each individual country. They spoke to 820 people in Spain, Italy, and Germany; 812 people in the UK; 804 in France; and 803 in Belgium. They don't say how many of these were men and how many were women. However, they do say that they spoke to representative quotas of people according to age, gender, profession, region, and marital status – so we can assume around 400 men and 400 women in each country.*

Each respondent in the survey was asked if they had 'ever been unfaithful (that is to have had sexual intercourse with someone other than with whom you were a couple)'. The numbers given above are the proportion of men and women in each country saying 'yes' to that question. Because there's more variation in male cheating, let's focus on the men's results. Figure 3.1 shows what they look like plotted on a bar chart.

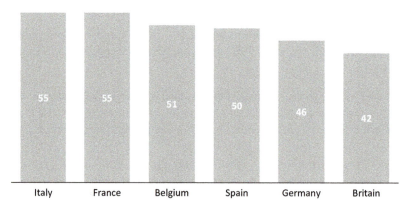

Percentage of men who say they have cheated on a partner

Figure 3.1 Bar chart visualising the results of the IFOP infidelity survey

From the previous section we know that each of the numbers in this graph is an <u>estimate</u> of what all the men in each country would say, and that each of these numbers has a <u>margin of error</u> around it. Because each sample comprises about 400 men, the margin of error is around 5 percentage points. This means, for example, that we can only be confident that the real number for France is somewhere between 50% and 60%. Crucially, you'll notice that the lowest point of this range overlaps the estimates for Belgium and Spain.

When the confidence interval for France overlaps the estimate for Belgium or Spain, it means **we can't be confident that the numbers for these countries are actually different in reality**. Remember, the number for each country is an estimate (guess) of what's going on in the

---

* An extra wrinkle is that these totals include some people who had never been in a couple before. Because you can't cheat on a partner you don't have, IFOP sensibly filtered these people out before producing the figures reported above. Unhelpfully, IFOP don't say how many people this was. However, I'm going to be generous and assume it wasn't many.

whole male population of that country: this is the point of the exercise. The confidence intervals for each estimate tell us the range within which we are confident the real number in that country falls. If the range for one country overlaps the estimate for another, we can't be confident that the two numbers are actually different. In statistical parlance we say that the difference between the two numbers is not <u>statistically significant</u>.

Figure 3.2 is what it looks like if you plot the confidence intervals onto the above graph as error bars.

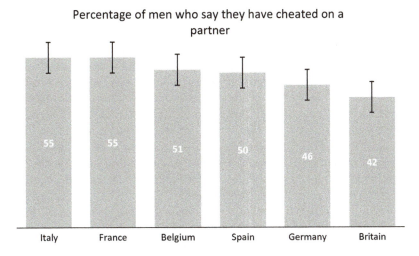

Figure 3.2 IFOP infidelity bar chart, with error bars added

These numbers can tell us some things. For example, we can be reasonably confident that British men are less likely to cheat (or at least less likely to admit to cheating) than Italian, French, Belgian, or Spanish men. We can also be reasonably sure that German men are more faithful than Italian, French, and Belgian (but not Spanish) men. However, we can't be certain of much else. The large margins of error mean that we can't be at all confident that the differences between many of the countries actually reflect differences in the real world. This makes the idea of a league table of infidelity meaningless. In the survey samples, France and Italy are tied for first, while Spain is fourth. In reality, these positions could be reversed. The margins of error are just too big for us to be sure.

This story is a harmless piece of fluff that is probably not worth getting worked up about. However, this problem is not just restricted to 'fun' stories like this. Any time people are comparing numbers from survey samples you have to ask yourself whether we can be confident that these numbers are actually different in the real population. This includes things like whether people who eat a lot of fish oil are less likely to get dementia, or if parents who move house a lot are damaging their children's health: stories that can have real impacts on important decisions people make in their lives.

Numbers other than percentages

Most of the numbers discussed in this chapter are percentages. What percentage of Americans know the earth goes round the sun? What percentage of British men would sleep with a robot? However, all the concepts we've discussed apply to other numbers as well, like **counts** (the number of people watching *The Walking Dead*, the number of people migrating to the UK) and **averages** (the average income of college graduates, the average number of calories people consume per day).

Counts are pretty straightforward: they are just extrapolations from a percentage. You can see this if you go back to the *Walking Dead* example. You start by finding out what percentage of your survey sample watches the show (we said 5% when we did this example), then you just work out how many people this would be if you applied it to the whole population. The US adult population is about 243 million people. 5% of that is 12.2 million. A lot of the specific numbers you see in the news come about this way. This includes official sounding things like the number of people who've been burgled this year, or (as we've already discussed) the number of people who are unemployed. But just because you've turned something into a count doesn't mean you can forget about margins of error. If the 12.1 million *Walking Dead* figure is from the Nielsen sample of 20,000 people, the margins of error would be plus or minus about 85,000 people either side.

The same logic applies to averages. Let's say you want to know the average salary of recent social science graduates in the USA (this might be of particular interest to some of you). There is no centralised record of what every single college graduates earns, so, again, we have to get this information from a survey. In this case the survey is called the National Survey of College Graduates and it shows that social science students who graduated between 2010 and 2013 were earning a median salary of $59,000 when surveyed in 2013. Because this is an estimate, we have to worry about margins of error. Working these out is a little different for an average than for a percentage, but the principle is broadly the same. In this case the margin of error is plus or minus about $2,000, so we can be confident that the real median salary is somewhere between $57,000 and $61,000.

Bad samples

I want you to put yourselves in the shoes of a young American couple – let's call them Sarah and Josh. Sarah and Josh are both 24. High school sweethearts, they got a little place together right after graduation. They both earn the average salary for Americans without a college education, which is a little under $30,000. They recently got engaged, so they do the first thing young couples these days are wont to do: put a picture of the ring on their chosen flavour of social media, and spend the next two hours obsessively checking for likes and comments.

The next day they sit down to work out how much the wedding is going to cost. How much are they going to need to save?

> *"The average cost of a wedding rose to $32,641 last year … "[7]*

This is from an article on CNN Money. If you Google 'wedding cost USA', it's one of the first articles that comes up.

This is bad news. CNN is a reputable source, but $32,000 is more than half what they both earn in a year. How are they ever going to save up that much money? Especially if their parents don't help out (Josh's mum's campaign to become a professional poker player is not going well, and Sarah doesn't speak to her dad since the incident with the raccoon and the medical marijuana).

At this point you know there's going to be something wrong with the $32,000 figure. I've not seized on this opportunity in a book about statistics to finally tell the tragic story of Sarah and Josh and their unaffordable nuptials. So let's take this number apart:

Step 1: Is this number a precise, definitive figure for the whole population, or is it an estimate from a smaller sample? This is pretty easy to work out. There's no way someone spoke to every American couple getting married in 2015 to ask them about their wedding costs – so it's the latter.

Step 2: Who is the population of interest? This is pretty easy too. The headline and the article don't say that they are talking about the average cost of a wedding among some specific group of people, so it must be 'all couples getting married in the USA in 2015'.

Step 3: What is the sample size? The CNN article tells us that the survey was conducted by a wedding planning website called *The Knot*, and that their $32,000 estimate 'was based on almost 18,000 responses from brides who were married last year'. 18,000 is a very big sample; much bigger than any of the surveys we've talked about so far (and much bigger than most surveys in general). A sample size of 18,000 is easily enough people to start saying reasonably accurate things about the population of people getting married in 2015. The CNN story doesn't give any information on margins of error, but with a sample this size they are going to be pretty small.

Step 4: What is the *nature* of the sample? Up to now we've only discussed samples in terms of their size. But there's actually something much more important than the size of a sample, and that is its *composition*. What type of person ended up in the sample? How much do these people resemble the people in the population you are trying to say something about?

This is where the wheels come off the wagon for *The Knot*'s wedding cost statistic. As we've established, the population they are trying to say something about is 'all couples getting married in 2016'. However, *they only sent the survey to people who were signed up to their website*. This is a specific group of people who are likely to be different from the general population of couples in some important ways. For example, people who sign up to use a wedding planning website might be richer on average than the general population, or more likely to live in expensive urban areas. The technical way of putting this is that the sample of people who filled in the survey (people signed up to *The Knot*) is not <u>representative</u> of the population of interest (all American couples marrying in 2015). The sample is likely <u>biased</u> towards the types of couples who spend more money on weddings. It's missing people who plan weddings just with help from friends and family, or people who just plain don't use the internet much (these people still exist). The $32,000 figure is therefore likely an overestimate of the real average cost of an American wedding.

Remember, taking a sample is a way of getting around the fact that you can't speak to every single person in your target population. You are speaking to a small subset of people in order to take an educated guess at what's going on in the population as a whole. If your sample is made up of people who are quite different from the general population (richer, poorer, more or less educated, disproportionately white or black, etc.), then your guess is not going to be very accurate.

Consider a hypothetical example. Let's say you are the editor of a Christian magazine, and you want to find out what percentage of Americans believe in the theory of evolution. You've got 130,000 subscribers: a massive potential sample of people you can send a survey to. Even if only half of them reply, this is bigger than any previous survey on this topic.

But any number you got back from this survey would be a bad estimate of what the general population think. Subscribers to a Christian magazine are likely to be different from the general population in a way that has a direct effect on what you are trying to measure. The sample is hopelessly biased. And when you have a bias like this, it doesn't matter how big the sample is. It can be 1,000 people, 100,000, or a million: the number will still be systematically distorted in a particular direction and will therefore be useless as a guess of what's going on in the population as a whole.

Spotting biased samples

Earlier I said that the media have, to some extent, learned that statistics based on tiny samples are not very newsworthy. Sadly, they have not learned the same lesson about *biased* samples. It's easy to look at a survey with a sample size of 100 and see that this is too few people. Understanding when a sample is not representative of the target population is a little harder. Consequently, we can't always trust reporters to shield us from dodgy samples. We're going to have to do this job ourselves.

There are three fundamental questions to ask when attempting to spot a biased survey sample:

1. What type of person would be most likely to fill in this particular questionnaire?

2. How might they differ from the population of interest?

3. Is this difference likely to make the number bigger than it would likely be in the population (an overestimate) or smaller (an underestimate)?

Self-selected samples

The most common type of bad sample is a 'self-selected' sample. Let's say you are an intern working for an American charity which campaigns for stricter gun laws. You want to find out what proportion of the public would support a complete ban on the sale of assault rifles (the sort of guns that have been used in several mass-shootings in the USA). By far the easiest thing to do would be to post the survey on your website. People showing up to your website will see the survey, and some proportion of them will fill it in. If you leave it there for a while, eventually you might end up with a decent-sized sample.

You will have spotted the problem with this immediately. Most of the people who end up on a pro-gun control website will be the type of person who already supports efforts to reduce the availability of guns. Any number you produce based on this sample will not be a good guess of what's going on in the population at large. If 90% of the people who come to your website support an assault weapons ban, this is not good evidence that 90% of the general population feel the same way.

What if you go beyond posting to your website? What if you post a link to the poll on social media (Facebook, Twitter, etc.)? This will indeed put your survey in front of a broader audience. However, the people who end up filling it in will still be 'self-selected'. They will be the fraction of people who (1) happen to see the link pop up in their feeds, and (2) are interested enough to follow it. This group is unlikely to be representative of the population as a whole (this is before we even get into the fact that social media users are already systematically different from the general population).

Surveys posted to websites and social media are an extremely popular way of collecting information from the public – for the simple reason that they are extremely cheap and easy to set up. However, because of the problems with self-selected samples, the statistics produced by these surveys are a terrible guide to what's going on with the population as a whole. Often these statistics are in service of some (relatively) harmless marketing exercise of the kind we discussed in the previous chapter. However, sometimes they purport to provide information on more serious topics. For example, in September 2017, a number of media outlets, including the *Wall Street Journal* and the *Washington Post*, wrote about a 'chilling' survey, apparently showing that American university students no longer support the fundamental right of free speech. One of the survey's most startling findings was, as the *Post* put it, 'A fifth of undergrads now say it's acceptable to use physical force to silence a speaker who makes "offensive and hurtful statements"'.[8] This would be pretty shocking if it were true of the general population of American undergraduates. And it feeds into a growing concern among many establishment figures on both sides of the Atlantic that university students are becoming increasingly intolerant of listening to people they don't agree with.

The trouble is that we really don't know if this statistic is a good estimate of what American students think about this issue. That's because the 1,500 undergraduates who filled in the survey were a self-selected online sample. And it's very easy to see how the sort of person who would click on a survey about offensive speech might also be the sort of person who has strict views on the subject. This problem did not stop the results of this survey from gaining an enormous amount of traction in the media and in political discussions around the future of free speech in America.

Scientific surveys

Self-selected surveys are so named to distinguish them from surveys in which the researcher, rather than simply hosting the questionnaire and waiting for people to stumble across it, purposefully selects who will be surveyed. This puts the researcher in control of what type of person is approached, giving them the opportunity to ensure that the sample is representative of the target population.

This can still go wrong of course. In the wedding cost example, *The Knot* could have purposefully emailed their survey to a selection of their customers, attempting to get a decent spread of people of different ages and ethnicities and from different parts of the country. However, the 'frame' from which they have selected this sample is still 'people who are registered on their website'. And this group of people is still different from the population as a whole, in all the ways we've already discussed.

So how do we actually go about getting a *good* sample, one that is genuinely likely to be representative of the target population? Somewhat counterintuitively, the answer is that we pick people at random. We start with a list of everyone in the population we are interested in, then we let a computer choose people at random from this list. Whoever the computer picks, that's who we send the survey to.

To understand why this works, let's shrink the problem down. Let's say you are a student in a high school of around 1,000 pupils. You want to find out what proportion of pupils think that there should be no school uniform – that kids should be able to wear what they want. You haven't got time to speak to all 1,000 of your fellow students, so you decide to ask a sample of 50. You take the register of all the students at the school and you let a computer choose 50 of them at random (you could also pick names out of a hat, or construct some kind of lottery ball device – but a computer is easier). The beauty of this approach, and the reason why it is the best way of getting a representative sample, is that *every kid in the school has a perfectly equal chance of being chosen.* Girls don't have a better chance than boys, older kids don't have a better chance than younger ones, rich kids don't have a better chance than poor kids, rebellious kids don't have a better chance than goody-two-shoes … and so on. This means your sample is much less likely to be biased towards a certain type of person. If, say, 60% of your sample think that the uniform should be scrapped, then you can be confident that this number is not being pushed up or down because you've got too many (or too few) smoking-behind-the-bike-sheds D students, or too many (or too few) straight-As, lunchtime chess-club kids.

This method is called <u>random probability sampling</u>, and it is what is usually meant when a story says that a survey was 'scientific'. For example, here is a story from *The Guardian* about the decline of religious belief in the UK:

> *"More than half the UK population has no religion, finds survey …*
> *The survey found that 53% of all adults had no religious affiliation,*
> *up from 48% in 2015" – The Guardian,* 4 September 2017

This story is based on data from the British Social Attitudes Survey (BSA). This is a biennial survey which attempts to discover what British people think about important social issues like welfare, racism, climate change, and religion. The researchers start out with a list of every household in Britain. A computer picks a sample of households from this list at random, and the BSA researchers interview a random adult from each of these households (they usually end up with about 3,000 people). Because the researchers have gone through this rigorous process, we can be pretty confident that the people who filled in the survey are a representative slice of the British population. Therefore, we can be confident that the figure of 53% is a reasonably good guess as to what the whole British public think (within a margin of error of course).

The key to this process is starting with a list of everyone in the population of interest. This is called the <u>sampling frame</u>. In the case of the school example, this was all the students at the school. In the BSA example, this was every household in Britain. If you select from a bad sampling frame, then random sampling is not going to help you. For example, if you had randomly selected students from a single form class, then your sample would still be biased. Or if the BSA researchers had decided to randomly sample people from Twitter, then their sample would be biased – because people on Twitter are systematically different from the general population.

Non-response bias

There's one final wrinkle to the sampling story, and it is that, as much as you might like to, you can't force people to fill in your survey. You can follow the BSA researchers and take a scientific approach, selecting a random probability sample from a perfect sampling frame. But the people in your sample don't have to say yes to filling in the survey – and many of them will say no. This doesn't matter so long as the people who agree are not too different from the people who refuse. If they *are* different – if a particular type of person (say, older people, or richer people, or people who support a particular political party) is more likely to agree to fill out the survey – then your sample is once again biased.

A famous example of this comes from a survey into women's sexuality conducted by a researcher called Shere Hite in the 1970s. She sent a survey out to a huge sample of 100,000 women, and found, shockingly, that 70% of the married women who responded said that they'd had sex outside their marriage (yes, we're back to cheating again).[9] You still sometimes see this statistic quoted by people who want to make a point about the inevitability of infidelity:

> "70% of married women have cheated on their partners ... Although society cherishes monogamy, the expectation of exclusive sexual activity is unsustainable for most couples" – Washington Post, 13 February 2012

100,000 is a big sample, and we'll give Hite the benefit of the doubt and assume that she used a good sampling method. However, the 70% figure comes only from the people who actually filled in the survey rather than throwing it in the bin. This was a grand total of 4,500 women. 4,500 is still a lot, but it's a tiny proportion of the 100,000 who were approached.

These 4,500 are the small fraction of women who got a survey in the post and were happy to fill it in with intimate details about their sex lives. The responses of this specific group are (to put it mildly) very unlikely to be a good estimate of what's going on with all married women in America.

Spotting non-response bias can be quite difficult because it can crop up even when the sample is quite large and the researcher apparently did everything right. However, there are a couple of things to look out for. The first is if the survey would clearly be of more interest to a particular type of person. Is it a survey about a sensitive subject that most people wouldn't want to answer questions on? Is it about a niche interest that a lot of people wouldn't care enough about to fill in a survey?

Sampling beyond surveys

So far in this chapter we've talked about samples purely in terms of surveys. But the basic logic of sampling – using a small subset of a population to represent the whole – extends far beyond this. For example, when we talk about 'populations' we don't necessarily have to be talking about *people*.

Let's say I wanted to find out what percentage of all Instagram photos are selfies. My bet is that it's a lot – but I want some quantitative evidence. Looking through every single photo on Instagram to work this out would take from now until the heat death of the universe. The best way to answer my question would therefore be to take a sample and make an estimate. The principle here is exactly the same as when we're taking samples of people – except this time the population of interest is not 'all British men' or 'all American couples', it's 'all photos on Instagram'.

Exactly as if I were doing a survey, I want my sample to be representative of the 'population' of all photos. This means I can't just take a sample of photos from, for example, the most followed users. These snaps are likely to be different in some important ways from the general population of Instagram photos (for example, more shots of movie premieres and fancy Hollywood parties). They would be a *biased* sample. The best way to approach this would therefore be to take a random sample of photos (and this time we don't have to worry about non-response bias – public photos can't refuse to be looked at).

All the other stuff carries over from surveys too. A larger sample would give us a more certain estimate, a smaller sample a less certain one. The calculations for margins of error work exactly the same as well.

You can use the logic of sampling for anything. Whenever it's impossible (or just really, really hard) to look at everything in your population of interest, you can make an estimate from a sample instead. This can be for newspaper articles, photos, video games, sofas, companies, hospitals, schools – anything that can be counted can be sampled.

The second thing to watch out for is a low <u>response rate</u> (this is the proportion of people who got sent the survey who actually agreed to fill it in). The lower the response rate, the more likely it is that the group of people who actually did fill in the survey are (for want of a better word) weirdos.

The magic of sampling

If I've made sampling sound very difficult, that's because it is. And it should be. You are trying to find out about an entire population by looking at only a tiny sliver of it. It's almost magical that it works at all – and we should not be surprised that it goes wrong more often than it goes right. The trouble comes when, lulled by the fact that sampling is so commonplace, you forget how difficult it actually is. You forget that the number in front of you is a sort of guess as to what's going on the real world, and that seemingly small, technical differences in sampling methodology make a big difference as to whether the final number is telling you something useful.

It would be easy to take this as an injunction to treat all statistics derived from samples as inherently suspect. But, as we've discussed before, this sort of easy cynicism would mean missing out on a lot of genuine insights. Sample surveys, when done well, can tell us extremely interesting things about the societies we live in. For example, the most recent US General Social Survey (a true scientific survey conducted by National Opinion Research Centre at the University of Chicago) found that 62% of Americans agreed that immigrants made the country stronger through their hard work and talents – useful information at a time when anti-immigrant sentiment is often in the news.

This is just one example from a potential list of thousands. Insights from well-conducted sample surveys are an invaluable resource to researchers, charities, governments, and all sorts of other organisations. Without them we would really know very little about how people actually live their lives – their fears and wants, their political and social attitudes, their experience of crime, even their income and working conditions. Using the concepts covered in this chapter, it's entirely possible to sort these good surveys from the bad.

 ## Summary

Many statistics come from samples. Many, if not most of the statistics you encounter in the media will be from samples. It's rarely possible to look at every entity (person, organisation, etc.) in a large population. Researchers must therefore collect data from a sample in order to make an estimate of what's going on in the population as a whole.

Estimates from samples have a margin of error. Statistics derived from samples are not concrete figures; they are estimates – educated guesses as to what is really going on in the population of interest. They should therefore be provided with a corresponding margin of error. The bigger the sample, the smaller the margin of error.

Samples can be biased. A sample is biased if it is composed of a different type of person (or organisation or object, etc.) than the general population of interest. For example, a sample composed entirely of Greenpeace activists would not tell us much about the general population's beliefs about climate change. Because biased samples produce bad estimates, even if the sample size is very large, issues of bias override any concerns about the margin of error.

The best way to ensure an unbiased sample is to use random probability sampling.

 ## Terminology used in this chapter

Census: A survey which collects information from every entity in the population of interest, rather than from just a sample. For example, the UK National Census is a survey completed by every household in the entire country.

Population of interest: The population a statistic is supposed to inform us about.

Margin of error: An indication of how uncertain our estimate is. A large margin of error indicates that, based on our sample, we are not really sure what the true number in the population actually is. A small margin of error means we are confident that our estimate is quite close to the real number.

95% confidence interval: (Roughly) the range within which we are confident the real number lies.

Statistically significant: Most commonly used to refer to the difference between two sample-based estimates. Statistical significance is related to the margin of error. Two numbers are statistically significantly different if their respective margins of error are small enough for us to be confident that the numbers are actually different in the real world.

Representative: A sample is representative of the population of interest if the characteristics of the sample match the characteristics of the population. For example, a national sample which comprised 50% men and 50% women would be (roughly) representative in terms of gender.

Self-selected sample: A sample which is not chosen by the researcher, but by the potential respondents themselves. For example, a survey hosted on a public website would attract a self-selected sample. Samples of this kind are often biased (see above).

Random probability sampling: A procedure by which a researcher randomly selects the elements of their sample (e.g. people) from a sampling frame (see below). Each entity in the sampling frame has an equal chance (probability) of ending up in the sample.

Sampling frame: A list of entities from which a sample is selected. For example, the UK Postcode Address File contains a list of all households in the UK. A random probability sample of UK households could be generated by picking randomly from entries in this list.

Non-response bias: Bias produced by a pattern in the type of person (or organisation, etc.) who responds to a survey. For example, a survey attempting to determine what proportion of the public want to see a remake of the classic 1993 Arnold Schwarzenegger action comedy *Last Action Hero* is sent out to a representative sample of the population. However, only people over the age of 30 bother to respond.

Response rate: The proportion of the sample that actually responds to a survey. A low response rate can indicate a potential problem of non-response bias.

Seeing beyond the headlines

In a court of law, you are innocent until proven guilty. But because it is so hard to get sampling right (and because so many surveys don't even try), numbers from surveys should be considered guilty until proven innocent. Here are three questions to ask of any statistic based on a sample survey:

1. HOW BIG IS THE SAMPLE?

Every number from a sample survey has a margin of error (uncertainty) around it. The smaller the sample size, the bigger the margin of error. Numbers from surveys of less than 1,000 people are pretty vague guesses. The only time this is not true is when the claim is being made about a small population of interest (e.g. if the claim is about Fortune 500 CEOs, then a sample of 1,000 is clearly a physical impossibility).

2. WHAT IS THE RISK OF SAMPLING BIAS?

Did the survey use a proper scientific (random probability) sample? Or was it filled out by a particular company's customers, or a self-selected sample of Twitter users, or some other group that is unlikely to represent the general population of interest?

3. WHAT IS THE RISK OF NON-RESPONSE BIAS?

Even if the sample is good, if only a small fraction of people replied (e.g. less than 20%), there's a good chance that they are not representative of the population of interest.

Example

CLAIM	HOW BIG IS THE SAMPLE?	WHAT IS THE RISK OF SAMPLING BIAS?	WHAT IS THE RISK OF NON-RESPONSE BIAS?	VERDICT
The average US wedding costs $32,641	18,000	HIGH: the sample comprised only customers of one wedding planning website.	Unknown. Response rate not given.	A biased sample means the number is unlikely to be an accurate estimate of what's going on in the population of interest.

 Exercises for Chapter 3

Exercise 1: Is it a good sample?

Pick a newspaper or magazine (online or in print). Read whichever articles interest you. Alternatively, just browse Twitter or Facebook. Keep reading until you find a statistic like the ones we've been discussing in this chapter ("one in five students think X", "the average score in a football game is Y", "More than 30 million people a year visit Z"). I guarantee it won't take long to find one.

Once you've found a statistic, see if you can answer the following questions:

1. Where does the statistic come from? Is it a piece of research that the author of the article has carried out themselves, or are they citing some research conducted by someone else?

2. Is the statistic something that is known precisely, or is it an estimate from a sample? If it's the former, how did the researchers manage to get information from every person or thing in the population of interest?

3. If, as is most likely, the statistic is an estimate from a sample:

   a. What is the population of interest?

   b. What is the sample size?

   c. Are there any important ways in which the sample is likely to differ from the population of interest? Think about sampling bias (who/what was selected to be in the sample? How were they selected?). If the statistic is based on a survey, also consider the possibility of non-response bias.

   d. If there are differences between the sample and the population of interest, how are they likely to affect the statistic? Do they mean that the statistic is likely to be too high or too low?

4. Taking all these questions into consideration, do you think the statistic tells us something useful about the real world? Or do you think it is bullshit?

Getting the information you need to answer these questions might require a bit of googling. Newspaper and magazine stories are (unfortunately) not in the habit of giving in-depth explanations of the methodology behind the statistics they quote. In many cases they don't even provide a link back to the original source of the number. If you're having trouble finding the original source of the statistic, try a search which combines (1) the name of the person or organisation who conducted the research (most articles do usually include this information), and (2) some key words from the claim itself.

Exercise 2: Surveying the headlines

Below are two real headlines based on statistics, along with some details about the research behind the numbers. Do you think these headlines are accurate or misleading? Give your reasons (on this book's companion website you can find the link to the original article, as well as the report and survey which the statistics are based on).

Headline 1: "Gays seven times more likely to take illegal drugs than the general population" – Daily Mail, 23 September 2012

- This story claims that 35% of gay people in Britain take illegal drugs compared with about 5% of the population.

- The 5% statistic for the general population comes from the Crime Survey for England and Wales. This is an annual survey carried out on behalf of the British government. This survey interviews around 50,000 randomly selected people in England and Wales.

- The 35% statistic for gay people comes from a survey conducted by the LGBT Foundation. They interviewed 4,000 gay and bisexual men and women. The majority (80%) of these people were recruited at Gay Pride events in English cities. The remainder were recruited through online and postal questionnaires distributed through LGBT organisations.

Headline 2: "Racism 'on the rise' in UK with 1 in 3 people admitting prejudice" – The Independent, 28 May 2014

- This story claims that nearly a third of people in Britain admit to being racist on some level.

- This statistic is based on the 2013 British Social Attitudes (BSA) Survey. This is a biennial survey which interviews around 3,000 randomly selected people in Britain.

- 30% of these 3,000 people said they would describe themselves as very or a little prejudiced against people of other races

---

www.macmillanihe.com/devries-critical-statistics
Go to the book's companion website for further examples, data, links, and other useful resources.

ONLINE RESOURCES AVAILABLE

---

4 MEASURE FOR MEASURE

Content warning: Readers should be aware that the first section of this chapter discusses differences between countries in rates of rape and sexual assault. These specific words are used frequently, and definitions of the concepts are discussed. However, the chapter does not contain any descriptions or discussion of specific incidents.

The dark side of immigration in open, generous Sweden

People on the left of the political spectrum often point to Sweden as something close to an ideal society. Sweden has high taxes, spends a lot on public services, and gives generously to people on welfare. And, on average, Swedes are healthier, happier, and better educated than almost any other population on earth.

Sweden has also proved itself to be open and generous when it comes to helping the victims of global crises. In the 1990s Sweden took in more than 100,000 people fleeing the conflict in the Balkans: a huge number for a country with a population only a little larger than London's. The recent wars in the Middle East have led to another refugee crisis; and again, Sweden has stepped up to do more than its fair share. However, this generosity appears to have had a steep price. Historically, Sweden has had relatively little serious crime. But over roughly the same period as the country was accepting increasing numbers of asylum seekers, rates of rape in Sweden skyrocketed. In 2004 there were 25 instances of rape for every 100,000 people in the country. By 2014 this figure had more than doubled to 65 per 100,000. In 2015 the rate declined a little, to 57 per 100,000. However, this still leaves Sweden with a higher rate of rape, not only than any other country in Europe, but *than any other country in the world* (with the sole exception of Botswana). This fact has not gone unnoticed by politicians and commentators who favour greater limits on immigration:

"In 2016 alone [Sweden] accepted more than 160,000 asylum seekers ... There was an absolute surge in gun violence and rape in Sweden once they began this open door policy" – Ami Horowitz on Fox News programme *Tucker Carlson Tonight,* 17 February 2017

"Sweden. They took in large numbers [of immigrants]. They're having problems like they never thought possible" – Donald Trump in a speech at Florida Rally, 18 February 2017[1]

"Sweden has taken more young male migrants than any other country in Europe. And there has been a dramatic rise in sexual crime in Sweden – so much so that Malmo is now the rape capital of Europe, and some argue, perhaps the rape capital of the world" – Nigel Farage on LBC Radio, 20 February 2017[2]

As we saw in Chapter 2, organisations with an axe to grind can very easily sell dodgy numbers to the media. And from there it's a short hop into the mouths of politicians and political activists. However, the Swedish rape figures do not come from some fly-by-night anti-immigration organisation. They come from the United Nations Office on Drugs and Crime (UNODC) – an official UN organisation responsible for helping member states coordinate their responses to crime.[3]

But just because the statistics come from an official source, it does not mean the numbers are saying what Trump, Farage, and others think they are saying. The key to this puzzle is that the figures I quoted above are from **police recorded offences**. That is, they are crimes people have reported to the police, which officers have then recorded in their files as rapes. There are several crucial factors which explain why Swedish police recorded many more incidents in 2015 than they did in 2004, and why they record far more incidents overall than police in other countries do:

- **Sweden has a broader legal definition of rape than many other countries**: Sweden's police record a wider spectrum of sex crimes as rape than police in other countries do. The legal definition of rape has also broadened several times over the period in question. For example, in 2005, the definition was broadened to include the sexual exploitation of people who were asleep, too intoxicated to consent, or in other vulnerable states. The police recorded rape rate consequently jumped from 25 per 100,000 in 2004 to 42 per 100,000 in 2005.

- **Swedish police record all incidents of rape separately**: Where perpetrators have committed multiple sex crimes against the same victim over a long period of time (for example, ongoing abuse against a spouse), each incident is recorded separately. In other countries, these incidents would tend to be grouped together as a single offence.

- **Swedish people may be more willing to report sex crimes to the police**: In many countries around the world, victims of sexual offences are hesitant to go to the police. The reporting process is often brutal, and police officers can be unsympathetic and dismissive. Sweden has higher levels of gender equality than many other countries. Trust in the police, and in public services more generally, is also higher. It is therefore plausible that Swedish victims are more likely to come forward after an offence than victims in other countries are. Research by the Swedish government suggests that willingness to report sex crimes has also increased dramatically in recent years.[4]

Together, these facts drastically change the interpretation of Sweden's relatively high rate of recorded rapes: the headline rate is measuring something fundamentally different in Sweden than it is in other countries. In the UNODC data, Sweden is counted as having 57 rapes per 100,000 people. India is counted as having 3 rapes per 100,000 people. This is not because a person in Sweden is more likely to be raped than a person in India. It's because the two countries are counting different things. Because the same words are being used, it seems like the numbers refer to the same thing, but they don't.

Anti-immigration commentators have made precisely the same mistake when interpreting high rates of criminal shootings in Malmo (Sweden's third largest city). Malmo has a smaller population than Stockholm or Gothenburg, but a far higher number of criminal shootings. In 2014 police recorded 89 shootings in Stockholm and 50 in Gothenburg. In Malmo, police recorded 122.[5] Malmo also happens to be a port city with a large population of immigrants and refugees. For many people, the natural explanation is that the influx of immigrants is driving an epidemic of violent crime.

However, once again, the difference in the number of shootings is almost entirely due to differences in what is being counted. In Stockholm and Gothenburg, police record an event as a 'shooting' in basically the way you would expect: someone has to have witnessed a gun being fired or there needs to be compelling forensic evidence that one was fired (a bullet found somewhere, gunpowder residue, and so on). In Malmo, police use a broader definition. Their figures include 'shootings' involving things that aren't guns; including bows, slingshots, and airsoft guns (toy air-powered guns that shoot pellets). They also have a lower threshold for forensic evidence. For example, a hole in a windowpane that looked like a bullet-hole might be counted as evidence that a shooting had taken place. Again, Malmo counts itself as having 122 shootings whereas Gothenburg counts itself as having 50 – but they are counting different things.

It is not my purpose here to take a position on immigration or the refugee crisis. You will have your own opinion about whether Sweden (or any other country) should seek to reduce levels of immigration, and on what constitutes an acceptable policy on refugees. However, arriving at an informed opinion requires the consideration of facts and evidence. And in this specific case, the evidence some have marshalled on the harms of immigration in Sweden is deeply misleading.

Define your terms

How you count things (and therefore the number you end up with) depends first and foremost on your **definition** of the thing you are counting. If you are trying to count shooting incidents, then a broader definition of what constitutes a 'shooting' (one that includes airsoft guns for example) will give you a bigger number than a narrower definition would. This sounds like an obvious point. But it's clearly not *that* obvious, because, as we've seen, people forget it all the time.

Before we start counting anything, we have to begin with a clear definition. This is true even for seemingly straightforward concepts. Think about this question:

"How many countries are there in the world?"

This seems like an almost childishly simple query. To answer it, we can just start looking around the world and counting. We know Spain is a country, so that's one. We know France is a country, so that's two. Japan is a country – that's three. And on we go …

… and after a while we hit a tricky one. Is Wales a country, or is the United Kingdom a country? Or maybe they're both countries, even though Wales is part of the UK? That doesn't sound right.

Is Palestine a country?

Is Taiwan?

The answer is that how many countries there are depends entirely on how you define a 'country'. You could define a country as a place with a permanent population, defined borders, and a government which has the ability to negotiate with other governments. By this definition there are probably more than 200 countries in the world. I say 'probably' because a lot of the terms in this definition are still debatable. For example, how do you strictly determine whether a government 'has the ability to negotiate with other governments'?

Another common way to define a country is simply to ask whether it is a member of the United Nations. This is a rough indicator of whether a country is recognised as such by other national governments (basically on the principal that you are a country if other people treat you like one). By this definition there are 195 countries in the world: 193 UN member states plus two 'observer states', Palestine and the Holy See (Vatican City). But this is obviously not a perfect measure of 'recognition by other states' because it includes places that other UN members *don't* recognise as legitimate countries. Japan and South Korea don't recognise North Korea as a country, for example.

This is a roundabout way of saying that it is impossible to count a thing without a clear definition of what that thing is, and that different definitions will mean you end up with different numbers. This is true not only for artificial, human things like countries, but also for things in the natural world, from plants to animals to planets. Consider the fact that if you were counting the planets in our solar system in 2004 you would probably have counted 9. If you were counting again in 2007 you might have counted 8. In 2017, you might count 9 again, or maybe 8 (or maybe 110). Nothing in the solar system has actually changed. Pluto didn't go whizzing off into deep space in 2006 (then maybe come back again in 2017 with 109 of its mates, ready to rough up the members of the International Astronomical Union). The only thing that changed is the popular definition of what makes something a planet.

The human, social world is messy. So is the natural world. Things don't naturally fit into tidy, discrete boxes. Objects in space exist on a continuum of different shapes, sizes, and orbital patterns. Populations have a kaleidoscope of different characteristics – of government, of population stability, of recognition by other states. Interactions between people can be measured on a range of different scales – of consent, of harm, of intent, and many others.

In order to start counting 'planets', or 'countries', or 'crimes', we need to start drawing clear lines and boxes on top of messy reality. We need to say 'Everything bigger than *this*, and rounder than *that* is a planet. Everything else is not a planet' or 'Everything conducted with a weapon that works *this* way is a shooting. Everything conducted with a weapon that works *that* way is not.' These lines and boxes are always going to be artificial in some way or another, but they are a necessary tool in helping us understand and communicate about the world.

Because the first step in counting anything is to define it, the first question to ask when confronted with any claim involving a number is 'how did they define that?'. This is true even if what they are counting sounds simple, like countries, or planets, or shootings (or households, or species, or students, or deaths in a war, or anything else).

Two is the loneliest number

Let's say we came across the following story about a piece of research on the effect of social media on young people:

> *"More than two hours of social media a day doubles your risk of feeling isolated ... Young adults who use social media feel more lonely, say psychologists"* – Daily Mirror, 6 March 2017

It's easy to feel like we understand the story, even from just this short quote. But without knowing exactly how each of the concepts it mentions was defined and measured, we're not getting anywhere near the full picture.

There are three key concepts at play in this story:

1) Young people

2) Social media

3) Social isolation (also described as 'loneliness')

The first one seems like the easiest, so we'll start there. The article explains that the study 'questioned 1,787 adults aged 19 to 32'. The upper end of this age bracket was a little older than I was expecting from 'young adult' (other newspapers that covered this story also used words like 'youths'). I'm 32 and it's been a while since I considered myself a 'young adult', let alone a 'youth'. Again, this shows how important it is to question the definitions of even seemingly simple concepts. Without checking, we might have gone away thinking the story was about teenagers, with their Snapchat selfies and cyberbullying; when actually most of the people in the study were of an age where their primary social media concern is that their Facebook feed is full of pictures of other people's babies.

The next concept is also seemingly straightforward: social media. It's probably safe to assume that Twitter, Facebook, Snapchat, and Instagram are included here, but after that it gets trickier. What about Reddit? Is that 'social media'? What about maintaining your own blog? Does that count? What about commenting on forums or under news articles?

The article explains that the study questioned adults 'about their use of the 11 most popular social media platforms at the time the research was conducted in 2014: Facebook, YouTube, Twitter, Google Plus, Instagram, Snapchat, Reddit, Tumblr, Pinterest, Vine and LinkedIn.' So Reddit *is* included, as is Google Plus (which, as far as I am aware, no human being has ever actually used), as is LinkedIn. The latter is perhaps a little surprising – given that it's a tool mainly used for business networking. But I suppose that *is* social, so I can see the argument for including it. For me, the most problematic inclusion here is YouTube. The article doesn't explain whether this only includes making your own videos, commenting on other people's, or otherwise participating in a YouTube community *or* whether it also includes simply watching videos. To me, watching two hours of music videos or video game Let's Plays doesn't really feel like 'using social media'.

This story originated with a press-release from the University of Pittsburgh, so I went back to see whether this explained the YouTube issue.[6] It did not. So I went to the original academic paper (published in the *American Journal of Preventative Medicine*).[7] The paper explains that participants were simply asked how much they used each site per day – meaning that simply watching YouTube videos *would* be counted as 'social media use'. You can decide for yourself if this changes your interpretation of the story.

Finally, we need to understand how the study defined 'feeling socially isolated'. The *Mirror*'s news article explains that the study used 'a standard technique called the Patient Reported Outcomes Measurement Information System (Promis)'. This is not much help unless you happen to be familiar with this particular tool. Going back to the original paper, we can see that this is a simple questionnaire made up of four questions. These questions ask respondents how frequently in the last seven days they felt 'left out', 'isolated from others', that 'people barely knew them', and that 'people were around them but not with them'. Participants answered on a scale from one (never) to five (always) and the scores were added up – higher scores mean more social isolation. The study defined people as socially isolated if their answers put them in the top third of scores. This seems basically reasonable to me – though, again, you can make up your own mind.

I'm not trying to say here that the specific definitions this study used were particularly bad (or particularly good). Just that in order to understand this seemingly simple story you need to understand (in a lot of detail) what those definitions were. The story that 'young people' who spend too much time on 'social media' are at twice the risk of being 'socially isolated' hangs entirely on how these three concepts are defined. Change any of the definitions and the story might change dramatically. Change 'young people' to mean 15–21 year olds and maybe social media would be beneficial. Or maybe it would be even more harmful – we don't know. Change the definition of social media to one that did not include watching YouTube videos or hustling on LinkedIn, and maybe the outcome changes again. Change the measure of social isolation – for example, to one which captured how frequently you saw people in real life, and maybe everything changes yet again. Only when we're given all the relevant information can we make up our own minds about what a story means and what it doesn't mean.

How to lie with definitions

Once you realise that there are many different ways of defining even quite simple concepts, and that different definitions can produce very different stories, this opens the door to a lot of mischief. Let's say you are a politician in America who is in favour of greater regulation on gun ownership. You want to highlight the damage guns do to American society, so you turn to statistics on the number of people who are shot each year. Here is Democratic Senator Tammy Baldwin doing exactly this in a tweet in January 2015 (Figure 4.1):

Sen. Tammy Baldwin @ @SenatorBaldwin · 24 Jan 2016
Over 32,000 people die from #GunViolence every year. Yet, @CDCgov is banned from researching ways to prevent this. baldwin.senate.gov/press-releases...

♡ 3   ⟲ 19   ♡ 9   ✉

Figure 4.1 Screenshot captured from @SenatorBaldwin Twitter feed

This number is accurate to the average number of gun deaths recorded by the US Centres for Disease Control (who source the data from death certificates). However, only *one-third* of these 32,000 deaths are due to homicide. The other 21,000 are mostly suicides (along with some accidents). Some of the power of Senator Baldwin's statement relies on the fact that a technical definition of gun violence differs markedly from what most people will understand the words 'gun violence' to mean. When I hear that 32,000 people die from 'gun violence' each year, I interpret that to mean that every year 32,000 people are purposefully shot by other people. I do not interpret it to mean that around 11,000 are shot by other people, and 21,000 commit suicide using a gun.* The key here is the difference between the natural interpretation (violence means gun murders) and the speaker's definition (violence includes suicides).

Once you start noticing this trick, you will see it everywhere. For example, here is former UK Education Secretary, Nicky Morgan, criticising the previous government's record on education on the floor of the House of Commons:

> *"If the shadow Secretary of State wants to see a failure to prepare young people for the life of work, he ought to be thinking about the fact that under the previous Labour Government* **one in three of our young people were leaving primary school unable to read and write.** *That is a shocking statistic."* – Nicky Morgan MP, House of Commons Oral Answers, 10 December 2014 (my emphasis)

A shocking statistic indeed. But only if you fail to recognise that Morgan's definition of 'unable to read and write' is quite different from the common-sense definition.

In the English school system, at the end of primary school (ages 10–11) children's reading, writing, and maths skills are given a 'Level' from one (the worst) to five (the best).** In 2010 (the end of Labour government to which Morgan is referring), 64% of children reached Level 4 in all three areas.

---

*   This is of course not to say that gun suicides are unimportant, or that the stricter gun laws Senator Baldwin advocates would not help to prevent some of these deaths (there is good evidence that they would).

**   These assessments were changed slightly in 2015, so the system now works a little differently. However, this was after Morgan made her claim.

By Morgan's definition, the 36% of children who didn't reach Level 4 across the board were 'unable to read and write'. This is where her 'one in three' figure comes from. You'll note that this includes children who reached Level 4 in reading and writing, but not in maths. However, even setting this aside,* the 'one in three' also includes children who didn't get to Level 4 in reading or writing, but *did* get to Level 3. To reach Level 3 these children had to be able to 'read a range of texts fluently and accurately' and 'make inferences from references in the text'. In other words, they had to be able to read a piece of text and then correctly answer questions about what it meant. By the definition Morgan – the person ultimately in charge of the English education system – is using, these children are 'unable to read and write'. Does this match your interpretation of what being 'unable to read and write' means?

By using a private, technical definition of 'unable to read and write' Morgan has been able to arrive at a much bigger number than would have been possible had she used any common-sense definition of this concept. Conveniently, this number makes it seem as if the previous Labour government left the country with an epidemic of illiteracy that her party's government must now clean up.

This is a trick politicians, journalists, and political activists have been using since time immemorial. In the 1950s Darrel Huff gave this facetious advice to would-be bullshit artists in his seminal book, *How to Lie with Statistics*:

> *"If you can't prove what you want to prove, demonstrate something else and pretend they are the same thing."*

If you can't prove that there are 30,000 gun murders a year, then prove that there are 30,000 gun *deaths* – then pretend they are same thing. If you can't prove that one-third of 10 year olds are illiterate, then prove that one-third do not reach a specific level in a test – then pretend they are the same thing.

George Orwell explained this succinctly a decade earlier in *Politics and the English Language*:

> *"Words of this kind are often used in a consciously dishonest way. That is, the person who uses them has his own private definition, but allows his hearer to think he means something quite different"*

The beauty of this method of deceiving the public is that, by your private definition, the statement you are making is *technically* accurate. If you are accused of lying, you can simply cite your definition (which you

---

* Morgan later said she misspoke and had meant to say 'unable to read, write, and add-up'.

never made clear) and watch the argument descend into a technical discussion which no one but diehard fact-checkers will follow. This is what makes the trick so appealing to anyone with a message to sell. In fact, we've already seen at least two examples of it in previous chapters:

- *The Sun*'s story on British Muslims' 'sympathy for Jihadis': If you can't prove that one in five British Muslims are sympathetic to ISIS (what you want people to hear), prove that they have sympathy for young, brainwashed recruits (your private definition).

- The Centre for the Study of Global Christianity's statistic on Christians martyrs: If you can't prove that 90,000 Christians a year are killed because of their religion (what you want people to hear), prove that 90,000 Christians die prematurely for some reason that could be loosely linked to their faith (your private definition).

We don't let people get away with this in real life. If your housemate Jane said that she had cleaned the flat, only for you to discover that her private definition of 'cleaned' was that she had moved a solitary beer can from the floor to the bin, you would probably be a bit peeved. Jane is fully aware that the message most people would take away from the statement 'I have cleaned the flat' is that the flat had, in fact, been cleaned. Not that some event had occurred which could be described, under certain technical definitions, as cleaning. However, politicians (and the rest) know that, as soon as statistics enter the picture, people's brains start to work differently. Change 'I have cleaned the flat' to 'Our government has cut child poverty in half' and all of a sudden people are less likely to notice that your definition of child poverty is very different to theirs.

Counting is hard

What if we are not interested in petty point-scoring? What if we are genuinely interested in discovering something useful about the real world?

In that case, *before we do anything else*, we need to come up with a clear, specific definition of the thing we want to find out about. If we want to find out about childhood illiteracy, then we need to define what we mean by 'illiterate'. If we want to find out about support for Islamist terrorism, then we need to define what 'support' means (and what we mean by 'Islamist' and 'terrorism').

Our next step is to come up with a measurement that matches this definition as closely as possible. If we are using a survey, then our survey questions should unambiguously target the concept we are trying to measure. In other words, if we are interested in support for ISIS, then we should ask about that, not about general sympathy for young people leaving to fight in Syria. This also applies when we are using pre-existing surveys. If we are interested in Christian martyrdom, then we should use a measure that specifically counts only Christians who were killed because they were Christians, not one that includes almost any Christian killed for any reason.

If I've made this sound easy, it's not. While being open and honest about what you're trying to measure (and how you're measuring it) is a lot easier than some people make it seem, actually coming up with good measures can be very difficult. Even with the best intentions, we are limited by practical realities – finite deadlines and budgets, people's willingness to answer questions truthfully, the nature of the data other people have collected, and so on.

To see this in action, let's think about how we would try to answer a perennial political question: to what extent is racial discrimination still a problem in American society?

Is racism a thing of the past?

Polls typically find that more than a third of white Americans think racial discrimination against black people is no longer a serious problem. Those who take this position often cite the election of Barack Obama as evidence that the USA has left its racist past behind. Some even argue that it is white Americans (and particularly white men) who now suffer the most discrimination – passed over for jobs in favour of minority candidates, denigrated online as the source of all the world's problems.

Depending on your perspective, the last paragraph will either have struck a chord, or it will have left you incredulous that anyone can still believe this stuff. But we don't have to settle for our gut feelings on issues like this. Discrimination is a real thing that happens in the world, and that means we can try to measure it – we can try to count up and compare how often black and white Americans experience discrimination in their day-to-day lives. This turns the political question of discrimination into an <u>empirical</u> one.

We'll start by defining what we mean by discrimination. We'll say that discrimination has occurred when someone has been treated in an inferior way *because they belong to a particular social group* (according to their race, religious belief, gender, sexuality, social class background, and so on). We could debate whether this definition is too broad (or too narrow), but to me this seems reasonable enough.

Now we need a way to measure discrimination in the real world. One possibility would be to follow a large sample of black and white Americans over the course of their lives, perhaps using hidden cameras. We could observe their interactions with others for signs of being treated in an inferior way because of their race. To do this we would probably need to hire a panel of experts to review the footage and make determinations (using clear, specific criteria) about when a discriminatory interaction had occurred.

Unfortunately this is where our ideal methods come face-to-face with inconvenient reality. A study like this would be almost impossible to conduct in the real world. Following a large enough sample of people for long enough would require ridiculous amounts of time and money. And any sort of covert surveillance would involve an unethical invasion of thousands of people's privacy.

The alternative, as is so often the case in social science, is a survey. Rather than follow people around for years on end, looking for signs of discrimination, we can simply ask them about their experiences. Several large US surveys include a question specifically designed to measure this. Below is a version from the US National Longitudinal Study of Adolescent to Adult Health ('Add Health' for short):

In your day to day life, how often do you feel you have been treated with less respect or courtesy than other people?

1. Never

2. Rarely

3. Sometimes

4. Often

In the absence of infinite time and money, this is the sort of survey measure we might use to try to compare the numbers of black versus white Americans who had experienced discrimination. However, you can see that the question is not ideal for this purpose. Crucially, *it relies entirely on the perceptions of the respondent themselves.* This has a couple of important consequences. First, any unnoticed instances of discrimination will not be recorded. This is important because a lot of discrimination is effectively invisible to the person being discriminated against. Let's say that a black family are looking for an apartment to rent. They are told by a building supervisor that there are no vacant units in her building. Unless they directly witness a white family being told something different, how are they to know that they have been discriminated against?

A subjective question like this also puts the work of definition entirely in the hands of the survey respondent. We (the researchers) might have a very clear idea of what we mean by discrimination, and how this is reflected in being treated with 'less respect or courtesy than other people'. However, respondents might have very different ideas. Some may interpret this in the way we intend – and only count instances where they have experienced inferior treatment due to their race, religion, etc. Others might count the times people have cut ahead of them in line at the store as an example of being treated with 'less respect or courtesy'.

These issues have a profound effect on how we interpret the numbers we get back. For example, in 2017 a group of American academics examined the data from the 2008 Add Health survey (this survey covered a nationally representative sample of about 15,000 people between the ages of 24 and 32). They found that 5.4% of black respondents said they were 'often' treated with 'less respect or courtesy than others'.[8] The figure for white respondents was very similar at 4.1%. Around a third of both black and white respondents said that they never experienced this sort of treatment.

It is tempting to interpret this as meaning that, in modern America, black and white people experience roughly the same amount of discrimination. In fact, a quick Google search will show you that many people have drawn this exact conclusion – with some citing the Add Health statistics as evidence that the problem of anti-black racism is drastically overblown. However, as we have seen, the survey question does not measure 'experience of discrimination' directly. Even if we are careful to describe the results as referring to 'perceived discrimination', we are not addressing the fact that people may not be interpreting the question as referring to the sort of discrimination we mean. A hint that this might be the case comes from a follow-up question in the survey which asks about the reason people thought they had been 'treated with less respect or courtesy'. Respondents were given nine possible options to choose from: Race/Ancestry/Skin Colour, Gender, Age, Religion, Height or Weight, Sexual Orientation, Education or Income, and Physical Disability. If people thought that none of these reasons applied, they could select an 'other' option. *More than half of all respondents* (58%) selected the 'other' option. This is a good indication that people were not necessarily equating 'less respect or courtesy' with the sort of discrimination we have been discussing.

In this example we didn't set out to deceive anyone. We had an important question and we tried to answer it using a fairly standard method (a sample survey). But measuring social factors (like discrimination) is hard. We often don't know whether the measure we've chosen is actually tapping into the thing we set out to investigate. This is why, when someone tells us that they have measured something human and social, like discrimination, or loneliness, or job satisfaction we have to think carefully about exactly how they measured it.

Asking the right questions

So far, we've established that when you are trying to count something, the number you end up with depends very strongly on how that something is defined and measured. This is something to keep in the front of our minds whenever we encounter a statistical claim. To make this easier, we can boil it down to a set of three questions:

1. What concept do the people making the claim say (or imply) is being measured? How is that concept defined?

2. What was actually measured in the real world?

3. Does it seem like what was measured in the real world actually matches up with the concept in question? (This question addresses an issue called <u>validity</u>, which is discussed in more detail in the box on 'Validity and reliability' below.)

Here is an example we can practise on:

> *"There are about 160,000 children that miss school every day out of fear of being bullied"* – bullyingstatistics.org

This quote is from the US anti-bullying website Bullying Statistics. The same statistic appears in a number of sources:

> *"Approximately 160,000 teens reportedly skip school every day because they are bullied"* – NOBullying.com

> *"Some 160,000 students stay home from school each day because of bullying"* – The National Education Association

> *"It is estimated that 160,000 children miss school every day due to fear of attack or intimidation by other students"* – Business Insider, 7 October 2013

So let's go through the questions in turn.

It's pretty clear that the concept they are measuring is 'skipping school due to bullying'. NoBullying.com (which bills itself as the 'World's Authority on Bullying') provides a definition of what bullying means:

> *"Bullying is present when there is a use of force or pressure in order to abuse or intimidate others … The definition of bullying is an undesirable, aggressive conduct among children that includes a real or perceived power imbalance and the behaviour is being or has been repeated over a period of time"*

This seems a little cumbersome, but otherwise reasonable. So the next step is to see how this was measured in order to reach the '160,000 children' figure. Working this out actually took a bit of sleuthing (which, if you are interested, you can read about in the box titled 'Tracking down the source of the "160,000" figure' below). However, to cut a long story short, the figure appears to come from a CDC (Centers for Disease Control) study called the Youth Risk Behavior Survey.[9] Looking through the questions asked in the survey, there appears to be only one question that could be interpreted as a measure of bullying:

During the past 30 days, on how many days did you not go to school because you felt you would be unsafe at school or on your way to or from school?

A. *0 days*

B. *1 day*

C. *2 or 3 days*

D. *4 or 5 days*

E. *6 or more days*

This is the most plausible source of the '160,000 miss school due to bullying' statistic.*

Tracking down the source of the '160,000' figure

None of the outlets I quoted above made it particularly clear where they got the '160,000 children' statistic from. NoBullying.com does not provide a source for the number. The *Business Insider* story (titled '11 Staggering Facts About Bullying in America') claims that their statistics come from a variety of sources, including 'the National Education Association (NEA), PACER Center, and Make Beats Not Beatdowns'. Unhelpfully, they do not specify which statistics come from which source. However, given that the NEA have themselves cited the statistic, they seem to be the most likely candidate (the NEA is the professional union representing American public school teachers).

A search of the NEA website yields a press-release which cites the statistic. The text contains a link which leads to the homepage of a website called bullyfree.com. This appears to be a service providing bullying resources for teachers, all of which are unfortunately hidden behind a registration page.

At this point I felt like I was going round in circles. So I went back to the first quote, from BullyingStatistics.org. They cite the 160,000 figure as coming from an ABC News story about a boy in Ohio who sadly committed suicide due to bullying. And it's this ABC story that finally got me somewhere. ABC report the statistic as having come from the National Youth Violence Prevention Resource Center (established by the CDC).

---

* A 2011 investigation by PolitiFact also identified the same source for this number.

They do not provide a link to a specific website or name a specific study (it's at this point that I begin banging my head on my desk), but this at least gives me something to go on.

A search of the CDC website does not yield a mention of the 160,000 figure specifically. However, the CDC do provide a number of other statistics, which all seem to be sourced from a survey called the Youth Risk Behavior Surveillance system. Luckily, the CDC provide a service by which you can directly examine the data from this survey online, and this, finally, is how I find the relevant question. Phew!

Now we can turn to the most important question: Does it seem like this survey question really taps into the concept of 'staying home due to bullying'? You can make up your own mind, but for me the answer is no. The crucial problem is that the question *does not mention bullying* – it only mentions the broader concept of 'feeling unsafe'. There are many reasons why students might feel unsafe at school (or on their way to or from school) that do not involve bullying. Perhaps they live in a dangerous area, or need to cross a busy road to get to school. Perhaps at school they are forced to play a physical sport (like rugby or American football), and they are worried about getting hurt. Just as in the examples from the beginning of the chapter, a broader measure (generally feeling unsafe) is likely to yield a higher number than one which focuses specifically on bullying.

By answering these three simple questions, we can see that the 160,000 figure doesn't necessarily mean what it seems to mean. And we can follow the same procedure to see behind any statistical claim, whether it's about gun deaths, discrimination, illiteracy, terrorism, or any other subject you can think of.

Validity and reliability

Validity is the technical term social scientists use to describe exactly what we've been talking about in this chapter – how well your measurement (for example, a survey question you've written) maps onto the concept you are trying to measure. A measure that does a good job of getting at the underlying concept you are studying has high validity. A measure that does a bad job (such as the bullying example above) has low validity.

There are a few ways to determine the validity of a particular measure. Let's take the concrete example of the 'PROMIS' measure we discussed at the beginning of the chapter. This comprised a series of four survey questions intended to capture social isolation. The questions were as follows:

How often, in the last seven days, did you feel the following:

I feel left out (1. Never 2. Rarely 3. Sometimes 4. Often 5. Always)

I feel that people barely know me (1. Never 2. Rarely 3. Sometimes 4. Often 5. Always)

I feel isolated from others (1. Never 2. Rarely 3. Sometimes 4. Often 5. Always)

I feel that people are around me but not with me (1. Never 2. Rarely 3. Sometimes 4. Often 5. Always)

Scores from each question are added up and can therefore range from 4 to 20, with higher numbers indicating a greater degree of social isolation.

The first way we can try to assess the validity of this measure is just by looking at it and using our own judgement. Do these questions seem to get at the concept of 'social isolation'? To me it seems like they do. I feel like someone who answered 'often' or 'always' to these questions would have to be very socially isolated; whereas someone who answered 'rarely' or 'never' would have to have a decent connection with other people. This process of looking at the measure and seeing if it makes sense on its face is called **face validity**. It relies on your subjective judgement, so it's not particularly scientific. However, it is an important first step (and you can improve on it by, for example, asking for other people's opinions as well).

As part of this process we can also examine the measure's **content validity**. Does the measure capture all the facets of social isolation, or does it miss some? Could someone score low on this measure but actually be socially isolated in other ways? Could they score high but actually be socially integrated in other ways? For example, this measure does not include any specific questions on relationships with significant others (for example, parents, or a spouse or partner). This is a potentially important element of social isolation that this measure doesn't capture.

The next thing we can do to evaluate this measure is to look at its **predictive validity**. Do scores on this social isolation scale predict things we would expect social isolation to predict? For example, we would probably expect socially isolated people to be less physically healthy. If we looked and found that people who scored high on the measure were actually just as healthy as people who scored low, we might start to wonder if our measure was really capturing social isolation.

Next we can look at the extent to which our measure is correlated with similar measures of the same concept. This is called **convergent validity**. In this case, we would look at the correlation between scores on our measure of social isolation and scores on other measures of social isolation that already exist. If people who score high on our measure also tend to score high on these other measures, this suggests that the measures are getting at the same thing.

Finally, we can look at the opposite of convergent validity – **discriminant validity**. Here we look at the correlation between our measure and measures of distinct but related concepts. In this case, we are trying to measure social isolation. This is a distinct concept from, for example, depression. We would expect some relationship between the two – we would expect socially isolated people to be more depressed. However, we don't want the correlation to be too high. If everyone who scores high on our social isolation scale is depressed, and everyone who scores low is not depressed, then our scale is not usefully measuring social isolation as distinct from depression.

* * *

In addition to validity, the other main test of a good measure is reliability. This is not about whether you are measuring the right thing so much as whether you are able to measure it *consistently*. If the thing you are measuring doesn't change, the score your measure gives you should not change either. Let's use the example of a set of weighing scales. If your weight stays the same, your scales should give you the same result every time you step on them. If they don't – if your scales tell you 70 kg on Monday, 85 kg on Tuesday, and 62 kg on Wednesday – then they are not measuring your weight *reliably*.

The same principle applies when measuring trickier concepts like social isolation. If our social isolation measure gave wildly different scores for the same person on different occasions, even if that person's circumstances had not changed much (they had not met or broken up with a partner, they'd not made or lost any friends), this would suggest it was not very reliable. Perhaps the way the questions were worded made it too susceptible to temporary changes in mood.

Reliability and validity are distinct concepts. It is possible for a measure to be highly reliable while also being utterly invalid. For example, you could decide to measure someone's sporting ability by measuring the length of their arms. This measure would be extremely reliable – you'd get the same results back every time – but this wouldn't make it valid.

Let's consider an alternative scenario. Having abandoned your arm-length measure of sporting prowess you decide on a more sensible approach. You develop a task intended to tap into manual dexterity and hand–eye coordination (good face validity). To examine whether this measure is reliable you administer it to the same group of people every day for a week. However, you find that people's scores on the task differ wildly from day to day, indicating low reliability. Given that reliability and validity can be examined separately, it's tempting to think that the measure could still be valid, if not reliable (you could still be measuring the right thing, just not very consistently). However, this actually can't be true. If scores on your task fluctuate this much – if your score today tells you nothing about what tomorrow's score will be – it can't be measuring *anything* very well, let alone the concept you are interested in.

* * *

In summary:

- **Unreliable** and **invalid** = inconsistently measuring the wrong thing
- **Reliable** and **invalid** = consistently measuring the wrong thing
- **Unreliable** and **valid** = can't happen
- **Reliable** and **valid** = consistently measuring the right thing

There's no such thing as a perfect statistic

At the beginning of this chapter I pointed out that even seemingly simple and straightforward concepts like 'planets' and 'shootings' can be harder to define and measure than we might think. Many of the things that social scientists care about (and that we as citizens care about too) are neither simple nor straightforward. We care about messy, human things like crime, the economy, people's health, attitudes, personalities, and beliefs. Because we care about these things, we want to count and measure them. We want numbers to tell us how well the economy is doing, how scared we should be of violent crime, or how much our diet increases our risk of heart disease. The media are keen to give us answers to these questions. However, while doing so they tend to conceal how difficult these things are to actually measure. They will report that 'A quarter of teenage girls are clinically depressed' but they won't tell you how this was measured, or discuss how the measurement affects the story. They will tell you that 'The number of lonely people has doubled in 20 years', but they won't explain all the guesswork and shortcuts that went into measuring loneliness. You will be left with the impression that counting cases of depression or loneliness is as easy as counting apples or bottles of beer.

Behind every seemingly clean, solid number is the blurry mess that is the real world. And between the real world and the number on the page there are researchers, journalists, politicians, and marketers making subjective, human decisions about how best to squeeze fuzzy reality into neat boxes that can be counted – how to define concepts, word survey questions, and assemble scales. If we forget this and treat the numbers as telling a clear and unambiguous story about reality, then we are apt to be deceived. Because all these human decisions and caveats are not just technical details. Change any one of them and, as we've seen, you can change the story dramatically.

One last example to illustrate the point. During her 2016 election campaign, Hillary Clinton famously said that 'to just be grossly generalistic, you could put half of Trump's supporters into what I call the basket of deplorables'. According to Clinton, half of Trump's supporters were essentially bigots: 'racist, sexist, homophobic, xenophobic, Islamophobic – you name it.' Her comments received widespread criticism. However, writing in *The Atlantic*, journalist Ta-Nehisi Coates came to Clinton's defence.[10] He pointed out that what had devolved in a political slanging match about whether Hillary Clinton was the real bigot, was actually amenable to the application of data. Clinton had claimed that 50% of Trump supporters (and by extension, large swathes of the American public) were bigots. So what did the data say? Coates pointed to a poll showing that 59% of Trump supporters thought that Obama was not born in the USA, and to another, larger poll showing that 'nearly half of Trump supporters described African Americans as more "violent" than whites, while 40% described them as more "lazy" than whites'.[11] If you consider these to be good measures of bigotry (and in the absence of knowledge of sampling issues) then Hillary Clinton was punished for merely speaking the truth. However, if you change the way in which you measure bigotry then the number will change as well. For example, data from the 2016 US General Social Survey suggests that, while a worryingly large proportion of Republican voters (around 36%) are willing to describe black people as lazy, a considerably smaller number (around 13%) are willing to describe blacks as unintelligent, and a smaller number still (around 10%) are willing to say that differences between blacks and whites are due to an 'inborn disability'. You may say that the latter are too strict as measures of bigotry in this case (and I would tend to agree). However, this shows how changing how we count 'bigots' can dramatically change our answer to a very important political question.

The message of this chapter is not that there is a perfect measure for any given concept, and that we should be critical of any measure that fails to reach perfection. The unfortunate fact is that there are no perfect measures, especially of messy human concepts like bigotry and loneliness. The best we can do is evaluate whether a measure is good enough to support the claim in front of us (and we've gone through some examples of this process). This judgement might change depending on the context: a measure of racism that works for evaluating the motivations of Trump supporters might not work in a court of law. A definition of gun deaths that includes suicide might be useful in conversations around public health, but not in debates about violent crime. It's up to us to make a judgement in each case. Which means it's also up to the purveyors of statistics – the politicians, researchers, journalists, and marketers – to give us the information we need to *render* that judgement: to be fully up front and open with us about what was measured and how.

Summary

To count something, you have to define it. Before you can count countries you have to precisely specify the boundaries of what is and isn't a country. The same is true for planets, crimes, and anything else you might want to count.

Different definitions produce different numbers. By one definition of 'planet' there are 8 planets in the solar system. By another definition there are 120. Don't assume that the person making a claim is using the same definition as you, even for familiar concepts.

The measure should match the concept. For a statistic to tell us something useful about, for example, racial discrimination, it should be based on a measure which clearly and unambiguously targets this concept.

There are no perfect measures. There is no single perfect measure for any given concept: there is no measure of bigotry or gun crime or loneliness that is ideal for all times and all contexts. Statistical claims should be evaluated on a case-by-case basis. Does the measure support the specific claim being made?

Terminology used in this chapter

Empirical: Research is empirical if it is based on data collected in the real world rather than, for example, pure theory or logical deduction.

Validity: The extent to which a measure measures what it is supposed to measure.

Reliability: The extent to which a measure measures the same thing consistently.

Seeing beyond the headlines

At the end of this chapter, I laid out three questions to help identify when a dodgy definition or measurement has produced a misleading statistic. Here are those questions again in table form, with two of the examples from the chapter filled in:

CLAIM	WHAT CONCEPT IS BEING MEASURED?	HOW HAS IT BEEN DEFINED AND MEASURED?	VERDICT: DOES THE MEASURE MATCH THE CONCEPT?
32,000 people die from gun violence every year	Deaths from gun violence	Count of all deaths from gunshot wounds, including homicides, suicides, & accidents. From death certificates	No – measure broader than concept
160,000 children miss school due to fear of bullying	Missing school due to fear of bullying	Answered more than 0 to Q: "During the past 30 days, on how many days did you not go to school because you felt you would be unsafe at school or on your way to or from school?"	No – measure broader than concept

Exercises for Chapter 4

Exercise 1

In 2015 the *Washington Post*'s *Wonkblog* published an article titled, 'The most racist places in America, according to Google'.[12] The article was based on an academic paper published in the journal *PLoS One*.[13]

The authors of this article measured racism in different geographical areas of the USA by looking at data on Google searches from 2004 to 2007. Their specific measure of racism was the proportion of Google searches that included the 'N-word' in singular or plural form. Colloquial spellings of the 'N-word' (i.e. those ending in '-a', rather than '-er'), were excluded.

1. Do you think that the prevalence of Google searches containing this word is a good measure of racism? If so, why? If not, why not?

2. Do you think that the Google search measure is a better measure of racism than a survey question which asks respondents if they have negative feelings towards African Americans? If so, why? If not, why not?

Exercise 2

You are working for a social research organisation. You are assigned to the following two projects:

1. Counting the total number of mass-shootings that have occurred in Europe and the USA over the last 50 years.

2. Counting the total number of homeless people living in your country of residence.

How would you:

1. Define an event as a mass-shooting?

2. Define someone as being currently homeless?

Search for definitions of these concepts that have been used previously by researchers and government agencies.

1. How do your definitions differ from theirs?

2. Which of the definitions you have found or come up with is likely to yield the largest/smallest final number?

---

www.macmillanihe.com/devries-critical-statistics

Go to the book's companion website for further examples, data, links, and other useful resources.

ONLINE RESOURCES AVAILABLE

---

5 WHAT DOES IT MEAN TO BE AVERAGE?

Average man

I learned about averages at school when I was around ten. I learned about the <u>mean</u> (add up all the numbers and divide by the number of numbers), the <u>median</u> (the man in the middle), and the <u>mode</u> (the most popular value). At the time, these were just terms I had to remember so I could answer questions on a test. I didn't really think about what an average was *for*. I also didn't stop to think that the concept of an 'average' was something that had to be invented. Someone had to be the first person ever to calculate an average. Who was it? And why did they do it?

We hear less about the origins of mathematical concepts than we do about other scientific advances. For example, I would bet that many more people have heard the story behind Darwin's theory of evolution than know anything about how Leibniz and Newton invented differential calculus. Partly this is because the journey of the HMS *Beagle* just makes for a more interesting narrative. But partly it's because mathematical insights aren't really the same as scientific discoveries. Evolution is something Darwin discovered about how the world works. Mathematical concepts like averages and calculus are more like tools people invented to help them do the discovering.

There is still a lot of disagreement about when the concept of the average was actually invented, and exactly what problem it was invented to solve. There are suggestions that some version of the average might have been used as far back as ancient Greece. However, people generally agree that prior to the 19th century the most prominent use of averages was in astronomy. Astronomy was the 'it' science in those days. The top astronomers got fancy royal titles and went to all the best parties, and countries couldn't show their face in polite society unless they had a really big telescope to wave around. A lot of inventions in mathematics and technology were therefore directed towards the problem of looking at faraway objects in space.

One of the things astronomers were interested in was measuring the speed of planets as they moved across the night sky. This helped them figure out their position and how they orbited the earth. To measure a planet's speed, they would mark two lines across the glass of their telescope, then use a stopwatch to time how long it took for the planet to move between the two lines. The problem was that the times they recorded varied not only due to the real speed of the thing they were measuring, but also due to the vagaries of human motor function and perception. Depending on how tired they were, or how much they'd drunk at their fancy party the night before, an astronomer could be faster or slower at starting and stopping the stopwatch.

The solution to this problem was to try to 'average out' the error. Let's say we are timing the movement of Venus between the two lines on our telescope. On the first try, we clock it at 3hrs 23m 3s. On the next attempt we make it 3hrs 22m 56s. On the third try we get 3hrs 23m 8s. We add up the figures and divide by three to get 3hrs 23m 2s. This is the mean average of our times, and it hopefully gives us a better idea of the actual speed of Venus. We still use the mean in this way today. Let's say someone is taking a statistics course at university. They take three tests over the course of the term. To get an idea of their statistical ability, we take the average of their three test scores. This average is likely to be a more accurate measure of their true ability than the score from any one particular test.

There is, however, another much more common way we use the average today. And for that we have to thank the 19th-century Belgian astronomer and mathematician Adolphe Quetelet. He saw the value of the mean average when measuring heavenly bodies, and he thought to apply it to a different problem – that of measuring and understanding *people*. Quetelet was fascinated by the idea of normality and abnormality in human beings. What was the 'normal' height or weight for someone to be? What was a 'normal' level of intelligence or moral rectitude? How tall or short, or bright or dull, or upright or dissolute did you have to be to be considered 'abnormal'? By answering these questions he hoped to investigate, and thereby potentially cure, the 'disease' of abnormality.*

Quetelet's first task was to work out 'what is normal'? Remarkably, before Quetelet embarked on his mission, no one had really tried to answer this question with actual data. You only have to look out onto a busy street to see that human beings are incredibly varied in hundreds of different ways. People thought there was no way you could pick a single height or weight or level of intelligence and say this was what was 'normal' or 'typical' for the population. This is kind of a tough idea to get your head around. We are so used to concepts like average height or BMI or income that it's hard to put yourself in the mind of someone who does not think this way. Kind of like how it's difficult to imagine not knowing what the earth looks like from space.

---

* A choice quote from him on the subject is 'If the average man were perfectly determined and defined, one could consider him the type (or model) of beauty, and, on the contrary, everything that instead of resembling his proportions or his way of being departed from them, would constitute deformities or diseases' (*A Treatise on Man and the Development of His Faculties*).

Quetelet's insight was that he could use the tools of astronomy – and specifically the mean average – to 'average out' all the variation between people and focus in on what was normal for a particular population. If he wanted to know the 'normal' weight for a professor at the Belgian Military School, where he taught, he could just add up all their weights and divide by the number of professors. People with weights higher than this mean average were abnormally heavy, and people with lower weights were abnormally light. Quetelet, perhaps understandably, did not actually start by measuring the weights of his colleagues. Instead he started with the chest circumference of Scottish soldiers. He considered the chest to be of particular importance in understanding people's health, and noted that the chest was also 'where the greatest malformations are most often to be observed'.

His research found that the average chest circumference of a Scottish soldier was 39¾ inches. This – more than a hundred years after the invention of calculus, and only a few decades before the invention of the lightbulb – was one of the first times anyone had *ever* calculated an average for any human characteristic.

After this groundbreaking start, Quetelet was unstoppable. He found averages for everything he could get his hands on: average height, average weight, the average age people got married, the average age people died, the average number of crimes committed by different age groups (young people commit more crimes – who knew?). He wrote up his theories and results in a book published in 1842 called *A Treatise on Man and the Development of His Faculties*.

Quetelet's findings kicked off a revolution in how we think about human populations. Rather than seeing an incomprehensible mess of variation – of tall people, short people, broad people, narrow people, smart people, stupid people – scientists could now use the average to identify trends and patterns. They could, for example, try to figure out what was 'normal' (in terms of physical or mental characteristics) for different groups of people: men and women, young and old, Scottish soldiers and Belgian professors.

And this is the way we predominantly use averages today: as a tool to provide a single number summarising some characteristic that varies in a population. A glance at the news media shows that we are voracious calculators of averages:

"The average American spends approximately $1,800 per year in online purchases" – Forbes, 25 October 2016

"The REAL cost of true love! The average person spends five years – and a whopping $20,200 – dating before deciding to settle down and get married" – Daily Mail, 14 March 2016

"The average student leaves university with £50,000 debt ... " – *Daily Telegraph*, 25 August 2017

"The average woman has sex for the first time aged 16 and will have eight sexual partners during her lifetime" – *Daily Mirror*, 17 July 2014

" ... around 100 different species of arthropod – the category that includes spiders, insects, centipedes, and mites – inhabit the average American home" – *Business Insider*, 19 January 2016

Quetelet would be proud.

The mean doesn't always mean what you think it means

Plucked from the mass of media stories about averages, here is one from 'gentleman's' magazine *GQ* (the magazine of choice for men who want to know which particular $15,000 watch will alleviate the crushing emptiness of their lives):

"US teenagers have an average of 150 [Instagram] followers. Among users generally, the average is somewhere north of 200" – *GQ* magazine, 1 November 2016

The natural way to read these numbers is exactly the way Quetelet himself would have done – 200 followers (or 150 if you are a teenager) is what a regular, normal Instagram user has. People who have more than 200 followers are abnormally popular. People who have less than 200 are abnormally unpopular.

Does this make you feel good or bad about your personal Instagram following? It should do neither – because even though we often use the mean to tell us what's 'normal' in a population, it's frequently a terrible tool for this purpose.

To understand why, let's shrink the Instagram example down to a more human scale. You and eight of your friends are comparing Instagram accounts. You have 60 followers. Riyadh and Andrew both have 12. Helen, Carina, and Jo have 41. Anthea and Malar both have 50, and Nik has 80. In your group, the mean average follower count is therefore 43 (60 + 12 + 12 + 41 + 41 + 41 + 50 + 50 + 80 = 387; divided by 9 = 43).

The next day you are walking around London and you bump into a familiar-looking dark-haired woman who seems lost. As you are helping her find her way, you realise, to your shock, that this woman is actually singer and actress Selena Gomez! Grateful for your assistance, and charmed by your sparkling personalities, she decides to spend the next few days of her trip hanging out with you all.

Now let's conduct the same exercise as we did before and work out the average number of Instagram followers in your now group of ten. Selena Gomez is the most followed Instagram user in the world, with a grand total (at the time of writing) of 128 million followers.* So now the sum looks like this:

$$\frac{60 + 12 + 12 + 41 + 41 + 41 + 50 + 50 + 80 + 128{,}000{,}000}{10}$$

This comes to a final figure of 12,800,038. Nothing has changed for the original nine members of your group. You are still scrubbing along with your tens of followers. However, adding Selena Gomez to the crew has made it so that the 'average member of your group' now has more than 12 million followers. This leaves you in a slightly odd situation: nine out of ten members of your group now have a 'below average' number of followers.

This is a particular problem with the mean average. Because of the way it is calculated, big, out-of-the-ordinary numbers like Selena's (in statistics these are called <u>outliers</u>) drag the average figure way up, so that it no longer represents what's 'normal' or 'typical' for most people. Of course, this can happen the opposite way too. If you'd met an unlucky soul with no followers at all, this would have dragged the group's average number of followers down (though not by such a crazy amount).

A good way of getting your head around how this works is to plot it out visually. Figure 5.1 is a chart showing the original situation with just you and your eight friends.

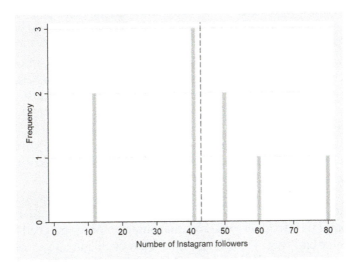

Figure 5.1 Histogram showing the distribution of Instagram followers in your group

---

* I say at the time of writing because her follower count went up by more than 400 in the time it took me to write this paragraph.

This chart is called a <u>histogram</u>.* The purpose of a histogram is to show how some quantity (in this case, Instagram followers) is <u>distributed</u> in a population (in this case, the population is your group of nine friends). Along the x-axis (the horizontal one) are groups of people defined by their number of followers. The value on the y-axis tells you the number of people in each group (this is called the 'frequency', because it tells you how 'frequent' each value is).

On top of the histogram I've added a dashed line showing the mean average number of followers in the group. As we already know, the mean is supposed to be an indication of the 'normal' number of followers. Another way of looking at it is that it gives you an idea of where the middle of the distribution is. This is why the mean (along with other types of average) is called a measure of <u>central tendency</u>. This is useful because it's difficult to hold all of the separate numbers together in your head at once. This becomes more and more true the bigger the group. In our tiny group of ten, we have some chance of simultaneously contemplating everyone's individual follower count. If we were talking about all Instagram users in the world, we would have no chance at all. This is why we need <u>summary statistics</u> like the mean average. They are single numbers that summarise something useful about a set of numbers too big to hold in our limited human brains (other examples of summary statistics include the highest and lowest values in the distribution).

We can see that, in the case of your group of nine, the mean is actually doing a pretty good job of pointing to the middle of the distribution. In other words, it's not a bad representation of what is a 'normal' number of followers in your group of friends. This is exactly as Adolphe Quetelet would have hoped.

Now imagine adding Selena Gomez to the chart. Her number of followers would be so far off the right of the plot that, if we kept to the same scale, we would need a piece of paper around 13,000 *kilometres* long to fit her in. That's more than half the length of the great wall of China. The line for the mean would be somewhere along the great expanse of empty space between your little huddle of bars on the far left, and Selena's bar on the far right. This line is most assuredly *not* a great representation of what is 'normal' in your group of nine-plus-Selena.

This is true even if we replace Ms Gomez with someone a little more realistic. Let's say that instead of Selena you bump into an actual friend, Anthony. His Instagram game is reasonably on point – some good brunch pics, some cute dogs – and he has 700 followers. Figure 5.2 is what the histogram would look like (again, with the mean plotted on top).

---

* The histogram was first introduced by English mathematician and statistician Karl Pearson. There is still some disagreement about why he called it a 'histogram'. One popular explanation is that it is from the Greek word 'histos', meaning mast or upright beam (as in a ship's mast). However, Karl himself didn't explain, so we may never know for sure.

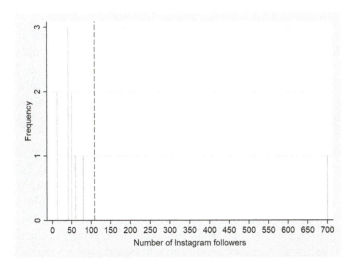

Figure 5.2 Histogram showing the distribution of Instagram followers in your group, plus Anthony

Again you can see that the mean average is doing a very bad job of representing the typical number of followers in your group. If we go by the mean, the average member of your group has 109 followers. However, just as in the Selena Gomez case, nine out of the ten of you have fewer followers than that.

Now we know why you shouldn't feel particularly bad if you have fewer than the average of 200 followers. The population of Instagram users includes a lot of regular people, but it also includes superstars like Gomez. Their massive follower counts are dragging the mean up, such that most people will end up 'below average'.*

Why doesn't everyone know this already?

The fact that the mean often does a poor job of representing 'the average' is actually pretty well known. In fact, the following is a famous joke among statisticians:

> "Bill Gates walks into a bar. Everyone cheers because, on average, they are all now millionaires."**

---

*   Of course the reverse might also be true. If the figures include, for example, thousands of bot accounts with zero followers, this would serve to drag the mean average down.

** After telling this joke in class, one of my students asked me who Bill Gates was. For my generation, Bill Gates, the founder of Microsoft, is the go-to reference for 'super rich guy'. But he left Microsoft in 2008. Most of my students were *nine* in 2008. I have never felt more like an old person.

Not a very funny joke, perhaps, but it illustrates the point.

Despite this problem being well known in the statistical community, the media nevertheless routinely treat the mean as a measure of what's 'normal' or 'typical'. We can see this in action if we go back to our wedding cost example from Chapter 3. If you cast your mind back, you'll remember that CNN pegged 'the average cost of a wedding' at an eye-watering $32,641. The claim was based on figures released by popular wedding planning website *The Knot*.

Almost all of the discussion around this figure treated it as evidence that the 'normal' cost of a wedding was more than $32,000. Even putting aside the problems with the sample (discussed in Chapter 3), this is clearly misleading. Spending on a wedding is one of those things which is likely to involve large outliers. There are people who spend truly vast amounts of money on their weddings. Add these people to the mix and you can see how the mean average would be dragged up above what is typical for the population.

Why, if the problems with the mean are so well known, did the articles covering this statistic all make the same mistake? And why do journalists and others keep making this mistake over and over again?

One obvious explanation is that the errors are intentional. The most common problem with the mean is for it to be much higher than what is really normal or typical. Bigger numbers often make for better headlines – so journalists might be choosing the mean intentionally, despite knowing it to be misleading. One can also see why a bigger number might be of interest to, say, a company which sells wedding planning services.

However, we should also allow for a more innocent explanation. As we've already discussed, few journalists (and politicians and marketers) have much in the way of statistical training. On reading a press-release which says, for example, that 'the average person spends £2,000 a year on online gambling' or whatever it might be, they may simply take the claim at face value. In regular English, the word average means 'normal', 'typical', or 'middle of the road' – he is average-looking, they grew up in an average neighbourhood, she earns an average salary – so that's the interpretation they go with. Even if they have an inkling that there might be something wrong, they probably don't have the time or the incentive to dig any deeper (for all the reasons we discussed in Chapter 2). After all, why wade into the statistics if the ultimate result would be to ruin a perfectly good headline?

The temptation to let well enough alone might be particularly strong when the natural (misleading) interpretation of the mean helps you score some points for your political team. This often rears its head in debates around tax – when supporters of one political party want you to think that the other party's plans will send your taxes through the roof. For example, during the 2017 UK General Election, the Labour leader,

Jeremy Corbyn, proposed a tax increase for people earning more than £80,000 a year. This increase would change the tax rate on incomes over £80,000 from 40% to 45%. It would also change the rate on incomes over £123,000 from 45% to 50%. Conservative newspaper the *Daily Telegraph* described the plans as 'the biggest tax raid the country has ever seen'. They noted that, for the 1.3 million people in the country earning more than £80,000 a year, the changes would mean 'an average [tax] increase of £5,300'.[1]

£5,300 sounds like a lot, even for people who are relatively well-off. But hopefully you are starting to see the problem here. Is £5,300 actually the *typical* amount by which taxes would rise for people earning more than £80,000? Or is there something else going on?

There are 1.3 million people in the UK who earn more than £80,000 a year (this is less than 3% of the total adult population). Of these 1.3 million people:

- 494,000 (38% of the 1.3 million) earn between £80,000 and £100,000 a year. This group would all see their taxes rise by less than £1,000 a year.

- Another 299,000 people (23%) earn between £100,000 and £123,000 a year. This group would see their taxes go up by less than £3,000 a year.

- Another 130,000 people (10%) earn between £123,000 and £150,000 a year. They would all see their taxes rise by less than £5,300 a year.

In total, this means that more than two-thirds of the 1.3 million people earning salaries of over £80,000 would pay less than the 'average' tax increase of £5,300. The reason for this is the same as in our Selena Gomez example. Extremely rich people, those with earnings in the seven figures, would see their taxes go up by *a lot*. The extra taxes paid by this group drag the average up above what most high-earners would be paying.

Once again, the mean average is not telling us much about what's 'normal' or 'typical' for a particular group of people. You can decide for yourselves if this was simply an oversight on the part of the *Telegraph* or a deliberate attempt to make Corbyn's tax policy look bad.*

The median: The mean's under-appreciated brother

We've established that, in many situations, the mean is bad at telling us what is normal or typical for a population. Luckily, we have an alternative waiting in the wings: the median. In a group of numbers, the

---

* Here I am talking about the print version of the article. To be fair to the *Telegraph*, they did provide a more detailed breakdown of the tax changes in the online version.

median is the middle one – the one with an equal number of values above and below it. The median has a much easier time dealing with outliers than the mean does. For example, the table below contains the numbers from our Instagram story (Table 5.1):

Table 5.1 Instagram followers per person in your group, plus Selena Gomez

	Instagram followers
You	60
Riyadh	12
Andrew	12
Helen	41
Carina	41
Jo	41
Anthea	50
Malar	50
Nik	80
Selena Gomez	128,000,000

As we discovered already, Selena's massive follower count drags the mean up into the millions. However, the median is not so strongly affected. It is simply the middle value – 41. Half of the people in the group have less than 41 followers, and half have more. This is much closer to what we would think of as the 'typical' number of followers in your group.

The median solves the same problem in real-world situations. For example, in 2012 the Canadian news magazine *Maclean's* published a story posing the eternal question 'How Canadian Are You?'.[2] They based their assessment of your Canadian-ness not on your consumption of maple syrup or your affection for trapper hats (look it up), but on how close your spending habits hewed to those of 'the average Canadian'. This is a surprisingly common genre of article, often trotted out by newspapers and magazines when they haven't got much else to write about. See for example:

"How average are you? What is the typical Brit like and how many people pick their nose?" – *Daily Mirror*, 17 July 2014

"Meet Mr Average Aussie who's 175.6 cm tall and weighs 85.9 kg – but how does he compare to Mr USA, Mr Japan, Mr Netherlands and Mr France?" – *The Daily Mail Australia*, 29 October 2014

"How Average Are You Actually? ... You probably fart nearly 10 times a day" – Buzzfeed, 5 October 2015

According to the data source cited in the *Maclean's* article,* the average Canadian apparently spends:

- $2,841 a year on clothes

- $504 on home entertainment equipment

- $905 on alcohol

- $155 on lottery tickets

- $120 on art and antiques

But these are mean averages. Let's see what happens if we use the median instead (Table 5.2):

Table 5.2 Average annual spending in Canada on various items

	Mean spending per year	Median spending per year
Clothes	$2,841	$1,880
Home entertainment equipment	$504	$120
Alcohol	$905	$360
Lottery tickets	$155	$25
Art & antiques	$120	$0

Source: 2009 Canadian Survey of Household Spending

In all of these cases the median is considerably lower than the mean. For example, according to the mean, 'the average Canadian' spends $2,841 on clothes. However, the median shows that half of Canadians spend less than $1,880 – a thousand dollars lower. Similarly, 50% of Canadians spend nothing at all on 'arts and antiques', but 'the average Canadian' spends $120. These are clear examples of where big spenders – the people who buy their clothes from Versace rather than Walmart, and who buy their antiques from somewhere rather than nowhere – are dragging up the mean. Consequently, the median is doing a much better job of telling us about the spending habits of 'ordinary' Canadians.

We can see the same thing in action if we again return to our wedding example. Back in 2013, tech journalist Will Oremus, of American

---

*   The 2009 Canadian Survey of Household Spending.

news magazine *Slate*, was suspicious of *The Knot*'s recently published wedding figures.[3] In 2012 they had put the average cost of a wedding at $27,427, and this figure had been dutifully repeated across the media (as it is every year), from *CNN* to the *New York Daily News* to the news agency *Reuters* (who, as Oremus pointed out, 'should know better').

Oremus immediately recognised the potential problem of the mean being dragged up by very expensive weddings, so he called up *The Knot* and asked them about it. They admitted that the *median* cost of a wedding in their survey was ... $18,086. Half of all the couples they sampled had weddings that were almost *ten thousand dollars* cheaper than the 'average wedding'. Here the median is doing a much better job of representing the typical cost of a wedding than the mean is.* Despite this, *The Knot* chose to publicise the higher number.**

So if the median is so great, why don't we use it all the time?

The unsatisfying answer is that we just got used to using the mean. When you are working with large sets of numbers, the median is more difficult to calculate by hand than the mean. So before everyone had supercomputers in their pockets, people used the mean for practical reasons. The mean became our default measure of the average, and, just like the QWERTY keyboard,*** we appear to be stuck with it due to a sort of cultural inertia.

This is not to say that the mean is entirely useless. There are (admittedly rare) occasions when the mean does a better job than the median of representing 'the average'.† What gets people in trouble is not 'using the mean when they should always be using the median' – it's not properly thinking through what they are trying to calculate. It's thinking

---

* Of course, this number is still likely to be an overestimate given the problems with the sample we discussed in Chapter 3.

** I implied earlier on that *The Knot* may have done this on purpose, in a cynical attempt to get people to spend more money on their site. However, when Oremus asked *The Knot* why they didn't publish both the mean and the median, their spokesperson defended the use of the mean by arguing that 'if the average cost in a given area is, let's say, $35,000, that's just it – an average. Half of couples spend less than the average and half spend more.' You may recognise this as the definition of the *median*, not the mean. *The Knot* is a $500 million company which publishes a statistical release every year, to blanket media coverage. On this evidence, their spokesperson does not know the difference between the mean and the median.

*** The QWERTY keyboard layout we all use today is harder to type with than it needs to be. For example, a lot of commonly used letter combinations are under your left hand. Try typing a normal sentence (maybe just copy this one out) and see how often you are just using your left hand. QWERTY evolved in the age of typewriters and no one quite knows why it's laid out as it is (the story that it was to slow typists down to avoid typewriters jamming is apparently a myth). And despite the fact that there are clearly better ways you could lay out a keyboard, everyone's just too used to QWERTY to switch.

† For example, when you have a small set of numbers a small change in one number can move the median quite a lot.

of statistics as a black box into which you insert data, and out of which emerges a number you can put in your newspaper. Using statistics effectively requires consideration of what a given statistic (a mean, a median, or any other figure) can actually tell you. If someone asked you to undo a screw, you wouldn't hit it with a hammer. You know what you want to achieve. You know what a hammer does. So you know that a hammer is not the right tool for the job. The same goes for statistics.

What is a 'distribution'?

Near the beginning of the chapter, I briefly mentioned the idea of a 'distribution': the histogram showed the 'distribution' of Instagram followers in your group of friends. 'Distributions' are an important idea in statistics, so it's worth spending a little more time explaining what they are. Fortunately, it's quite simple – and quite close to our plain language understanding of the term 'distribution'.

Imagine it's the day after Halloween, and you are giving out leftover sweets in your office. A total of 100 people work in your office, and you give each them a number of sweets depending on how much you like them. Sophie in sales gets 5, Mark in accounts gets 3, and Gary in tech support gets 0. The number of sweets each person has at the end of the process is the 'distribution' of sweets in this population.

Now imagine that instead of giving out sweets, you are measuring how much people weigh. In the same way we can talk about the distribution of sweets, we can also talk about the 'distribution' of weights – how many people there are at each point in the weight scale.

We could visualise this as a histogram (Figure 5.3).

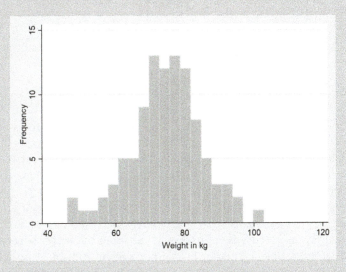

Figure 5.3 Histogram of a hypothetical distribution of weights

Exactly as in the Instagram example, each bar represents the number of people in each weight range. There are 12 people who weigh between 79kg and 82kg, and 6 people who weigh between 58kg and 61kg. In the parlance of histograms, these ranges are called 'bins'. The height of each bar tells you how many people are in each 'bin'.

One of the most immediately recognisable things about this graph is the shape. This shape – lots of people in the middle, fewer people at the edges – is called the <u>normal distribution</u>. It's called that because it applies to a lot of different things, from weight to intelligence to shoe size. To understand why this is so, consider the following example. Let's say I asked you and 99 other people to run a timed lap of 100m track. Which of the following do you predict would best represent the distribution of times? (Figure 5.4).

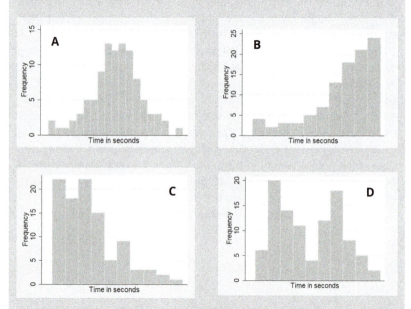

Figure 5.4 Histograms of possible distributions of 100m times

Personally, I would predict graph A. Graph D would suggest that around half of the sample are very fast, half are very slow, and very few are in the middle. Graphs B and C would predict that most people are either very slow or very fast, respectively. Graph A on the other hand shows that a few people are very fast, a few are very slow, but most people are somewhere in the middle. In this, as in the weight example and in many other situations, it makes sense that most people are in the middle and that there are progressively fewer people as you move out to the extremes.

If we measure something in the population and the distribution looks like this, we would say that it is 'normally distributed'. In this situation, both the mean and the median give you a good idea of central tendency – they are equally informative about what is 'typical' for the population. In the case of B and C, the mean would be too high or too low to be fully informative – and therefore the median would be better. However, in situation D the story is different. Graph D is the distribution you might see for customer ratings of a restaurant that only served Marmite, or of an Uber driver who sang showtunes. Some people would love it, some would hate it; very few people would be lukewarm. In this neither the mean nor the median would tell you anything particularly useful about what the 'typical' person thought.

Averages are not real

The real world is a messy complicated place. Too messy and too complicated, for our tiny human brains to understand in full. Take even something simple like height. I could conceivably hold the heights of maybe nine people together in my head at once (I don't mean remember, I mean keep in mind simultaneously). Maybe you could do better – but you probably couldn't manage 100. Certainly not 1,000. And definitely not the whole population. Our brains just can't work with this much raw data. Instead we have to *summarise*; to build a simplified picture of the real world. Fundamentally that's what all statistics are – simplified pictures (models) of a messy underlying reality. This includes averages, but also things like percentages and relative risks (which we'll be discussing in the next chapter). Just as an estate agent's floorplan is a simplified picture of your home, mean population height is a simplified picture of people's varying heights.

This process of summary and simplification is essential. We need to be able to think and talk about people's incomes, spending, heights, weights, IQs, and any number of other things. And the only way we can do this is by working with summaries. This is all perfectly fine (and necessary). It only becomes a problem when we forget we're working with summaries, and start to confuse the simple picture with real life.

You can see this mistake at its worst when people use statistics to make essentialist judgements about different groups of people. There are plenty of real examples, but for the sake of clarity we'll use an imaginary one. You are the captain of a starship on a search for new life, and new civilisations. You find an alien planet with two different sentient, humanoid species. Call them the Bingons and the Cromulans (hi Paramount, please don't sue me!).* You manage to learn their languages

---

* To preserve my geek cred, if I was talking about *Star Trek* (which, again, for the benefit of Paramount's lawyers, I'm definitely not) then I know the Klingons and the Romulans don't live on the same planet. Just go with me here.

well enough to administer some tests and you find that, on average, the Cromulans score a few points higher on IQ tests; whereas the Bingons score a few points higher on tests of aggressiveness. As a consequence, you start thinking of the Cromulans as 'the smart ones' and the Bingons as 'the aggressive ones'. By forgetting about the complexity of the underlying reality, you have started to engage in a sort of species essentialism.

Figure 5.5 is what the distribution of IQ scores among Bingons and Cromulans might look like.

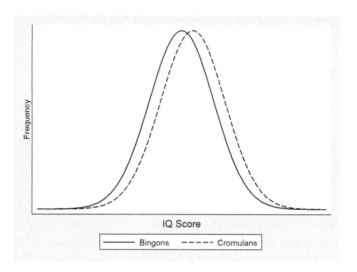

Figure 5.5 Histogram of hypothetical IQ distribution among Bingons and Cromulans

The averages here are indeed different, but there is a huge amount of overlap in the distribution of intelligence. The majority of both Bingons and Cromulans fall into the same range of intelligence. Another way of thinking about this is that if you picked a representative from each group at random, there's an almost 50:50 chance that the Bingon would be more intelligent than the Cromulan. Yet another way of thinking about it is that there is much more variation in intelligence *within* each group than there is between them. A focus on the averages alone – forgetting that averages are just *summaries* – conceals the extensive variation within groups, and the high degree of similarity between the groups.

You don't have to look far to see this kind of thinking going on in the real world. People are extremely quick to translate small differences in summary statistics into big theories about inherent differences between groups. This does not mean that statistical summaries are not useful (in fact they are vital). It just means you should never forget the messy real world hiding beneath the summary.

The mode

You might be wondering why I haven't mentioned the third type of average you typically learn about in school – the mode. The mode, in case you don't remember, is the most popular value in the distribution. In the case of the Instagram followers example, this would be 41 (three people have 41 followers – more than have any other individual value).

The reason I haven't devoted a section to the mode is because it's not really used that often, either in social science or in the media. There are benefits to the mode (it's sometimes helpful to know the most popular value). However, they are outweighed by the fact that it can very easily end up being a bad representation of the centre of a distribution. To see why this is the case, imagine you measure the heights of 50 people. Everyone in the sample has a slightly different height except the two very tallest people who happen to be the same height – 6'5". Is the mode a good representation of what's 'normal' for this group of people?

This problem means the mode is relegated to being a back-up player. You might use it in addition to the mean or the median, to give you some extra detail about whatever it is you are measuring, but you would never send it out there on its own.

 ## Summary

Averages are summaries of distributions. Averages are a tool for summarising a <u>distribution</u> of continuous values. They are a single number intended to give us an idea of the mid-point of the distribution.

The mean average is calculated by taking the sum total of all the numbers in a set and dividing it by the number of numbers in the set. It is strongly affected by <u>outliers</u>, and in the presence of outliers it is not a good measure of what is 'normal' or 'typical' in a population.

The median is the middle value in a set of numbers. 50% of the numbers in the set are below the median, and 50% are above. It is less affected by outliers than the mean, and is therefore often a better representation of what is normal or typical.

The mode is the most popular value in a set of numbers. It is rarely used because in many cases it is a bad representation of what is normal or typical.

Averages are not real. All averages are summaries that give us only a narrow view of what is going on in a given population. Don't forget the underlying variation.

Terminology used in this chapter

<u>Histogram</u>: A histogram is a type of chart. Each bar on the chart represents the number or proportion of entities (e.g. people) that fall within a given range on some measured quantity (e.g. weight or height). Together, the bars show how this quantity is distributed in the data.

<u>Distribution</u>: How a measured quantity (e.g. weight or height) is distributed across entities (e.g. people) in the data. For example, the distribution of height in a population means the number of people there are of each different height.

<u>Central tendency</u>: The rough mid-point of a distribution. All of the averages listed above are measures of central tendency.

<u>Summary statistics</u>: A summary statistic is a single number intended to summarise the information from a larger set of data. Averages, counts, ranges, and percentages are all examples of summary statistics.

<u>Outlier</u>: An unusually large or small value in a set of values. For example, an unusually rich or poor respondent in a survey of people's incomes.

<u>Normal distribution</u>: A distribution in which most people are clustered near the middle and there are relatively few people at either extreme. Many things you can measure about people follow a normal distribution (including height and weight).

 ## Seeing beyond the headlines

As you have seen in this chapter, 'the average' often doesn't mean what we think it means. Here are three questions that help to determine when an average might be leading us astray:

1. WHAT TYPE OF AVERAGE IS BEING USED?

When critiquing a claim involving an average, the first step is to determine what sort of average is being used. Is it the mean, the median, or the mode? (If the claim doesn't specify, it's almost certainly the mean.)

2. ARE THERE LIKELY TO BE LARGE OUTLIERS?

This is particularly relevant if the average is a mean. Does it seem likely that whatever is being measured would include unusually large or small values? If so, is that likely to make the mean higher or lower than what's actually normal for the population?

You might be able to check this directly (if you have access to the underlying data). If not, you're going to have to speculate. HINT: anything involving money (income, spending, taxes, etc.) is likely to have large outliers.

3. IS THE AUTHOR 'ESSENTIALISING'?

Remember that any average is just a single number summarising a whole distribution. Is the author using the average as if it says something about everyone in the population? For example, the following would be an instance of an average being used to draw an essentialist conclusion: 'Women, on average, score higher than men on tests of the Neuroticism personality trait. Therefore, women are not suited to high pressure jobs.'

Example:

CLAIM	WHAT TYPE OF AVERAGE IS BEING USED?	ARE THERE LIKELY TO BE LARGE OUTLIERS?	IS THE AUTHOR 'ESSENTIALISING'?	VERDICT: A USEFUL AVERAGE?
The average person spends $20,200 on dates before getting married	Not stated: therefore likely the mean	YES. Some people spend **a lot** on dates	Not strongly	No. The mean average is likely being dragged up by big-spenders, and is therefore unlikely to represent the 'normal' amount people spend on dates

Exercises for Chapter 5

Exercise 1

In November 2015 the website *Business Insider* published a story about America's profligate spending on Christmas gifts.[4] The story noted that US adults were planning to spend about $830 on average on gifts, up from $720 in 2014.

The story was based on an annual survey conducted by the polling organisation Gallup. The survey asked respondents 'Roughly how much money do you think you personally will spend on Christmas gifts this year?'

Gallup's full report on the results of the survey can be found at the following address:

http://www.gallup.com/file/poll/186632/Christmas_Spending_ Estimate_151116%20.pdf

Use the report to answer the following questions:

1. What figure does the report give as the <u>mean</u> spend for adults in 2015?
2. What does it give as the <u>median</u> spend for the same year?
3. Why are these numbers different?
4. Is the mean figure likely to be representative of 'normal' spending for US adults in 2015?

Exercise 2

Choose a social group to which you belong: this could be based on nationality, gender, ethnicity, home-ownership (renters, home-owners), generation (Millennials, Generation Y, Baby Boomers, etc.), pet-ownership, hobbies or activities (surfers, cinema-goers, Twitter users) – whatever you want.

Search the internet for the following phrase 'the average [insert group]' (make sure you use quotation marks).

You are almost guaranteed to find at least one news article giving an average statistic for your group.

See if you can trace this story back to the original source of the data.

1. What sort of average is being used?
2. Is it likely to be an accurate representation of what's 'normal' for your group?

---

www.macmillanihe.com/devries-critical-statistics

Go to the book's companion website for further examples, data, links, and other useful resources.

ONLINE RESOURCES AVAILABLE

6 FRACTION OF A MAN

There are two kinds of data in the world

In the previous chapter we dealt with the question of averages. Averages are the tools we use to summarise what is called <u>continuous data</u>. Continuous data covers things that are measured on a smooth, continuous scale: things like height in centimetres, weight in kilograms, IQ scores, income in pounds (or dollars, or Euros, or Flanian Pobble Beads), and so on.

Not everything we're interested in can be measured this way. Let's say we want to know how people feel about women with young children going back to work. A brief glance at the headlines yields lot of strong opinions on both sides of the issue:

> *"Working mothers risk damaging their child's prospects" – Daily Mail,* 16 March 2001

> *"Author calls for women to prioritize mothering for the first three years after giving birth" – Fox News Blog,* 11 April 2017

> *"It should be illegal to be a stay-at-home mum ... we should make it a legal requirement that all parents of children of school-age or older are gainfully employed" – Daily Telegraph* (Australia), 20 March 2017

> *"Men staying at home to look after children should be cultural norm, claims minister" – Daily Mail,* 8 January 2008

You will have your own personal view on this. Maybe you think that young children need their mothers around as much as possible, and therefore that women with small children should work only part-time or not at all. Or maybe you think it's best for the mother's emotional and financial well-being for her to be able to return to full-time work as quickly as possible (and what's stopping the father from staying home instead?).

But what do the public (rather than the media) actually think about this? Luckily, we have the data we need to answer this question. Every six to ten years, the International Social Survey Programme (ISSP) asks a nationally representative sample of people from a variety of countries the following question:[1]

Do you think that women should work outside the home full-time, part-time or not at all ... when there is a child under school age?

1. *Work full-time*

2. *Work part-time*

3. *Stay at home*

4. *Can't choose/don't know*

The table below gives you an idea of what the responses to this survey would look like when entered into a spreadsheet:

idno	Q3a Should women work: Child under school age
1157AA	Part-time
1138BC	Part-time
1295AE	Full-time
1892CF	Stay at home
1354FQ	Full-time
...	...

In this table, each row is a person and each column contains some information about that person. The first column identifies each survey respondent via a unique code (survey data is – or at least should be – stored anonymously, so codes are used instead of people's names or other identifying details). The second column gives each person's response to the question about whether women should work when they have a child under school age. In quantitative research, we would call the information in this column a <u>variable</u>. A variable just means some measurable thing that varies between the people (or countries, or organisations, or whatever you are looking at) in your data.

In the real spreadsheet there are thousands of rows (one for each person) and hundreds of columns, with each column containing responses to one of the questions in the survey.* As with the examples in the previous chapter, this is too much information for us to hold in our brains at once: therefore we need to summarise it.

If this were continuous data – for example if we were measuring people's height in centimetres – we could take an average. But even if we

---

* You can download the real spreadsheets for free from the ISSP website at https://tinyurl.com/yc69zc7v. Or search Google for doi:10.4232/1.12661 stored people's responses to this question as numbers rather than words (1. standing for full-time, 2. for part-time, and so on), it clearly wouldn't make sense for us to calculate the mean or the median. Excel (or whatever programme we are using) would compute an average if we asked, but the result would be meaningless. What would an average response of, say, 2.3, or 4.5, even mean?

What we are dealing with here is <u>categorical data</u>. We are not measuring something that exists on a continuous low-to-high scale, like height or weight; we are measuring something that is split up into **categories**. If we want to summarise this data, we therefore need a different tool than the average.

The most obvious tool is a simple count. Just count up how many people are in each category (how many people picked each option). Table 6.1 gives these figures for the Netherlands.

Table 6.1 Frequency table of responses to the maternal employment question in the Netherlands

Should women work when they have a child under school age?	Frequency
FULL-TIME	70
PART-TIME	751
STAY AT HOME	335
TOTAL	*1,156*

Source: 2012 ISSP

In statistics this is called a '<u>frequency table</u>' because it tells you how frequent each response was. These results tell us that, of the 1,156 Dutch people who filled out the survey, a lot of them (751) thought that women with pre-school age children should only work part-time. A decent chunk (336) thought such women should stay at home. Only a few (70) thought they should work full-time.

These numbers tell us something. But they are a little bit difficult to work with. Of the 1,156 people, how big a chunk does 751 represent? How much bigger of a chunk is this than 70 or 335? The solution to this problem is to move beyond the raw counts and express these numbers as fractions of an easily understandable <u>common denominator</u>. We'll tackle this in the next section.

What's the point of percentages?

What does it mean to express something in terms of a 'common denominator'? You may remember from school that the denominator is the number below the line in a fraction: for example, in the fraction $\frac{4}{5}$, the denominator is five. In the case of our survey question, the denominator is the total number of people who answered the question. So when we say that 335 out of 1,156 people thought that women should stay at home to look after small children, the denominator is 1,156.

As we've already noted, 1,156 is not an easy number to work with. So what we'll do is reduce this number down. Instead of saying that 335 out of 1,156 people think mothers should stay home, we could say that 2.9 out of every 10 people think this. If we do this for the other numbers, the number for part-time becomes 6.5 out of 10, and the number for full-time becomes 0.6 out of 10. Shrinking down the fractions has made them a bit easier to interpret and compare.

One of the most important things this process of manipulating factions allows us to do is to compare numbers between populations of different sizes. For example, let's say we want to compare responses to the working mums question between the Netherlands and the UK. Table 6.2 gives the frequency of responses from the UK version of the survey.

Table 6.2 Frequency table of responses to the maternal employment question in the UK

SHOULD WOMEN WORK WHEN THEY HAVE A CHILD UNDER SCHOOL AGE?	FREQUENCY
FULL-TIME	50
PART-TIME	415
STAY AT HOME	330
TOTAL	*795*

Source: 2012 ISSP

If we just left the numbers as they were, we could say that 330 people in the UK think that mothers with small children should stay at home, compared to 335 people in the Netherlands. These numbers are very close. Does this mean that people in the UK think basically the same way as people in the Netherlands when it comes to the question of maternal childcare?

The answer is no. The reason being that there are many fewer people in the British Survey than in the Dutch one (795 vs. 1,156). *Proportionally*, 330 is a bigger chunk of 795 than 335 is of 1,156. But exactly how much bigger of a chunk is it?

Here is where manipulating fractions helps a lot. If we do the same thing for the UK as we did for the Netherlands – reduce everything down to fractions out of ten – 330 out of 795 becomes 4.2 out of 10 (people thinking that mothers should stay at home). We can now compare this directly to the 2.9 out of 10 people in the Netherlands who felt the same way. Reducing the numbers from both countries to a *common denominator* (10) has made it much easier to see that people in the UK are more likely than people in the Netherlands to think that mothers of young children shouldn't work. In other words, British people have more conservative attitudes than Dutch people when it comes to gender and childcare.

Per (out of) cent (a hundred)

The common denominator I used in the above example is 10. However, this is not the modern convention. The modern convention is to express things out of 100. So instead of saying 2.9 out of 10 for the Netherlands and 4.2 out of 10 for Britain, we would say 29 out of every 100, versus 42 out of every 100. In this day and age, expressing things 'out of 100' has become so commonplace that we have a special word for it: a **percentage**.

The reason I have taken such a long-winded route to get to the seemingly obvious answer of 'we should express these numbers as percentages' is because, although we take percentages for granted, there is nothing necessarily special about expressing things out of 100. Rather than expressing things per 100 (Latin: *per centum*), we could just as easily use per 20 (*per viginti*) or per 1,000 (*per mille*), or any other number. Up to the 15th century people used a lot of different numbers. Per 100 only came into fashion when people started having to deal with large amounts of money. As 'per 100' started to be used more and more often, *per centum* got abbreviated to 'percent'. Then, like Prince in the nineties, it got its own special symbol – the % sign.

Taking things back to first principles – understanding *why* we express numbers as percentages – also helps us to avoid simple mistakes. The sorts of mistakes that are still made by people in high places, who should know better.

Do we need a White Lives Matter?

On 6 July 2016, a school kitchen assistant named Philando Castile was shot and killed by a police officer during a routine traffic stop in St. Paul, Minnesota. Castile was black. The officer, Jeronimo Yanez, was not. This incident is one of the many troubling police shootings which have inspired the Black Lives Matter movement.

Three days after Castile was shot, former US presidential candidate Mike Huckabee appeared on Fox News to argue against the idea that such killings were racially motivated:

"More white people have been shot by police officers this past year than minorities" – Mike Huckabee on Fox News, 9 July 2016

According to the *Washington Post*'s database of fatal police shootings,* Huckabee's statement is correct. In 2015, 990 Americans were shot and killed by police. 494 of the victims were white, 258 were black, and the remaining 238 were of other ethnicities or their ethnicities were not known. Figures for 2016 were similar: of the 900 fatal police shootings that year, 465 of those killed were white and 233 were black.

Taken at face value, this seems to strike at the heart of the complaints of the Black Lives Matter movement. If the number of white victims of police shootings is almost double the number of black victims, isn't this compelling evidence that police racism is not the problem it's being made out to be? A cursory Google search shows that many people have drawn this exact conclusion: countless YouTube videos, blog posts, and news articles have used the *Washington Post* figures to 'debunk' the Black Lives Matter campaign.

These articles make exactly the same mistake we would have made if we had used the raw figures to compare Dutch and British attitudes about maternal childcare. 335 people in the Dutch sample said that women should stay at home, compared to 330 people in the British sample. Therefore, more Dutch people think that women should stay home. The problem with this statement is obvious – overall, more Dutch people took the survey. If you count the number of times something happens in a large group of people, you will naturally tend to get a bigger number than if you count the same thing in a smaller group. If you count the number of Ed Sheeran fans with IQs over 140 and compare it to the number of rocket scientists with similar IQs, you will find that the former number is bigger than the latter. This does not mean that Ed Sheeran fans are smarter than rocket scientists. It's just a natural consequence of the fact that (unfortunately) there are more Ed Sheeran fans in the world than there are rocket scientists. To properly compare numbers from populations of different sizes, we need to look at proportions, not at raw counts.

Huckabee's mistake with the police shooting figures should have been just as obvious. There are many more white people in the USA than there are black people or people from other minority groups (this is what the word 'minority' means after all). Of the total US population of 323 million people, 197 million (61%) are white,** and 43 million (13.3%) are black*** (with the remainder being of other ethnicities).

---

* Which you can download for yourself from https://github.com/washingtonpost/data-police-shootings.

** This does not include white Hispanics or Latinos. The American Census Bureau classifies Hispanic/Latino as a separate type of ethnicity. So one can be classified as both white and Hispanic/Latino or both black and Hispanic/Latino.

*** This includes black Hispanics/Latinos.

To compare the number of police shootings properly, we need to express the numbers as proportions of the relevant populations. The 258 black people shot by police in 2015 represents 0.0006% of the total black population, or 0.6 for every 100,000 people (here is an example where we need to use a bigger denominator than 100 to get a manageable number). By comparison, the figure for white people is 0.25 per 100,000. In raw terms, more white than black people are shot by police each year. But comparing proportions shows us that black people are 2.4 times more likely to be shot and killed by police than white people are.

There are complications to this straightforward story. There is disagreement about the extent to which one should factor in relative crime rates and numbers of interactions with police. However, none of these disagreements contradict the fundamental fact that we need to use proportions to make these sorts of comparisons. Using the raw figures is just not very informative – and in this case, is actively misleading. I expect my first-year students to know this. Though, given past form, perhaps it is a little much to expect from US presidential candidates.

Does gun violence mean the USA is deadlier than a warzone?

Late US senator Frank Lautenberg (Democrat, New Jersey) was never a presidential candidate. He did, however, make exactly the same mistake as Huckabee when he made the following claim in July 2012:

> *"Guns have murdered more Americans here at home in recent years than have died on the battlefields of Iraq and Afghanistan. In support of the two wars, more than 6,500 American soldiers have lost their lives. During the same period, however, guns have been used to murder about 100,000 people on American soil"* – NorthJersey .com, 30 July 2012

As with Huckabee's claim, the underlying numbers are accurate. As *PolitiFact* noted in their critique of Lautenberg's statement,[2] FBI figures show that more than 95,000 people were murdered with a gun in the ten years between 2001 (the beginning of the Afghanistan war) and 2011 (the year before Lautenberg's claim). US Department of Defense figures also show that the 6,500 figure is correct.

On its face, the senator's statement seems reasonable. Shouldn't we expect fewer civilians to be shot at home than soldiers shot in an actual war? However, the Ed Sheeran/rocket scientist comparison shows us that the answer to this question is actually no. If you measure something in a large population you are almost bound to find a larger number than if you measure the same thing in a smaller population. Comparing the number of civilians shot on US soil to the number of soldiers shot in

Iraq and Afghanistan is like comparing the number of people who are violently assaulted every week in New York City to the number assaulted every week in the country's most violent supermax prison. The former number will be larger than the latter, but this doesn't tell you much about how safe or unsafe you should feel walking around New York on a Saturday night.

If we were genuinely interested in the risk of being shot for a regular US civilian compared to a soldier deployed in Iraq or Afghanistan, we would need to compare proportions. Research into US military deaths has put the hostile death rate (deaths due to combat) of soldiers in Iraq and Afghanistan in the range of 300 to 400 deaths per 100,000 troops per year.[3] By contrast, the gun homicide rate on US soil is closer to 3.5 per 100,000 – around 100 times lower. As we would expect, the battle-field is a much more dangerous place than America's towns and cities.

Percentages – backwards and forwards

Before we close out our discussion of percentages, it's worth spending some time on a mistake that's often made even by people who recognise the need to use percentages to make comparisons. To illustrate this mistake, I'm going to go back to our analysis of the ISSP data on maternal childcare.

As well as asking what proportion of the population think that women with young children should either stay at home, work part-time, or work full time, we could also ask how opinions on this subject differ for different groups in the population. For example, we could ask whether younger people are more likely to think that it's OK for women to go back to work full-time. Given that younger people are generally more socially liberal, we might expect that this would be the case.

Table 6.3 gives the raw numbers of people giving each response, separately for people over and under 65 (this is using the data from the Netherlands).

Table 6.3 Cross-tabulation of age and responses to the maternal employment question in the Netherlands

	UNDER 65	65 AND OVER	*TOTAL*
FULL-TIME	52	18	*70*
PART-TIME	523	228	*751*
STAY AT HOME	185	150	*335*
TOTAL	*760*	*396*	*1,156*

Source: 2012 ISSP

A table like this is called a <u>cross-tabulation</u> (cross-tab for short), because it cross-tabulates one variable (measured thing) against another. In this case, response to the maternal employment question are cross-tabulated against age group. You may also see cross-tabs like this described as <u>joint frequency tables</u>.

We already know that to properly compare the number of people who think that women should stay home, we need to use percentages. However, there are a few potentially relevant percentages we could pull from this table:

- 335 people think that women with young children should stay at home rather than going out to work full-time or part-time. Of this more conservative group, 185 (55%) are under 65 and 150 (45%) are 65 or above.

- 760 respondents are under 65. Of this younger group, 185 (24%) think that women with young children should stay at home. 396 respondents are 65 or over. Of this older group, 150 (38%) think that mothers of young children should stay home.

Only the second of these comparisons actually helps us answer our question. The first comparison *seems* like it might be relevant. It shows that the majority of people who think women should stay home are under 65. However, this actually tells us very little. The majority of *the sample as a whole* is under 65. Therefore, the majority of people giving *any* of the responses is also under 65. Most people who think women should stay home are under 65, but so are most people who think women can work full-time or part-time.

By contrast, the second comparison actually tells us something useful. Here we are percentaging the table in a different 'direction' – we are using the column totals (the total number of people in each age group) as our denominators instead of the row totals (the total number of people giving each response). By doing this, we can see that a greater percentage of older people (38%) than younger people (24%) think that mothers of small children should stay home – exactly as we expected.

These two comparisons are drawn from the same table and use a lot of the same words, but they tell us fundamentally different things. Confusing the two is easy to do, but it can lead us to deeply misleading conclusions. Some examples to help you keep this in mind:

- The percentage of students who take drugs is not the same as the percentage of drug takers who are students.

- The percentage of clowns who are scary is not the same as the percentage of scary people who are clowns.

- The percentage of statistics in the *Daily Mail* that are misleading is not the same as the percentage of misleading statistics that appear in the *Daily Mail* (as opposed to other newspapers).

Risky business

In the previous section, we compared the proportion of older people (38%) who thought that mums should not work with the proportion of younger people who thought the same (24%). How should we quantify this difference? One way would be to simply take the absolute difference in terms of percentage points (see the 'Percentage points' box in Chapter 3): older people are 14 percentage points more likely than younger people to think that women with young children shouldn't work.

An alternative is to use something statisticians call <u>relative risk</u>. If we divide 38% by 24%, we get a figure of about 1.6. This is the 'relative risk' that older people will think that mums should stay home with the kids. Older people are 1.6 *times* more likely than younger people to think this. Another way of saying '1.6 times more likely' is to say '60% more likely'. These are exactly the same figure, just expressed in different ways.*

Relative risks are a very commonly used statistic in the media. They are most frequently deployed when talking about things that affect your health. For example, if a new study finds that 10% of people who watch the *Great British Bake Off* (an extremely popular British cooking show) develop diabetes within the next five years, compared to 8% of non-viewers, the relative risk associated with watching *Bake Off* is 10 ÷ 8 = 1.25. In other words, people who watch *Bake Off* are 1.25 times (25%) more likely to get diabetes. The resulting headlines might read 'Watching *Bake Off* increases risk of diabetes by a quarter'.

All about that base

If you spend any time at all reading the news, the 'x raises/lowers risk of y' headline will be something you've seen a lot. Here, for example, is a collection of headlines reporting on a study of the risks associated with an expanding waistline:

> *"Skirt size increase linked to breast cancer risk, says study ... Women who went up a skirt size every decade after their mid-20s had a 33% greater risk of breast cancer"* – BBC News website, 25 September 2013

---

* We performed the same calculation when comparing the rate at which black vs. white people were shot by police.

"Increasing skirt size linked to breast cancer risk ... going up a skirt size over a period of 10 years after age 25 was linked with a 33 percent increase in the risk of breast cancer" – Fox News website, 25 September 2013

"Women who go up a skirt size 'raise breast cancer risks' ... Going up a skirt size with each decade could raise the risk of breast cancer by one third, according to a new study" – The Telegraph, 25 September 2013

But what do these results actually mean? The numbers involved seem to suggest that getting a bit wider as you get older is *really* bad for you. A 33% increased risk of getting breast cancer seems extremely serious. However, there is a crucial piece of information missing from these headlines. Without this information, it's very difficult to interpret what a '33% increased risk' actually means. Just now, I told you that to work out the relative risk, you divide the risk in one group (in this case women who go up a skirt size every 10 years) by the risk in another group (in this case, women whose skirt size stays the same). Now look at these headlines again. What information is missing?

Before you answer that, I want you to imagine that someone has rung your doorbell and is attempting to sell you special shoes that have been scientifically proven to reduce the risk of slipping on a banana peel by 90%. What are you thinking? I'm thinking that I've never slipped on a banana peel in my life, and nor has anyone I know outside of a cartoon. A 90% reduction in a risk of zero is ... zero – so I'll probably take a pass on the shoes.

In this somewhat ridiculous scenario, I was presented with a statistic – a 90% reduction in the risk of slipping on a banana. To interpret this statistic properly, I first needed to consider the *baseline risk* of the event happening in the first place – i.e. the risk for people who *don't* have the special shoes. Only when I know this baseline risk can I understand what a 90% reduction in risk actually means.

The same issue applies to the skirt size story (and to any story about increased or decreased risks). In order to interpret a 33% increased risk of breast cancer for women who gained skirt sizes as they got older, we first need to know how likely you are to develop breast cancer in the first place.

The study on which the above headlines are based was conducted in the UK.[4] The figures come from interviews with more than 92,000 women aged 50 and over who had no previous history of breast cancer. In the interviews, women were asked what their current skirt size was, and what it had been during their twenties. The researchers then checked back in with the women five years later to see how many had developed breast cancer. 1.63% of the women whose skirt sizes had stayed the same since their twenties got breast cancer. Another way of saying this is that the five-year absolute risk of getting breast cancer in this group was 1.63%.

Now we are in possession of the baseline risk figure, we are much better equipped to interpret what a '33% increased risk' actually means. If you start with a 1.63% risk of getting breast cancer, then a 33% increase would bring your risk up to 2.17%. To me this sounds a lot less scary than 'increasing your risk of breast cancer by a third'. You can decide for yourself if going from a 1.63% risk to a 2.17% risk is enough reason to stress about middle-age spread.

Stories about risk are an extremely common feature of the news media. Here is just a smattering from a random Google search:

> "Taking common painkillers like ibuprofen 'increases your risk of cardiac arrest by a THIRD'" – The Sun, 15 March 2017

> "White bread, bagels and rice INCREASE the risk of lung cancer by 49 per cent, experts warn" – Daily Express, 9 March 2016

> "One cup of coffee a day reduces the risk of death from all causes by 12 percent" – Pravda, 11 July 2017

> "Two glasses of wine a day increase the chances of bowel cancer by 21% – Survey" – The Star (Kenya), 5 July 2017

Journalists love these stories because they grab people's attention. Everyone wants to know what is going to kill them or keep them healthy. And these stories almost always report the relative risk – how much more or less likely are you to get lung cancer if you eat white bread every day – while failing to provide the straightforward risk information that would help you understand how much difference cutting out white bread would really make.

There are lots of reasons why newspapers do this: relative risks provide big eye-catching numbers; the journalist may not really understand the statistics; the underlying figures may not have been provided in the press-release. Whatever the reason, the upshot is that the newspapers and the internet are full of needlessly scary health stories.

One solution to this is just to tune out health stories completely. As my mum used to say, 'if you listened to everything they said you'd only ever have bread and water' (she hadn't heard the bad news about bread). But complete ignorance is rarely the best policy. In the 1950s and 1960s it would have left you blind to the hazards of smoking. In the 1970s you would still have been happily insulating your house with asbestos. Rather than a blanket policy of avoidance, far better to actually think about the numbers in the claim. How big is my risk of lung cancer to begin with? What does an increase of 49% mean in that context? Is it enough to make it worthwhile to change your behaviour? After all, in the immortal words of Ben Goldacre: 'You are 80% less likely to die from a meteor landing on your head if you wear a bicycle helmet all day.'[5]

Likert scales

On a scale of 1 to 5, where 1 means 'agree strongly' and 5 means 'disagree strongly', to what extent do you agree with the following statement: 'The media can be trusted to report statistics accurately.'

Chances are that you've been asked questions like this before – if not on this particular topic, then at least in this format. You are asked a question, and then asked to respond in a scale of 1 to 5, or 1 to 7, or 0 to 10. These are called Likert scale questions, named for their inventor, psychologist Rensis Likert. They are typically used to measure people's attitudes and beliefs: To what extent do they support a particular government policy? To what extent do they believe that climate change is caused by human activity? And so on.

If this question format seems like something too obvious to need an inventor, then you should know that in the early 20th century psychologists and sociologists were not convinced that attitudes could be measured with numbers at all. How on earth could you quantify how much someone supported the Republican Party, or how much they favoured the prohibition of alcohol? Early pioneers in psychometrics (the measurement of psychological phenomena) like Likert and Louis Thurstone changed all that (Thurstone wrote a famous article in the *American Journal of Sociology* in 1928 titled simply 'Attitudes Can Be Measured').

In terms of statistics, Likert scales are intended to be just that – continuous scales. As such, it is possible to summarise responses to Likert scale questions by means of an average. For example, let's say we ask 10 people the question at the top of this box, and we get the following responses back:

Person number	Response
1	5
2	3
3	5
4	4
5	5
6	3
7	4
8	5
9	5
10	1

If we calculate the mean average here, we get 4. So, on average, people are generally of the opinion that the media can't be trusted (good on you, fictional respondents!).

Although calculating an average here is perfectly legitimate, in many cases, researchers will instead collapse the scale into two categories and work out percentages. In this case, instead of saying that the average response was 4, we might say that 70% of respondents had a score of 4 or above. If we wanted to fit this into a headline, we might drop the mention of the scale and just say '70% of people thought the media could not be trusted to report statistics accurately'. Here we have collapsed everyone responding with a 4 or above into a category and labelled them as 'thinking that the media cannot be trusted'. If we had drawn the line at 5 instead of 4, this would have given us a different result: 50% distrusting the media instead of 70%. For me, it makes less sense to do this than to draw the line at 4, but there are no hard and fast rules.

Because so much of our data comes from surveys, and because so many surveys use Likert scale questions, a fair number of the statistics you'll see in the media will have come about through this sort of process. It's therefore worth digging about to see if you can see what the original scale was, and where the researchers (or the journalist) have drawn the line demarcating the categories.

Statistics aren't real

In the previous chapter, I talked about the fact that averages are summaries. They are models of the underlying reality, not the reality itself. The same is true of percentages. When we are talking about complicated things like people and societies, reality is always much messier and blurrier than a black and white percentage would suggest.

One of the most important things to remember about categorical data (and therefore about percentages and risk ratios too) is that it comes from putting people (or things) into discrete boxes (this is something we also covered in Chapter 4). For example, to determine people's views on maternal childcare, the ISSP survey forced people to choose between three rigid options: women with young children should stay at home, they should work part-time, or they should work full-time. No doubt many of the people who participated in the survey had more nuanced views than these categories would allow. For example, perhaps they would say that it's preferable for women to work part-time, but that it's OK for them to work full-time if that's what makes the most sense for them financially. Or they might say that at least one parent should stay at home, but that it doesn't matter if it's the mother or the father. Neither of these is a possible response to the survey question (or rather, both would be bracketed together into the 'can't say/don't know' category). This is something that is always worth remembering when you see headlines claiming that 'Nine per cent of Americans support neo-Nazis',[6] or that '75% of Britons support the legalization of assisted suicide'.[7] These headlines may or may not be accurate descriptions of the survey findings – but in either case they certainly conceal much of the complexity of people's actual views.

This is true in cases where a survey has forced people to fit themselves into narrow boxes. It is also true in cases where the researcher has come along later and drawn the boxes onto the underlying data. For example, in Chapter 4, we discussed the example of a study which investigated social media and loneliness. The study was reported in the press as showing that 'more than two hours of social media a day doubles your risk of feeling isolated'.* If you remember, the researchers measured loneliness using a series of four questions, each of which were measured on a five-point scale. However, rather than looking at participants' total scores out of 20, the researchers drew a box around the top third of scores and called everyone in that box 'socially isolated'. This allowed them to work out how much more 'at risk' people who used a lot of social media were of being socially isolated, versus people who used social media less often. However, this comes at the cost of lumping together people who might have very different life experiences – people without a friend in the world with people who maybe just feel a bit misunderstood and left out of things.

Whenever we split people up into categories and calculate percentages (or frequencies, or risk ratios), we are inevitably imposing an artificial structure onto a messy underlying reality. The only time this isn't true is when nature has served up truly clear-cut categories – for example, whether someone is alive or dead is a pretty concrete distinction (though perhaps not as concrete as you might think). As in the case of averages, this does not make the statistics arising from these categories useless. In fact they are often vital. We need to be able to talk about how many people are lonely, or how many people think assisted suicide should be legal, or how many people think women should stay home to look after the kids. We just need to make sure we don't forget that our averages and percentages are summaries which gloss over a great deal of the variation and complexity of the real world – that when we say that some firm percentage of the public think something, or feel something, or support something, that these percentages contain multitudes.

---

*   Note the lack of baseline risk information.

Summary

There are two types of data in the world. Continuous data comes from things measured on a smooth, continuous scale. Weight in kg, IQ score, age in years, height in cm, price in dollars: all of these are examples of continuous data. Categorical data comes from things measured in discrete categories. Eye colour, ethnicity, country of origin, favourite sports team, Facebook relationship status: these are examples of categorical data.

Raw counts vs. percentages. Raw counts are the simple count of the number of entities (e.g. people) meeting a certain description – for example, the number of people picking a particular response to a survey question. Percentages are raw counts expressed as a common fraction. For example, the number of people picking a particular response for every 100 people who answered the question.

Cross-tabs provide information about the relationship between two categorical variables. For example, you could use a cross-tabulation of age group and support for the death penalty to determine whether older people are more in favour of this type of criminal punishment than younger people.

Relative risk figures tell you how much more at risk of some event one group is than another. A relative risk is calculated by dividing the risk of something happening to a member of Group A, by the risk of the same thing happening to a member of Group B. For example, if 1 out of every 1,000 people in Group A contract Hedwards syndrome (an unexplainable attraction to BBC newsreader Huw Edwards), compared to 2 out of every 1,000 people in Group B, then the relative risk of members of Group B contracting the disorder (which is known to be fatal) is 2. In other words, members of Group B are twice as likely to get Hedwards as members of Group A.

Percentages are summaries. Splitting people into categories is often necessary, but almost always involves a simplification of the real world. Bear this in mind when interpreting what percentages (and relative risks) actually mean.

Terminology used in this chapter

Variable: A measurable factor that varies between the cases (e.g. people, countries, schools) in your data. For example, if you recorded the height and weight of 100 people in a spreadsheet, the spreadsheet would contain two variables: height and weight.

Frequency/Frequency table: How common a particular value is in a set of data. For example, how many people say 'Yes' to a survey question asking whether they voted in the last national election could be described as the frequency of 'yes' responses.

A frequency table is simply a table of these frequencies. For example, a table separately listing the number of people who responded 'yes', 'no' and 'don't know' to the voting question.

Common denominator: A denominator is the bottom half of a fraction. For example, in the fraction 3/4 the denominator is 4. When you are dealing with multiple fractions with different denominators, it is often helpful to convert them all to use the same (i.e. a common) denominator. For example, we could express the fractions 3/4 and 4/5 as 15/20 and 12/20, respectively.

Joint frequency table: A cross-tabulation of frequencies for two categorical variables (see above).

Likert scales: A Likert scale is a type of survey question which allows responses along a numbered scale. The most commonly used form of Likert scale is a scale of agreement from 1 (strongly agree/disagree) to 5 (strongly disagree/agree).

Seeing beyond the headlines

As this chapter has shown, percentages, counts, and risks can be deceptively tricky. Here are some questions to ask when dealing with these types of statistics:

1. IS A COMPARISON BEING MADE IN TERMS OF RAW COUNTS WHEN PERCENTAGES (OR ANOTHER PROPORTION) WOULD BE MORE APPROPRIATE?

Sometimes it's OK just to count things. But when you are making comparisons, it's often better to use proportions. For example, based on the raw counts, the number of people who become pregnant while using a condom is much larger than the number of people who become pregnant while using herbal contraception. This does not tell us that the former is less effective than the latter.

2. IS THE RIGHT PERCENTAGE BEING USED?

If the author is making a claim on the basis of calculating percentages, do you agree with their calculations? Are they looking at the right categories? If they are comparing two percentages (e.g. from a cross-tab), have they 'percentaged' the table in the right direction?

3. IF THE CLAIM IS ABOUT AN INCREASED OR DECREASED RISK, HAS THE BASELINE RISK BEEN PROVIDED?

Is the claim about the effect of an exposure (like taking herbal contraception pills) on the risk of something happening (like becoming pregnant, or getting liver disease)? If so, you need information about the baseline risk. What would your absolute risk be if you were not taking the pills? What would that risk become if you did take them?

Examples:

CLAIM	RAW COUNTS WHERE PROPORTIONS BETTER?	RIGHT PER-CENTAGE?	BASELINE RISK PROVIDED?	VERDICT: A USEFUL STATISTIC?
More white than black people shot by police each year	YES. The statistics involve comparing groups of different sizes. So the counts should be expressed as proportions of the total in each group	N/A	N/A	NO. The statistic does not tell us whether black or white people are more at risk of being shot by a police officer
Common painkillers like ibuprofen increase the risk of heart attack by a third	NO. Relative risk based on comparing proportions	YES. Proportion of people taking NSAID painkillers who suffered heart attacks compared to proportion of people not taking these painkillers who suffered heart attacks	NO. Only relative risk increase provided	NO. Without knowing the baseline risk, we do not know whether a risk increase of a third is meaningful

Exercises for Chapter 6

Exercise 1

Despite robust evidence of their safety and efficacy, anti-vaccine campaigners believe that vaccines (such as the combined Measles, Mumps, and Rubella – MMR – vaccine) are harmful. On Facebook, you see an anti-vaccine organisation post the following message:

> *FACT: The numbers show that more vaccinated than unvaccinated people get measles.*

This statement is plausibly true. If the measles vaccine is less than 100% effective, some number of vaccinated people will go on to contract measles. This number may be larger than the total number of unvaccinated people who contract measles.

Would this represent good evidence that vaccines don't work? If not, why not?

Exercise 2

In June 2016, President (then candidate) Donald Trump gave a speech in Virginia in which he emphasised the importance of increasing the employment rate among young African Americans:

> *"If you look at what's going on in this country, African-American youth is an example: 59 percent unemployment rate; 59 percent".*

Table E6.1 gives the most recent available employment figures for African Americans aged 16–24 at the time of Trump's speech:

Table E6.1 Frequency table showing the employment situation of African Americans aged 16–24

Number not in employment	3,426,000
Of which unemployed and seeking work	559,000
Of which not in the labour force	2,867,000
(This includes school and college students, disabled people, and stay-at-home parents)	
Number in employment	2,434,000
Total	5,860,000

Source: US Current Population Survey, May 2016

Use the information in the table to answer the following questions:

1. Where does Trump's 59% figure come from?

2. Is this figure an accurate representation of the percentage of young African Americans who are unemployed?

---

www.macmillanihe.com/devries-critical-statistics

Go to the book's companion website for further examples, data, links, and other useful resources.

ONLINE
RESOURCES
AVAILABLE

---

7 CAUSE AND EFFECT

I have a confession to make. I am addicted to newspaper advice columns. I open my browser, fully intent on catching up with the important news of the day – world events, the latest political developments, important scientific advances – but instead I inevitably find my cursor hovering over the latest Dear Abby (or Dear Prudence or Dear Mariella). The economic impacts of Brexit can wait – Confused in Colorado wants to know if she should keep her stepbrother's baby.

If you spend enough time reading these letters, you'll quickly notice certain kinds of problem coming up again and again. One popular genre is the 'did I do something wrong?' scenario. A typical letter might go something like this:

> *Dear Abby,*
>
> *I've been messaging back and forth with this great guy I met on Tinder, and we were getting to the point of arranging to meet for a date in person. But a couple of weeks ago he seemed to just completely lose interest. His messages went from long and flirty to short and non-committal ('yeah can't do this week but sometime would be good'). Then last week he just completely ghosted. I've been trying to figure out what happened and the only thing I can come up with is that in my last message before he went cold I mentioned that I'd been hanging out with my new niece (my sister just had a baby) and it made me realise how much I want kids someday (someday!). Did I scare him off with the baby talk?*
>
> *– Ghosted in Green Bay*

Of course the answer to the letter writer's question is: maybe ... but maybe not (I'd make a terrible advice columnist). Maybe the guy was looking for something casual with this girl and the reference to kids did scare him off. But there are also plenty of other potential explanations. Maybe he was on Tinder after a breakup and his ex just came back into the picture. Maybe he's just been diagnosed with a terminal illness. Maybe he's actually a 12-year-old boy with a fake account. I could go on. The point is that just because she mentioned wanting kids and then he ghosted does not necessarily mean that her mention of kids is what *caused* him to ghost.

What we are trying to do here is something scientists do all the time. The technical term for it is <u>causal inference</u>. We can see that two things (call them X and Y) are related: in this case the X is the letter writer's mention of kids, which was immediately followed by Y, the disappearance of her Tinder correspondent. We are trying to figure out (infer) whether X actually *caused* Y.

In our daily lives this is something we're generally pretty good at. If you tell your friend that you've got a really bad hangover today and you suspect the kebab you had before you went to bed, they might offer some alternative causes (such as the three tequilas you had in the club, or the eight beers you sank to keep them company). If you've lost a bit of weight recently, you might speculate as to exactly what caused it: is it the fact that you've started taking the stairs to the office rather than the lift? Or is it because you've kicked your 3am kebab habit?

Unfortunately, this ability to recognise that events can have multiple possible causes, and that just because two things are associated does not mean that one caused the other, often falters when we move out of our direct experience and into the world of numbers and statistics. Take the following quote from a 2017 Trump TV* segment touting the president's economic achievements:

> *"Overall, since the president took office, President Trump has created more than 1 million new jobs ... President Trump has clearly steered the economy back in the right direction"* – 'Trump TV' video published on Trump's official Facebook page, 4 August 2017

Here Republican National Committee spokesperson Kayleigh McEnany is making a *causal* statement. Since Trump took office, the American economy has added a million new jobs: therefore Trump *caused* these new jobs to be created – he has 'steered' the economy in the right direction. Trump is not the only one to make this kind of claim of course. It's a particular disease of politicians to claim credit for any positive movement in the economy under their watch. For example, during her campaign, Hillary Clinton credited her husband Bill with the 1990s economic boom (the 1990s also happened to be when the internet was invented).

The problem with all claims of this nature is that there are many potential causes of economic growth or changes in the employment rate. A national economy is a complex machine with many millions of moving parts. There are any number of things that can cause it to move in one direction or another; from the price of oil, to changes in the economies

---

* Trump TV is an online video news outlet created by the Trump team to combat 'fake news' in the mainstream media.

of other countries, to technological developments. It is entirely possible, for example, that if Hillary Clinton had won the election, or if Donald Trump was replaced by a sentient geranium, the jobs numbers would have grown in exactly the same way. Donald Trump is exactly like the letter-writer with her Tinder beau. He has taken some actions while in office, and a million new jobs have been created. But we have no idea if the former *caused* the latter.

This is a fundamental rule of statistics: **just because two things are associated does not mean that one of them caused the other**. This is often abbreviated to '**correlation does not equal causation**'. It's an easy rule to remember. Remembering to actually *apply* it is much harder. Trump's supporters conveniently forgot to apply it when crediting him with 'saving' the economy. And I fully expect that his critics will also conveniently forget it when they blame him for any economic problems down the road.

Kill or cure

Another situation in which the fundamental rule of 'correlation is not causation' is often forgotten is when we talk about health. And, as we've already discovered, the media *loves* to talk about health. On any given day, the international news media publishes a roughly infinite number of stories about things that might kill or cure us. Open almost any newspaper and you will inevitably find a story about some everyday thing that will give you cancer or heart disease, or will make you fat or will make your children fat (or stupid, or both). Or you will find a story about some miracle nut or berry or diet that will *stop* you from getting cancer or heart disease, or make you thin or give you smooth skin like a baby mole. Here are just a few headlines published on the day I sat down to write this section:

"Increase in the popularity of oral sex blamed for rising rates of throat cancer in New Zealand men" – Mail Online, 7 August 2017

"High-fat diet linked to lung cancer risk" – ABS-CBN News, 8 August 2017

"Daily Tipple Raises Risk of Skin Cancer, Study Suggests: Drinking just one glass of beer or wine a day could give you skin cancer ... " – Huffington Post UK, 7 August 2017

"Weekend lie-ins may be bad for your heart AND waistline: Habit found to increase chance of an early death from heart disease by 11%" – Mail Online, 7 August 2017

"Does Tap Water Cause Acne? Here's Why Some Dermatologists Are Saying Yes" – StyleCaster.com, 7 August 2017

This is just a smattering – there are hundreds more I could have included from just this 24-hour period. Try it for yourself. Go to Google's news tab and type 'cancer' or 'heart disease' (or diabetes, or stroke, or 'lose weight', or whatever you want). The result will be a cascade of articles which, taken together, claim that almost every food, drink, activity, or inanimate object on earth will in some way harm or improve your health.

Many of the claims made in these articles appear to be based on legitimate scientific studies. But this does not mean they can be taken at face value. All these studies will have often found is that two things are associated – which, as we've established, is not strong evidence of a causal relationship.

Let's look at a specific example. In 2011 a group of researchers found that women who drank coffee regularly were less likely to become clinically depressed.[1] News outlets around the world wrote up this story as evidence that drinking coffee helps prevent depression:

> *"Coffee can cut depression risk in women"* – NBC News.com, 26 September 2011

> *"Coffee may prevent depression"* – *BBC News* website, 27 September 2011

> *"Coffee is good for you: Women who drink four or more cups a day are less likely to be depressed"* – *Mail Online*, 27 September 2011

One potential reason why women who drink lots of coffee are less likely to get depressed is because coffee is indeed beneficial. Perhaps caffeine alters the brain's chemistry in some way that helps prevent depression over the long-term.

But it could also be that the coffee itself does nothing, and that instead women who drink coffee are less likely to get depressed for other reasons. Maybe women who drink coffee regularly are richer than women who don't drink coffee, or maybe they have more rewarding jobs. These might be the reasons why they are less likely to get depressed. If that's the case then starting to drink a lot of coffee is not going to help prevent depression – because it's not actually the coffee that's helping, it's being rich (or having a good job).

This is perhaps easier to understand if we use a hypothetical example. Imagine we run a study looking at the relationship between life expectancy and owning a pool. We find that people who own a pool live longer, on average, than people who don't own a pool. This might be because owning a pool is good for you (swimming is good exercise after all). But it's more likely to be because people who own pools are rich. And rich people tend to live longer regardless of whether or not they own a pool.

There is also another potential reason why coffee drinkers may be less likely to become depressed: people who already have emotional problems (who are more likely to subsequently become depressed) may tend to avoid coffee because they don't like what it does to their mood. This type of explanation is called <u>reverse causation</u> – because we thought that coffee drinking affected depression, but actually it might be the other way around.

Again this may be easier to grasp with a hypothetical example. At our imaginary bad science university, we conduct another study and find that people who spend a lot of time on Instagram are more likely to worry about their looks. This *could* be because spending time looking at the beautiful people of Instagram makes you more insecure about your appearance. However, causation could also flow the other way: it could be that people who are already worried about how they look are drawn to spending more time on Instagram.

Why does all this matter? Good statistical principles tell us that we shouldn't infer causation from the simple fact that two things are associated. But we don't abide by this rule just for the sake of being pedantic. We abide by it because inferring a causal effect where none exists can cause real harm to real people. People really do change their behaviour because of what they hear in the news. They hear that coffee helps ward off depression, so they start drinking more coffee. They hear that tap water gives you acne so they start wasting money on bottled water. Not such a big deal maybe. But then they hear that vaccines cause autism, so they decide not to vaccinate their children. Or they hear that divorce causes children to go off the rails, so they stay in a relationship that's making them deeply unhappy. The rule about correlation and causation isn't just important to statisticians, it's important for anyone who wants to make informed decisions about their (or other people's) lives.

CSI: Causation

So we know that two things being associated with each other does not mean that one caused the other. That leaves us with the same choice we've faced a few times now. Either we can assume that all causal claims are bullshit to be ignored – the newspaper says that sugar is bad for your heart, that's probably rubbish; the government says that a new prison policy helps stop people reoffending, that's probably rubbish too, and so on and so on. *Or* we can actually try to figure out for ourselves if the claim is true or not. This process need not involve any fancy maths, or even any numbers at all. All it requires is a little detective work.

Imagine there have been a series of grisly murders in your small town. You have a suspect in your sights. All of the bodies were found dumped in a particular spot at a nearby lake – somewhere concealed from the road, accessible only by a dirt track. The hikers who found the bodies saw the suspect's car parked a short way down the track. Other witnesses have since come forward to say that they have seen his car there at other times. What's more, a strand of the first victim's hair was found in the boot of his car.

So far this seems like pretty compelling evidence. But you know that it wouldn't necessarily lead to a conviction in court – where you need to prove that the suspect is guilty *beyond reasonable doubt*. The suspect having committed the murders is one explanation for the evidence you've collected. But there are others. For example, the lake is a popular fishing spot and fishermen sometimes park on the dirt track to avoid parking fines. The suspect is also a minicab driver, and his car is therefore often parked in many different places for entirely innocent reasons. The fact that the suspect drives a taxi also presents a plausible explanation for how the victim's hair might have come to be in the boot of his car: he may have been taking the victim somewhere and the hair might have got in there while they were depositing or extracting their luggage.

These are plausible alternative explanations for all the data you have at hand. In order to prove guilt beyond reasonable doubt, you need to rule out these alternative explanations, until the only plausible explanation left is that the suspect committed the crime. This will require you to collect more evidence. For example, you might ask the cab company for the suspect's booking records. If the victim never booked a ride with him then this removes one innocent explanation for their hair being in his car.

This is precisely the same process we need to apply to identifying causation in other scenarios – both in everyday life and in science. Let's go back to the example of hangovers. Many people have the belief that some specific drink, or combination of drinks, is particularly likely to give them a bad hangover. For example, you may have observed that your hangovers are especially unpleasant if you've drunk tequila the night before. You may therefore identify tequila as your particular nemesis. This is a causal hypothesis: tequila *causes* bad hangovers. However, there are a number of other potential explanations for the pattern you've observed. Maybe the nights where you drink tequila are also the nights where you stay out later than you normally would. Maybe they are the nights where you also drink more alcohol overall. In order to identify tequila as the culprit, you would need to rule out these other explanations.

One thing you could do is to start measuring the length of your nights out and the overall volume of alcohol you consume. If you find that the nights where you drink tequila generally end at the same time and involve the same amount of overall alcohol consumption as your other nights out, then you have excluded 'lateness' and 'overall volume of alcohol' as explanations for the association between tequila and bad hangovers. It's starting to look more plausible that it's a causal effect of the tequila itself.

Something else you could do is conduct an experiment. On some nights out where you would normally have drunk tequila, switch to rum – keeping everything else the same. Compare the strength of your hangovers on the rum nights vs. the tequila nights. By doing this, you've excluded the other explanations for why your hangovers from tequila nights might be worse.

This is a frivolous example, but the principle is the same when we're talking about real scientific findings. If you see that two things are associated – like coffee and depression – your first step should be to list all the plausible reasons why this association might exist. These include reverse causation (depression affects coffee drinking rather than the other way around) and other differences between coffee drinkers and non-coffee drinkers (such as age, wealth, and occupation). Only when these differences have been definitively ruled out can you reasonably conclude that coffee itself does indeed help to prevent depression.

This process of excluding alternative explanations is particularly important in the development of new medicines. We want to make very sure that new drugs actually *work*. That means making sure that they actually cause the effects that have been attributed to them – whether that is reducing blood pressure, improving mood, or killing an infection. The techniques medical researchers use to test drugs are therefore a good illustration of how the whole process of causal inference works in practice.

The habits of highly successful people

- Former US Secretary of State, Condoleezza Rice, claimed to get up at 4.30am every day to go to the gym. Tim Cook, the current CEO of Apple, starts his day at 3.45am. Former CEO of Yahoo!, Marissa Mayer, says she only needs around five hours of sleep a night. Donald Trump says he only needs three or four.

- Marc Cuban, owner of the Dallas Mavericks, reads for three hours a day. Warren Buffett, one of the world's richest investors, reads for five hours a day. CEO of Tesla, Elon Musk, read for 10 hours a day as a child.

- Mark Zuckerberg dresses the same way every day so he doesn't waste mental energy deciding what to wear.

- Steve Jobs was apparently so good at maintaining eye contact with people that he created a sort of 'reality distortion field' which led people to buy into whatever he was saying.

What do these facts have in common? They have all been cited as habits or qualities that helped these ultra-successful people get to the very top of their fields. Every year, an army of success coaches, personal development gurus, and 'life transformation strategists' package up facts like these into books, articles, and motivational lectures and sell them as lessons for success.

This is an example of an entire industry built almost wholly on the correlation/causation fallacy. Tim Cook gets very little sleep and is very successful. Is he successful *because* he barely sleeps? Would he be less successful if he slept a little more? Steve Jobs was great at eye contact and made a lot of money. Would he have been substantially less successful if his eyeball game wasn't always on-point?

The answer is that we have no idea. All the evidence we (and the life-transformation strategists) have available to us is that two things are associated. As to whether one caused the other, we are pretty much clueless. Correlation does not imply causation. An easy rule to remember – but an even easier one to forget, especially if you are charging punters $100 a ticket to hear you talk about the secrets to success. Or if you are a rich person who is keen to put your success down to a lack of sleep rather than simple good luck (or the $50 million you got from your dear old dad to get you started).

Now you know to look out for it, you'll start seeing this logic everywhere. Someone or something becomes a success, and people will start scrabbling around for 'lessons' as to why. A new horror movie about a killer bear has become a surprise hit? It must be because people are fed up of supernatural jump-scares and want a return to old-school killer animal movies. A sitcom became super-successful after they removed the laugh-track, so people must prefer their comedies without laugh-tracks.*

Maybe these conclusions are right. Maybe the movie did become a hit because people like killer animals again. Maybe Mark Zuckerberg did become successful partly because he doesn't care what he wears. But maybe not. There are plenty of other potential explanations. But people who are desperate to make a buck do not want to hear about other potential explanations. They see a clear bright line between X and Y, so goddammit they are going to greenlight this movie about killer sloths and they are going to start wearing the same black t-shirt & jeans combo every day. Maybe when the movie flops, or they see a nice pink shirt they like, then they'll listen the next time someone tells them that correlation is not evidence of causation.

---

* The same process also works in reverse. *Catwoman* and *Elektra* flopped, so audiences must not like superhero movies with female leads. Then *Wonder Woman* becomes the fifth biggest superhero movie of all time …

The drugs don't work

Imagine you've invented a pill that you think makes people smarter. Not movie superhero use-100%-of-your-brain-and-you-can-read-minds-and-time-travel smart.* Just smarter in an everyday way – a bit better at retaining information, a bit quicker on the uptake. This is plausibly possible. We know that long-term use of chemicals like alcohol can permanently damage the brain. It's possible that other chemicals could do the opposite – for example, by helping the development of brain tissues like myelin, or by altering the brain's chemistry in other ways.

This is an active area of research. Millions of government and pharmaceutical company dollars are currently sloshing around high-tech labs in pursuit of brain-enhancing chemicals. But you, in your shed in the garden, think you've cracked it. You've isolated a chemical that you think will substantially improve the development of important brain tissues. You give your pill a fancy name: 'Sagacium' has a nice latin-y ring to it (sagacity means 'wisdom'). Now you just need to see if it works.

Study 1: A Case study If your pill functions by improving brain development, it makes sense that it would work best on children – because their brains are still growing. You really decide to lean into the 'mad scientist' vibe by testing it on your own child first. Every morning, while your husband is not looking, you add some ground up Sagacium to your kid's breakfast cereal. And what do you know, her grades start to improve! She was getting mostly Cs and Ds before and now she's getting As and Bs.

Given what we've discussed so far, it should be clear to you that this experiment does not represent good evidence that your drug works. You have observed that X (taking Sagacium) and Y (improvement in grades) are associated. However, there are plenty of alternative explanations for your results that don't involve the drug actually doing anything. An important one that we've not discussed so far is **coincidence**. It's entirely possible that little Grismelda's grades were about to start going up anyway, and your illegal child experiment just happened to coincide with that.

Study 2: An observational study The only way to remove coincidence as a possible explanation is to try the drug on a lot more kids. If one child's grades improve after taking the drug, that could be a fluke. But if 1,000 kids' grades go up after taking it, that's a different story. So you start mass-producing Sagacium and selling it online. To determine if it's working you take a random sample of 1,000 of your

---

*   As we noted in Chapter 2, the idea that you only use 10% of your brain is actually a myth. Pretty much every part of your brain shows some level of activity all the time – even when you're asleep.

customers and compare their grades to a random sample of 1,000 kids who are not taking Sagacium. The kids taking the drug are called the <u>treatment group</u>. The kids who are not are called the <u>control group</u>. You find that, on average, the kids taking Sagacium are getting substantially higher grades than the kids who aren't. This is very unlikely to be coincidence.* So does this mean the drug works?

Not necessarily. The reason being that there are still other explanations for why the kids in the treatment group are doing better than the kids in the control group. For example, it might be that more of the kids taking Sagacium are from wealthy families – after all, their parents are spending a lot of money on brain pills. They might therefore be getting better grades not because of your drug, but because of the other benefits of coming from a wealthy home, like private tuition.

In statistics, this is called <u>confounding</u>. The apparent relationship between Sagacium and better grades is actually due to some external factor that is related to both – in this case, wealth. It's often helpful to think about confounding visually:

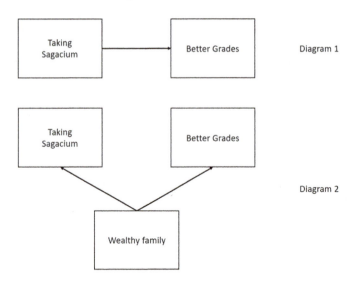

Diagram 1 shows what we initially thought might be happening: the better grades are due to Sagacium. Diagram 2 shows the alternative explanation for our results: kids from wealthier families are more likely to get the pill and are also (for other reasons) getting better grades. In order to prove that Sagacium actually works, we would need to definitively rule out this alternative explanation.

---

* See Chapter 3 for why it's important that the samples be random and also for an explanation of how differences between groups can be due to chance.

Another explanation we would need to rule out is one we've already talked about: <u>reverse causation</u>. It may not be that Sagacium is causing kids to get better grades, but that kids with better grades already are more likely to take Sagacium. Maybe parents whose children are already doing well academically are more likely to buy your drug to give their kids an extra edge. You could represent this visually on the diagram by drawing an arrow from grades back to Sagacium.

Study 3: A randomised experiment The best way to rule out these potential explanations is to decide for yourself who gets the pills and who doesn't, rather than leaving people to make their own decisions. That way you can make sure that the kids taking Sagacium are not already smarter, are not wealthier, are not getting more help with their homework – are not different in any way that would make them more likely to get better grades. What we're trying to do is eliminate every difference between the treatment and control groups *except for* whether they are taking Sagacium. If this is the only thing that's different between the groups and you still see that the Sagacium kids go on to get better grades, then the Sagacium *must* be the cause.

The easiest way to achieve this is to let a computer choose randomly which kids will go in the control group and which will go in the treatment group. This might seem a little bit counterintuitive: shouldn't we deliberately pick who goes in which group, so we know the groups are the same? This makes sense in theory, but it's actually almost impossible to do in practice. We can pretty easily make sure that the kids in both groups are the same age, gender, wealth, have the same existing IQ, and so on. However, there's just no way we can think of, and manually equalise, every possible difference that might be important. Letting chance decide removes this problem. The computer (or dice, or deck of cards, or whatever) is completely blind to the characteristics of your subjects. Which group a kid ends up in therefore can't be affected by family background, the school they go to, their favourite subjects – or anything else for that matter. Randomisation is therefore your best shot at equalising all the important differences between the groups.

Randomisation also prevents you, the experimenter, from cheating. You know the result you want: for the kids taking Sagacium to do better than the kids in the control group. You might therefore be tempted (consciously or unconsciously) to stack the deck in your favour. Maybe you pick the bright-looking kids for the treatment group and the dumb-looking ones for the control group. If a computer is making the decisions randomly, you can't get up to these sorts of shenanigans.

Now you're ready for your experiment. You bring a sample of kids back to your lab. You randomly allocate half of them to take Sagacium and the other half to sit and do nothing. After a while you give them all intelligence tests and you find that the kids who have taken the pill do substantially better. Eureka! You've got a big sample, so this is not likely to be coincidence. You've assigned kids to the groups randomly, so it's unlikely to be because the Sagacium kids were already brighter, or had some other advantage. Your drug works! You're going to get so rich! Maybe you should buy a volcano base, or a big laser, or …

… not so fast. Even after all this, there's still one more explanation you haven't ruled out. The kids in the treatment group *knew* they were getting a pill that was supposed to make them smarter. The kids in the control group knew they weren't getting anything. Maybe just feeling like they were getting a drug made the kids in the treatment group try harder, or made them more confident when they took the test. This is called the <u>placebo effect</u>, and it can be very powerful.

Study 4: A randomised controlled trial The only way to rule out the placebo effect as an explanation for your results is to do another study. This time you need to give the kids in the control group a pill too – a fake one with nothing in it. And, crucially, you need to make sure that the kids don't know if they are getting the fake pill or the real one. Ideally you would also make sure that *you* didn't know which pill each kid was getting until you'd crunched the numbers. Again, this is so you can't cheat. This is called a 'double blind' trial, because neither the participant nor the experimenter knows who is in the control group and who is in the treatment group.

In all of the previous studies, there were potential differences between the treatment group and the control group that were nothing to do with Sagacium getting into their bloodstreams. And as long as there are other differences, *they* could be the cause of any improvement in cognitive function. But in this final study, the only difference between the treatment and the control group is the presence or absence of the drug itself. If you still find that the kids taking Sagacium do better, you can therefore be confident that the drug actually works. This type of study is called a <u>randomised controlled trial</u> (RCT for short) and it is the way all new medicines need to be tested before doctors are allowed to prescribe them.

If this seems like a lot of unnecessary hassle, consider this: in the 1940s and early 1950s doctors thought it was a good idea to administer high concentrations of oxygen to premature babies, to help them recover. They were so convinced that this was a good idea that testing oxygen treatment in an RCT was considered unethical – because the infants in the control group would be deprived of a beneficial treatment. However, against these protests, an RCT was carried out. It showed that, not only was the oxygen treatment not helpful, it was actually making babies go blind. Around 10,000 babies were blinded because doctors were sure they didn't need an RCT to prove that oxygen treatment worked.[2] The medical literature is replete with examples like this. Even the experts aren't immune to seeing causation where there is none.

Postscript – fish brain

The Sagacium example is entirely fictional. However, in 2008 a group of people in Durham, England did think they had found a way to boost children's mental abilities using a pill. What was in these pills wasn't a drug per se; it was fish oil. Durham County Council's education team thought that omega-3 fish oils would have a beneficial effect on children's brains, thereby improving their exam performance.* In collaboration with an educational psychologist, they designed an experiment to see if this was true. They gave 3,000 teenagers six fish-oil pills a day for several weeks. 832 of these children did what they were told and took the tablets regularly. These 832 children did better in their exams than children of the same age, gender, and previous school performance who did not take the pills. I'll leave it to you to decide if these subsequent headlines were justified:**

> "Why a daily dose of fish oils 'can boost your GCSE grades'" – Daily Mail, 26 September 2008

> "'Proof' – Fish oils make you smart" – Northern Echo, 25 September 2008

'Have smartphones destroyed a generation?'

Testing Sagacium was tricky. It was only when you had eliminated every other possible difference between the people who took it and the people who didn't that you could be confident the drug actually worked. Now imagine that, instead of a drug, you are trying to determine whether smartphones are damaging young people's mental health.

This is a question posed by American psychologist Jean Twenge in an influential article for *The Atlantic* magazine.[3] In the article, she paints a bleak picture of young people raised in the age of social media and the iPhone. Despite being physically safer than any previous generation, today's teens are far sadder, lonelier, and more anxious than those that

---

*   This is entirely reasonable. Omega-3 fatty acids are one of the key building blocks of brain tissue, and could plausibly have a beneficial effect on brain development and neurotransmission.

** If you are interested, you can also read Ben Goldacre's extensive coverage of this story at badscience.net.

came before. Twenge describes us as being on 'the brink of the worst mental health crisis in decades'. And she lays the blame squarely on the little rectangle of metal and glass that, chances are, you have in your pocket right now:

> *"the twin rise of the smartphone and social media has caused an earthquake of a magnitude we've not seen in a very long time, if ever. There is compelling evidence that the devices we've placed in young people's hands are having profound effects on their lives – and making them seriously unhappy"* – The Atlantic, September 2017

No previous generation has, from their earliest teenage years, had a portal in their pockets through which they receive non-stop updates as to exactly what all of their friends and peers are saying and doing. No generation's behaviour has been as 'on display' as this one's is – as if they are all Z-list celebrities being followed by a miniature army of paparazzi. This, Twenge argues, has drastically exacerbated normal teenage worries about being judged and left out, leading to unprecedented levels of anxiety and depression.

It's a compelling argument. It's also a causal one: smartphones (twinned with social media) are *causing* young people to become depressed and anxious. If this hypothesis is correct, it has dramatic implications for our society. In countries like the USA and the UK, almost every teen has a smartphone. If they are doing such profound harm to young people's mental health, then we should be thinking seriously about ways to limit or repair the damage. So how do we work out if what Twenge is saying is actually true?

When you wanted to find out if Sagacium worked, you had to get people into your lab to assign who got the drug and who didn't. This is called <u>experimental research</u>. Experimental research is when you, as the researcher, deliberately manipulate X so you can see what happens to Y. In this case, X is not a pill, it's a piece of technology (actually, it's more like a complex interaction of hardware, software, and behaviour). If we wanted to take the same approach we did with Sagacium (i.e. conduct an experiment), we would need to take a large group of kids in their early teens and split them up into two groups.* Kids in the first group would have free use of their smartphones. Kids in the second group would have their smartphone use strictly controlled (let's say no more than half an hour's use per day). We would then track these children's development up until their early twenties. Were the children with less access to smartphones mentally healthier than the children who could use them as much as they wanted? If so, we have some decent evidence

---

*   By random assignment of course.

that smartphones have a causal (and detrimental) effect on young people's developing mental health.*

This study would be basically impossible to carry out in real life. It would require parents in both groups to adhere strictly to the terms of the study. For almost a decade, parents of children in the 'restricted smartphone use' group would have to precisely monitor their child's behaviour every single day. If too many of these parents, forced to endure their child's constant complaining, decided to be a bit more lenient in enforcing the half-hour limit (or if too many parents in the other group got fed up of seeing their kid's nose in their phone and decided to implement some restrictions of their own), then the experiment wouldn't work.

Because this study is so unworkable, we're instead going to have to rely on <u>observational research</u>. This is exactly what it sounds like. You observe what's going on with X and Y in the real world and you try to draw conclusions from that. Twenge marshals two key strands of observational evidence to support her hypothesis. First, she points to national surveys showing 2012 (when smartphone ownership reached 50% of the population) as an apparent inflection point in teenage attitudes and behaviour. Second, she compares young people who spend a lot of time on their phones to those who spend less:

- '[Teens] who spend 10 or more hours a week on social media are 56 percent more likely to say they are unhappy than those who devote less time to social media.'

- 'Teens who visit social-networking sites every day but see their friends in person less frequently are the most likely to agree with the statements "A lot of times I feel lonely", "I often feel left out of things", and "I often wish I had more good friends".'

- 'Eighth-graders who are heavy users of social media increase their risk of depression by 27 percent, while those who play sports, go to religious services, or even do homework more than the average teen cut their risk significantly.'

- 'Teens who spend three hours a day or more on electronic devices are 35 percent more likely to have a risk factor for suicide, such as making a suicide plan.'

These are interesting results, but by now you should recognise that this observational research does not constitute strong evidence that smartphones *cause* loneliness or depression or feelings of exclusion. Unlike

---

* This study is not perfect. There are other differences between the groups that aren't directly due to the use of smartphones. For example, group two are having their behaviour controlled in a way that group one aren't. This control in itself might create mental health differences between the two groups. Maybe not being able to do what you want all the time is character building.

your Sagacium experiment, this research has not eliminated all other potential explanations for the increased mental health burden of heavy smartphone/social media users.

One of the most obvious alternative explanations is reverse causation. Maybe the kids who are already excluded at school are drawn to spending their evenings with their face pressed up against the window of social media, while the happy, popular kids use it more sparingly. If smartphones disappeared, maybe the unhappy kids wouldn't get any happier – they would just spend their time doing some other lonely activity instead.

There are also plenty of other potential differences between heavy smartphone users and other kids that might explain these results. For example, maybe kids experiencing a lot of conflict at home retreat to their rooms with their phone rather than spending time with their families. Or maybe they just live further away from their school friends – with this physical distance making them feel more isolated and also forcing them to communicate through their phones rather than in person. In both of these situations, there is a clear association between smartphone use and sadness – the kids who use their smartphones a lot are less happy. However, the smartphones themselves are not the cause of the problem.

These alternative possibilities do not mean that Twenge is definitely wrong. She could well be right. It's certainly plausible that carrying out your social life on constant public display through a device in your pocket is deeply unhealthy, and that it's causing permanent damage to the next generation. But, with the evidence we have available, we can't be anywhere near *sure* that this is true. And it's important to remember that we can't be sure. Because if smartphones *aren't* the culprit, then we risk wasting a lot of time, energy, and worry solving the 'smartphone problem', when we could have been addressing the real reason teens are suffering.

Establishing causation is *really* hard

Because it's often so hard to study social phenomena under lab conditions, we're forced to rely on purely observational evidence more than we might like. As a consequence, we actually know a lot less about how the world works than most people think. Ever wondered why advice on diet seems so changeable? Fat is bad. Or maybe carbs are bad and fat is fine. Gluten is bad. Or maybe it's not. Cholesterol will *definitely* kill you. Oh no, wait, it probably won't. We've been doing science on food for a long time. Shouldn't we have figured all this out by now?

The reason we still have such a loose grasp on the harms or benefits of specific foods is the same reason we're not sure if smartphones are bad for us. The best way to find out if, say, kale was good for you would be to kidnap 2,000 people and randomly assign them to a kale-rich or a kale-poor diet; keeping everything else about their diet and lifestyle exactly the same. But we can't do that because it would be 'illegal' or 'immoral' or whatever. Instead we are stuck with observational evidence. We observe what people eat (actually we usually just ask them and trust that they'll be honest, which comes with its own set of problems), then we keep a check on their health. If we observe that people who eat lots of kale are less likely to get heart disease, is that because kale is good for you? Or is it because the kind of people who eat kale are also the kind of people who go running a lot and wouldn't enter a McDonald's if their life depended on it? There are ways to try and rule out these alternative explanations, but none of them are perfect (we'll go through this in the next section). The upshot is that a lot of dietary advice is an exercise in educated guesswork.

The same issues lie behind ongoing arguments about some of the most important questions in social science. After years of research we're still not *completely* sure how much widespread gun ownership pushes up the murder rate. There is still vast scientific disagreement as to whether various left- or right-wing economic policies help the economy or hurt it. We don't fully know if capital punishment helps deter crime. The list of unanswered questions goes on and on.

We can't bring a bunch of countries into the lab and randomly assign half of them to have their guns taken away, or to raise or cut their top rate of tax. So instead we're stuck with observational evidence. For example, we can see that US states where fewer people own guns have fewer murders (proportional to their population) than states where gun ownership is more common. It's highly probable that guns have something to do with this – but there *are* other potential explanations. For example, many of the states with lots of guns and high murder rates also tend to be those with high rates of poverty and inequality. Maybe that's what's ultimately causing the murders, not the guns.

This is not a council of despair. Just because we can't always do a randomised controlled trial does not mean we should give up on ever knowing how people or societies work. It just means that we have to be a lot more cautious and patient than we usually are before we conclude that X definitely causes Y. We have to be cleverer with our research, and we have to keep our detective hats on and our eyes sharp for alternative explanations for the patterns we observe.

In the final section of this chapter, we'll go through some ways in which social scientists try to figure out if one thing causes another when they can't do an experiment.

Establishing causation is not impossible

Natural experiments

Does hanging out with a bad crowd make you more likely to start behaving badly yourself? If we go by every film ever made about teenagers then the answer is definitely yes. But, unfortunately, Hollywood movies don't count as good evidence of anything (if they did, all we'd need to do in the event of nuclear war is find the nearest fridge ...).

This is another example of a situation where we can't really do an experiment. It would be practically impossible (not to mention unethical) to randomly assign kids to hang out with either the kids in the chess club or the kids smoking behind the bike sheds. However, a group of US social scientists came up with a clever solution to this problem. They were interested in what made young people more likely to drink and do drugs in college.[4] Unlike in many other parts of the world, first-year students in American colleges tend to share their dorm-rooms with another student. And, unlike movie colleges, which assign roommates strictly in order to maximise odd-couple hilarity, real American colleges assign roommates on a purely random basis. This means that, regardless of their own proclivities, some students will be assigned hard-drinking, hard-partying roommates, where others are assigned teetotal bookworms (and all points in between). This allowed the researchers to measure whether the students who were assigned the 'bad' roommates were more likely to start behaving badly themselves. And contrary to what you might expect, they found that roommates did not have much of an effect. Students who did not do drugs or drink heavily before college were no more likely to break bad if they had a hard-partying roommate than if they had a roommate whose nose was more often in a book than a pint.

This type of research is called a <u>natural experiment</u>: natural because it is not the researchers themselves who are assigning people to groups, but some process that was happening anyway (in this case, college roommate assignment). The crucial difference between this and observational research is that the process by which 'nature' is allocating people to groups is entirely random. If we simply observed that students whose friends drank and did drugs were more likely to drink and do drugs themselves, we would not be able to rule out the possibility that this was due to students choosing who to hang out with, rather than who they hung out with having an effect on their behaviour. However, because roommates are randomly assigned, it *can't* be that hard-drinking students choose roommates similar to themselves. Any difference we see between people assigned 'bad' versus 'good' roommate therefore has to be an effect of the roommate.

Eliminating alternative explanations using statistics

Natural experiments are great. They give you something approaching the power of an experiment in situations where a real experiment would be difficult or impossible. For a social scientist, discovering a clear natural experiment is therefore something of a eureka moment. That's because nature serves up the circumstances for a good natural experiment only very rarely. The rest of the time we have to settle for something a bit more humdrum.

Let's say we wanted to answer one of the questions we posed in the previous section: Does more people owning guns lead to more murders? We start from the observation that US states where gun ownership is less common, like Hawaii and Massachusetts, have fewer murders (per head of population) than states where more people have guns, like Louisiana and Mississippi. There are a number of explanations for why this might be the case (besides the possibility that gun ownership itself is to blame):

- *Poverty*: States where a greater proportion of the population own guns also tend to be poorer, and poorer places tend to have higher rates of violent crime, regardless of how many people own guns.

- *Unemployment*: Closely related to the issue of poverty, states where more people own guns are also states where more people are unemployed. States with lots of unemployed people also tend to have higher rates of crime.

- *Alcohol consumption*: Drunk people kill each other more often than sober people do. People living in states where gun ownership is more common also tend to drink more. These states might have a higher murder rate, not because of the guns, but because of the drinking.

As we've already discussed, we can't do an experiment to rule out these explanations. It would be nice if there were a natural experiment – for example, if the guns in some random states all broke for some reason – but that doesn't seem very likely. So instead we have to find some other way to rule out these alternative explanations.

The most common way this is done is by using something called a regression model. I'm not going to go through the maths, but essentially what a regression model allows you to do is calculate how the outcome you are interested in (in this case, the murder rate) is related to a number of different things independently. Basically, it allows you to estimate what would happen to the outcome if one of these things changed but not the others. For example, we could use a regression model to estimate what would happen to the murder rate if the level of gun ownership changed, but the levels of poverty, unemployment, and alcohol consumption all stayed the same.

A group of researchers at the Harvard School of Public Health did exactly this in a paper published in 2002.[5] Using a regression model, they found that, even if you separated out the effects of all the other factors we've mentioned, states with more gun owners still had significantly more murders. So poverty, unemployment, and drinking are not the reason that people kill each other more often in states where more people have guns.

This is better than just knowing that gun ownership is correlated with the murder rate. But if you've kept your detective hat on you'll have thought of some other explanations that the authors haven't ruled out here. One example, suggested by other researchers in the field, is so-called 'Southern honour culture'. Most of the states with the highest rates of gun ownership are in the South. And some sociologists have speculated that a lot of the violence in these states is due not to the availability of firearms, but to the extreme way Southern culture encourages people (especially men) to respond to perceived slights and moral infractions. The Harvard study does not rule out this potential explanation.

Reverse causation is also a possibility. It may not be that people owning guns increases the risk of people killing each other, but that people in states where a lot of killing is happening are more likely to buy a gun to protect themselves.

Later studies have tried to account for these explanations, and have tended to find that there is still an effect of gun ownership. But it's always possible that there are other explanations we just haven't thought of. This is how a lot of social science progresses. One study will observe that two things are associated, and try to rule out some explanations for why that might be. Then another group of researchers will come along with some more explanations that they've thought of, and try to rule those out. This carries on until eventually, hopefully, we are satisfied we know what's going on. It's a process that can take a *very* long time.

The rush to infer causation

It would be great to know for sure if smartphones were bad for children's mental health, just like it would be great to know if tap water caused acne, or if tax cuts were the best way to end a recession. Because it would be great to know these things, people are keen to quickly get to the point where we *do* know. This, basically, is the reason why people are so quick to forget the rule that correlation does not imply causation. Remembering the rule means remembering the slow, careful accumulation of evidence that is actually required to establish that X causes Y. It means being stuck at 'we don't know' for a lot longer than we'd like. A health reporter who remembered the rule would not be able to write that story about how hazelnuts prevent diabetes, or about how yoghurt causes cancer. In fact, they probably wouldn't have much to write about at all. A politician who remembered the rule would have to admit that they weren't sure that their new tax policy was actually going to work.

Establishing causation is like a long, gruelling trek up a treacherous mountainside. Someone making a causal claim is telling you they've made the trip. And maybe they have. But you should ask for some very compelling evidence before you believe them.

 ## Summary

Understanding causation is vital in science and in everyday life. We need to understand what causes what in order to understand *why* things happen, and to have some idea of what *effects* our actions will have. Will this new drug reduce your risk of having a heart attack? Will banning assault weapons reduce the number of mass-shootings? These are both important *causal* questions.

Correlation does not equal causation. Just because X and Y are related does not mean X causes Y.

They key to establishing causation is ruling out alternative explanations. In order to determine whether X does in fact cause Y, you need to rule out other explanations for why X and Y might be related.

One of the best ways to rule out alternative explanations is through a controlled experiment. In a controlled experiment, you change X while keeping everything else the same. If Y then changes, it must be because you changed X.

Keeping everything except X the same is harder than it looks. This is why medicines and other interventions should be tested using randomised controlled trials.

We can't always do a controlled experiment. In the real world, we often can't conduct experimental research for ethical or practical reasons. In these cases, we have to rely on other ways of ruling out alternative explanations for the relationship between X and Y. These alternative methods include natural experiments and regression models.

Terminology used in this chapter

Causal inference: Figuring out whether one thing causes another.

Reverse causation: The relationship between X and Y arises not because X causes Y, but because Y causes X.

Treatment group: In an experimental study of an intervention, the group which actually receives the intervention. For example, in a drug trial, this would be the group that actually receives the drug.

Control group: In an experimental study of an intervention, the group which *does not* receive the intervention.

Confounding: An external factor which produces an association between X and Y – representing an alternative explanation for why X and Y are related.

Placebo effect: An effect produced by people's *expectation* that an intervention will produce a result, rather than by any effect of the intervention itself. For example, in a drug trial, people taking the pill may get better not because the pill works, but because people *expect* the pill to work, and this expectation makes them feel better.

Randomised controlled trial (RCT): A specific type of experimental study in which a treatment group receiving a particular intervention are compared to a control group (who receive a different intervention, or no intervention). A random procedure is used to allocate participants to the treatment or control groups.

Experimental research: Research in which the researcher themselves intentionally manipulates X to see what will happen to Y.

Observational research: Research in which the researcher does not manipulate X. Instead the researcher observes the naturally occurring relationship between X and Y.

Natural experiment: A specific type of observational study which takes advantage of the fact that an existing process (for example, college roommate allocation) has randomly assigned people to treatment and control groups.

Regression model: A type of statistical model which attempts to determine the relationship between a particular outcome (for example, health) and one or more potentially explanatory factors (for example, pool ownership). Regression models are often used to account for potential confounding factors. For example, to exclude wealth as a potential explanation for a positive relationship between pool ownership and health, a researcher might use a regression model to estimate what would happen to someone's health if their pool ownership changed but their wealth stayed the same.

Seeing beyond the headlines

Establishing whether one thing causes another is difficult. Causal claims should therefore be subjected to special scrutiny. Here are three questions to ask any time someone implies that X causes Y:

1. IS THIS A CAUSAL CLAIM?

For the most part, journalists, politicians, and the like have heard the 'correlation is not causation rule'. They can therefore be wary of making it too obvious that they are making a causal claim. Look out for active words like 'boost', 'cut', 'harm', 'affect', and 'damage'. These words all imply that something causal is happening. You should also look out for any recommendation that people should change their behaviour. For example, if readers are being advised to cut down on their smartphone use in order to improve their mental health, this necessarily implies that smartphones have a causal effect.

2. WHY MIGHT X AND Y BE ASSOCIATED?

Broadly, there are four reasons why X and Y might be related:

i.   ***Coincidence.*** *For example, the number of people who drown in pools in the USA in a given year is strongly correlated with the number of Nicolas Cage films released that year.[6] This is probably a coincidence.*

ii. ***Reverse causation.*** *X doesn't cause Y, Y causes X. For example, people who don't drink alcohol are more likely to be seriously ill. This is not because alcohol protects you from serious illness, but because people with serious illnesses tend not to drink.*

iii. ***Confounding.*** *X doesn't cause Y. Instead there exists some other factor that is related to both X and Y. It is this third factor that causes X and Y to appear related. For example, people with Ferraris may be less likely to get diabetes. This is not because Ferraris are good for you, but because people with Ferraris also tend to be rich, and rich people are generally less likely to get diabetes.*

iv. ***Causation.*** *X really does cause Y.*

3. WHICH EXPLANATIONS HAVE BEEN RULED OUT? WHICH EXPLANA-TIONS REMAIN?

To establish that X causes Y, you need to rule out all other plausible explanations for why they might be associated. Ways of ruling out explanations include conducting an experiment, exploiting a natural experiment, or controlling for confounding factors in a regression model.

If the claim is based on an experiment, check the methodology. Is there a control group? Have participants been assigned to the control and intervention groups randomly? Have the control group been given an effective placebo?

In the case of observational research, what factors have been controlled for? What factors have not been controlled for? What has been done to eliminate the possibility of reverse causation?

After you have listed all the explanations that have been ruled out, is a causal effect of X on Y the only plausible one remaining?

Example

CLAIM	IS THIS A CAUSAL CLAIM?	WHY MIGHT X AND Y BE ASSOCIATED?	WHAT EXPLANATIONS HAVE BEEN RULED OUT?	VERDICT: CAUSATION ESTABLISHED?
Young people who use social media a lot increase their risk of depression by 27%	YES. 'increase their risk' implies a causal effect	Reverse causation (unhappy people may spend more time on social media) Confounding (e.g. people with few real-life contacts may spend more time on social media) A genuine causal effect of social media use	The figure comes from a large study and is unlikely to be just coincidence Not an experiment. No statistical controls listed. Therefore no other explanations ruled out	NO. There are still many other potential explanations for why heavy social media users may be at higher risk of depression

Exercises for Chapter 7

Exercise 1

You are having lunch with a friend and she tells you about a ridiculous present someone bought her for her recent birthday. It's called a 'portable wine lanyard' and it's basically a necklace that holds your wine glass upright, freeing your hands up to hold a plate, or do whatever you want to do with your hands (this is a real thing).

After the conversation, you think no more about it. But the next day, you start seeing adverts for this gadget appear in your Facebook feed. Searching around, you find a YouTube video that purports to explain why this is happening: the Facebook app on your phone is using the microphone to listen to your conversations. It picks up on the names of products (or categories of products) and then shows you adverts for those products – in much the same way that Google and Facebook track the websites you visit to show you relevant ads.

Is this the only possible explanation for the association between your conversation with your friend and the appearance of the ads? Or are there other possible explanations?

Exercise 2

In December 2010, the left-wing US news website *Alternet* published a story under the headline 'Study Confirms that Fox News Makes You Stupid'.[7]

This claim was based on a survey of American voters conducted by researchers at the University of Maryland (you can find the link to the original study on this book's companion website). The study's principal finding was that people who watched Fox News were more likely than viewers of other networks to believe a series of false statements about politics (for example, that Barack Obama was not born in the USA).

Use the toolbox to determine whether the evidence from this survey supports the claim given in the headline.

---

www.macmillanihe.com/devries-critical-statistics

 ONLINE RESOURCES AVAILABLE

Go to the book's companion website for further examples, data, links, and other useful resources.

---

8 BAD GRAPHICS

Electioneering

I'm hoping that by this point in the book you are starting to develop a taste for spotting dodgy statistics. And for connoisseurs of statistical bullshit, there is one event that is like all our Christmases, Hanukkahs, Eids, and Baisakhis all rolled into one: a national election. Politicians engage in statistical trickery all year round, but at election time they really kick it up a notch. They are desperate, *ravenous* for your vote – and if they have to torture a few numbers to death to get it, then by god they'll do it.

Even in the age of social media, one of the main tools candidates still use to get their message out is physical leaflets. And it's here, next to a picture of their big smiling face, that the juiciest statistical bullshit can often be found. Bullshit like the graph* in Figure 8.1 from James Barber, a candidate for the Liberal Democrats in the 2015 UK General Election.

Figure 8.1 Photograph of James Barber's election leaflet

*Source: electionleaflets.org***

---

*   In this chapter I'm going to use the words 'graph' and 'chart' as if they are synonymous. If we're going to be pedantic about it, pretty much all the examples I use in this chapter are charts (graphical representations of data) rather than graphs (diagrams of mathematical functions). However, most people use terms like 'bar graph' and 'bar chart' interchangeably, so for the sake of ease of understanding that's the approach I'm going with too.

**   electionleaflets.org is an excellent crowdsourced public archive of the leaflets British people get through their doors at election time.

Before we dig into the problems with this graph, it's worth taking a moment to think about what a graph is actually *for*. Why turn numbers into a picture in the first place?

The main reason to do this is that most people are much better at understanding visual differences – size, shape, colour – than they are at understanding raw numbers. Reading a table of percentages, we can get a reasonable idea of which numbers are bigger and which numbers are smaller. But displaying the figures as, for example, bars of different heights, gives us a much more intuitive feel for what's going on. It makes the 'story' of the numbers much clearer.

The little note about who 'Can't win here' is a clue to the story James Barber wants his graph to tell. The numbers in the graph are the proportion of the vote each party in his constituency got in the previous general election. The message here is that people who don't want the Labour Party to win should vote for the Lib Dems, rather than for one of the other non-Labour parties. This is a very common tactic used in elections the world over. Here, the Lib Dems are trying to portray themselves as the only party with a chance of beating Labour. It's the same argument many of my American friends used on Gary Johnson voters during the 2016 US elections. Johnson can't win, so a vote for him is wasted. If they want to make sure Trump doesn't win, they should switch their vote to Hillary.

Unless you have an inherent distaste for tactical voting, there's nothing wrong with this argument. What is wrong in James Barber's leaflet is that the graph he is using is completely misleading. Look at the numbers: in the last election the Conservatives got 22% of the vote, the Lib Dems got 27%, and Labour got 46%. Now look at the height of the bars in the graph. The bar for the Conservatives is about two-thirds the height of the Lib Dem bar; whereas the height of the Lib Dem bar is very close to the height of the Labour bar. The graph is presenting the **5 percentage point difference** between the Conservatives and the Lib Dems as much bigger than the **19 percentage point difference** between the Lib Dems and Labour!

Figure 8.2 shows the numbers from the graph plotted accurately.

You can see that the real story of the numbers is that Labour is way ahead, and that the Lib Dems and the Conservatives are pretty close to each other. This story doesn't really do James Barber's campaign any favours, however – hence the distorted graph that actually appears on the leaflet.* (In the end, Labour won the seat with 54% of the vote and the Conservatives came second with 23%. The Lib Dems came third on 10%.)

---

*   I'm being slightly unfair in picking on poor James here. This exact problem is extremely common in campaign leaflets in the UK and elsewhere.

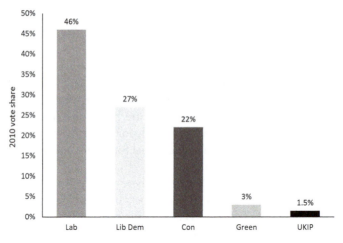

Figure 8.2 My corrected visualisation of the figures provided in the Liberal Democrat leaflet

Charts as a collection of 'visual metaphors'

As we've already discussed, the point of any chart is to present numerical information visually. To this end, designers have lots of visual elements they can play with, including shape, colour, size, and position. Any element that can be made to look different on the page can be used to convey information: varying the size of an element (like a bar in a bar chart) can be used to indicate bigger or smaller numbers, varying shape or colour or can be used to separate data from different groups, and so on.

In bar charts like the one we've been discussing, the main visual element a designer has to work with is the **height of the bars**. In this specific case, the height of the bars is proportional to the percentage of the vote each party received in the 2010 election. Taller bars indicate a larger vote share, shorter bars indicate a smaller one. Another way of saying this is that the height of the bars is a <u>visual metaphor</u> for vote share. The title on the left-hand side of my version of the graph tells you this, and the scale allows you to read off exactly what bars of each height mean. This scale (the <u>y-axis</u> of the graph) is essential. Without it, all sorts of problems can happen. If the graph on the leaflet had included a proper y-axis, it would have been impossible for the bars to be distorted the way they were.

There are other visual elements here that could be manipulated to convey additional information. In fact (though you can't see this in the black and white image), the graph does use colour to differentiate the political parties (red for Labour, blue for Conservative, etc.). However, the party labels make this information redundant. If you wanted to, you could also use the width or area of the bars to carry information. For example, you could scale the width of the bars to be proportional to the speed at which each party's candidate could run 100m. I have no idea why you would do this, but you could if you wanted to. As the designer of a chart it's up to you what information each visual difference in your chart conveys. Sensibly, the designer of this chart has chosen not to use 'width of bar' as a visual metaphor for anything, and has therefore kept all the bar widths the same.

A brief history lesson

In Chapters 5 and 6, we talked about the fact that things like averages and percentages were invented as tools to solve particular problems. The same is true of graphs. People in Ye Olden Days* couldn't just load up Excel and pick from a list of chart types. If they wanted to make a big table of numbers easier to absorb by turning it into a picture, they would need to make something up from scratch. For example, in the 1780s Scottish engineer William Playfair wanted a way to visualise Scotland's imports and exports to and from various countries. So he came up with the idea that the length of some bars on a piece of paper could be used as a visual metaphor for the number of pounds of goods being imported from and exported to each country (Figure 8.3).

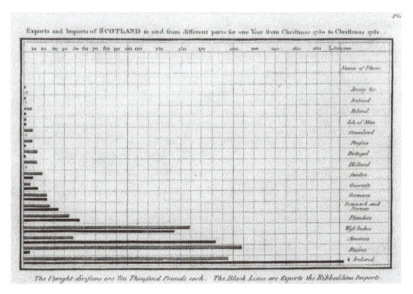

Figure 8.3 William Playfair's bar chart of imports and exports in Scotland

Source: First published in Playfair's 1786 'Commercial and Political Atlas and Statistical Breviary'

---

* People in those olden days didn't actually say 'ye'. They said 'the' like we do now. In old English, the 'th' sound was represented by a letter called 'thorn', which looked like this: Þ. But early printing presses were all made in Germany and Italy and they didn't have this letter. So when people needed to print the letter thorn they used the letter 'y' instead. If they'd used another letter (say 'p', which actually looks a lot more like thorn than y does), we'd all be saying things like 'Pe Olde Curiosity Shoppe' and 'Pe Olde Pub'.

Even though what he created might be the first ever bar chart, it has everything you would want out of a visualisation. You can see exactly what is being measured, and the scale is clear and consistent. There is even another visual metaphor being used here, in addition to length: the shading on the bars ('black' or 'ribbed') indicates whether the number is for imports or exports. In a way, this graph is so good it's depressing. Most inventions are improved over time – but this 230-year-old graph is better than most of what passes for visualisation in the age of Excel.

After Playfair (who also invented the line graph and the pie chart), there were many innovators in the field of visualising data, with one of the more noteworthy pioneers being none other than Florence Nightingale. During the Crimean War of the 1850s (which pitted Russia against an alliance comprising France, Britain, Sardinia, and the Ottoman Empire), Nightingale managed a team of nurses tending to wounded British soldiers. She was also responsible for compiling statistical reports about the health of the soldiers to send to the government back home. As a rule, the politicians couldn't really cope with raw statistics (some things don't change), so she needed to present them in a more intuitive way. This led her to invent several different types of charts, with perhaps the most famous being the 'polar area diagram' (Figure 8.4).

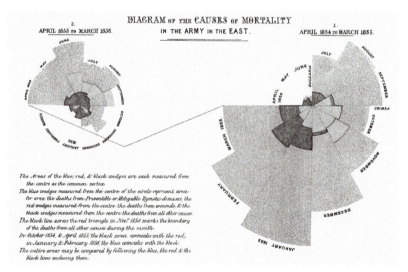

Figure 8.4 Florence Nightingale's polar area diagram of the causes of death of British soldiers in the Crimean war

Source: First published in Nightingale's 1858 report 'Notes on Matters Affecting the Health, Efficiency, and Hospital Administration of the British Army'

Here, the total **area** of each wedge (not just the length) is a visual metaphor for the number of soldiers killed in a given month. Bigger wedges mean more deaths. The outermost section of each wedge (which was blue in the original image) represents deaths due to infectious diseases, the plain light grey sections (red in the original) represent deaths due to wounds, and the black parts represent deaths from all other causes. Unlike the Lib Dem graph with which I began this chapter, the story of the numbers comes through clearly and accurately here: many more soldiers were dying due to infectious diseases than were dying of wounds sustained in battle. This message resonated strongly with the government back home, and encouraged dramatic improvements in hygiene and sanitation. Nightingale's statistical insights are credited as saving many thousands of lives. Despite this, chances are that statistics are not what you think of when you hear her name. Popular portrayals (at the time and since) have generally represented Nightingale not as a manager and statistician, but as tender-hearted, dedicated nurse: 'The Lady With the Lamp.' I'll leave it up to you to speculate as to why this might be.

After this wild and woolly period of early invention, data visualisation settled down into some standard forms: a few types of charts (with consistent visual metaphors) that did the job in most situations. These are the same types of charts you will still most often see in the media (and in science).

Bad charts: A spotter's guide

In this section, I'll go through the most common types of graphs you'll come across in everyday life: in the media, in marketing, in politics, and in science. I'll describe what they're good for when used properly, but also how they can be distorted to sell you a misleading message.

Bar charts

What are they used for?

Bar charts are used to convey differences between groups in some quantity. Each group gets its own bar and the height of the bar is proportional to the quantity being measured. The groups can be anything from countries, to age groups, to sports teams, to seasons of a TV show. The quantity being measured can be anything that it's possible to measure on a **continuous** scale: from salaries, to heights, to ratings, to personality traits. For example, the bar chart in Figure 8.5 gives the worldwide box office take for the five Transformers movies released to date, along with the worldwide take for the movie that won the Best Picture Oscar in the same year.

This is a slightly different sort of bar chart to the one we began with. It's called a 'clustered' bar chart because each year has a 'cluster' of bars. In this case, each year has two bars, one representing the year's Transformers movie, and the other the Best Picture winner. Here the pattern

Figure 8.5 Box office receipts of Transformers movies and best picture winners

Source: Statistics from Box Office Mojo*

on the bars tells us which movie each bar represents. The legend underneath the graph tells us which pattern represents which movie (solid grey for Transformers, light grey for Best Picture winner).

The story of the graph is that every Transformers movie has attracted vastly more viewers than the Best Picture winner for the same year. The highest grossing Oscar winner on the list, the Coen Brothers' *No Country for Old Men* (2007), made three times less money than the lowest grossing Transformers movie (2017's dismal *The Last Knight*). The graph therefore also shows that we need to burn civilisation to the ground and start again from scratch. You can be in charge of re-inventing graphs.

Bar charts are useful whenever you are comparing something between groups. And because this is a situation that comes up a lot, bar charts are probably the most common type of chart you will encounter in the media. As we'll see below, even things that don't look much like charts at all are often secretly bar charts in disguise.

Bar chart or column chart?

Searching around the internet, you'll often see charts like the ones above described as 'column' rather than bar charts. This is because it is sometimes useful to make a distinction between charts where the bars lie horizontally ('bar charts') and charts where they stand up vertically

---

* *Box Office Mojo* is a box office tracking site. The Oscars for a given year are held in February or March of the following year (for example, the Oscars for films released in 2007 were awarded in February 2008). It should be noted that the comparison for 2017 is a little unfair, given that, at the time I put this graph together, the Oscar winner (Guillermo del Toro's *The Shape of Water*) was still playing in theatres in some territories.

('column charts'). Microsoft Excel makes this distinction. However, the principles behind these charts are exactly the same, and can be grouped together under the generic heading of 'bar charts'.

What makes a bar chart misleading?

The easiest way to end up with a misleading chart is to, accidentally or otherwise, mess with the visual elements people perceive most strongly. In a bar chart, the main message comes through comparing the heights of the bars. You therefore need to be very careful with the message these bars convey. Figure 8.6, for example, is a chart from the Fox Business TV show *Cavuto*, broadcast in 2012.

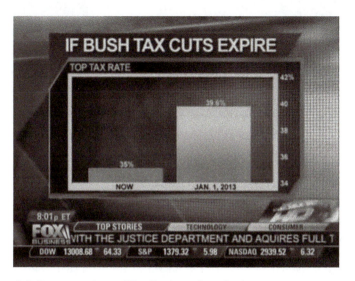

Figure 8.6 Screen capture of Fox Business bar chart

Source: Media Matters for America

While he was president, George Bush cut the top rate of tax in the USA (the rate paid by the richest households) from 39.6% to 35%. This tax cut was temporary, and in 2012 the Obama administration had to decide whether to allow the cuts to expire, or to keep them in place. The purpose of this chart is to illustrate how much the top tax rate would go up if the cuts were allowed to expire. The chart should therefore aim to give the viewer an accurate feel for the magnitude of the difference. Just by looking at the graph, it feels like taxes are going to go up by a lot – the bar on the right is more than five times taller than the bar on the left! But if we look at the *y*-axis, we can see that the scale starts at 34% and ends at 42%. This restricted scale vastly exaggerates the apparent size of what is in reality a less than five percentage point difference. This is a case in which the viewer would have a much better idea of what was going on if they closed their eyes and just listened to the numbers.

Another way in which problems can arise is when different visual elements of a chart are telling fundamentally different stories. Figure 8.7 is from a *Gizmodo* article titled 'Holy F*ck, the New iPad Has a Gigantic 70-Percent Larger Battery'.[1]

Figure 8.7 Screen capture of *Gizmodo*'s comparison of iPad battery sizes

Source: Gizmodo*

It may not look like it, but this is actually a bar graph. It's common practice for media outlets to try to pretty up bar graphs by replacing the bars with something more 'exciting' (in this case, pictures of batteries ... with unicorns floating in them for some reason).

As in a regular bar graph, the height of the bars (batteries) is functioning as a visual metaphor for battery capacity. The first problem with this chart is that, unlike in the Fox News example, there is no *y*-axis. The *y*-axis should provide a numbered scale we can use to read off the heights of the bars. The title of the axis should also tell us exactly what is being measured. In this case, this information is contained in the article itself: capacity is measured in watt-hours, and the numbers for the old and new iPads are 25 and 42.5, respectively. But the point of a chart is to present numerical information concisely and intuitively. If the only way to get all the information is to look at the graph *and* read chunks of the article, then what's the point of the graph? As a general rule, a good chart should give you all the information you need, without requiring you to read the accompanying text.

* Hat tip to *Business Insider*. This chart appears on their list of the '27 Worst Charts of All Time'.

Now we get to the real problem with this chart. From my rough measurements (which, again, would have been a lot easier with the help of a *y*-axis scale), the battery on the right is indeed 70% taller than the battery on the left. However, it is also a lot *wider*. This means that the *area* of the battery on the right is much more than 70% larger than the area of the battery on the left. This visual difference gives you the impression that the new iPad battery is actually something like *three and half times* (350%) bigger than the old one.

There are two visual elements that people could 'read' from this chart: height and area. The height of the batteries is telling the true story of the data (the new battery is 70% bigger than the old one). The area is telling an untrue story (the new battery is 350% bigger). Unfortunately, the latter is much more visually striking than the former. This may have been intentional (maybe some Apple exec slid some money under the table), but the likely explanation is more innocent. The designer wanted the heights of the bars to convey the relevant information, but they also didn't want the battery on the right to look skinny and weird. Whatever the reason, the result is the same – a very misleading chart.

A good rule of thumb for reading any bar chart (or any chart at all really) is to first think about the visual metaphors. Which visual elements of this graph (height, width, colour, etc.) are supposed to be communicating information? What story are these elements telling? You can then compare this story to the actual numbers: does this story seem true to the message of the data?

Pie charts

What are they used for?

The purpose of a pie chart is to illustrate proportions. If we are measuring something that can be split up into categories, what share does each category take up of the whole? For example, let's say we're arguing with a friend about the representation of women in movies. Our friend says that, sure, movies used to be all about men, but that's a thing of the past. Now it seems like basically every blockbuster has a female protagonist: from *The Hunger Games*, to *Wonder Woman*, to *Rogue One*, and *The Force Awakens*.

This is not an 'agree to disagree' sort of situation. Either modern blockbusters are still dominated by men, or they aren't. And luckily there is data to help us answer this question. In a 2017 report Dr Martha Lauzen of San Diego State University crunched the numbers.[2] Of the top 100 grossing films of 2016, she found that 54% had a male protagonist, 29% had a female protagonist, and 17% did not have an identifiable 'main' character (*Suicide Squad* would be an example). Figure 8.8 shows these figures plotted on a pie chart.

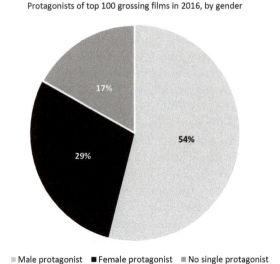

Protagonists of top 100 grossing films in 2016, by gender

■ Male protagonist   ■ Female protagonist   ■ No single protagonist

Figure 8.8 Pie chart showing the gender breakdown of movie protagonists

Source: Data from Lauzen (2017)

Arguably, presenting the numbers as slices of a pie gives us a more intuitive feel for how many more films star a male protagonist than star a female one. We can see that a decent chunk of the top movies of 2016 had a female main character, but the majority of these films still had a male protagonist.

However, the advantages of the pie chart are not quite as obvious as those of the bar chart. In fact, the pie chart gets something of a bad rap among data scientists. Many would argue that a pie chart is taking up a lot of space trying to visually communicate something (a small batch of percentages) that is already quite easy to understand. Why not just write the numbers out, or put them in a table? One of the leading lights of data visualisation, Professor Edward Tufte, describes pie charts as 'dumb' and says that they 'should never be used'.[3]

I don't know if I would go quite that far. It seems to me that pie charts can help give us a visceral feel for proportions – particularly those of us who are uncomfortable with numbers. However, the debate about pie charts does help illustrate the fact that you should always think about the *purpose* of a graph. If it's not doing anything to help illustrate the real story of the numbers, then it's a waste of time and page space – even if it looks pretty.

What makes a pie chart misleading?

Pie charts are so simple that it's actually quite difficult to create one that is genuinely misleading without being really obvious about it. Really the only option you have is to make the chart 3D, then play around with perspective until the slice you want appears bigger or smaller. For example, Figure 8.9 is a 3D version of the movie chart, rotated so that the 'Male protagonist' slice appears much bigger than it should. I've also removed the numbers so the trick is less obvious.

Protagonists of top 100 grossing films in 2016, by gender

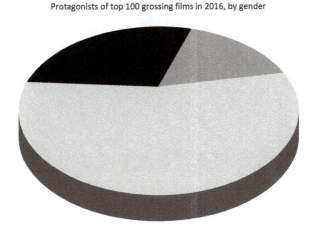

⬚ Male protagonist ■ Female protagonist ▦ No single protagonist

Figure 8.9 Pie chart showing the gender breakdown of movie protagonists, now three-dimensionalised

Source: Data from Lauzen (2017)

Looking at this chart it seems like movies are much more strongly dominated by male protagonists than they actually are.

Much more common than misleading pie charts like this are ones that just don't mean anything. The media loves a pie chart, but sadly they don't always understand how to make them. Figure 8.10 is a classic example from our friends at Fox News.*

This chart shows the results of a 2009 poll asking viewers their thoughts about potential Republican Party nominees for the 2012 presidential election. The numbers are pretty close: 70% backed Palin, 63% backed Huckabee, and ... wait, we're already over 100%. Add the 60% backing Romney and we're at 193%.

The reason for this is that the poll asked people whether or not they had a favourable opinion of *each* of the three candidates. So it was quite possible for people to say they supported all three. There's nothing wrong with asking this sort of question of course. The results just don't belong on a pie chart.

---

*   To be fair this is the Chicago Fox affiliate, not the national station.

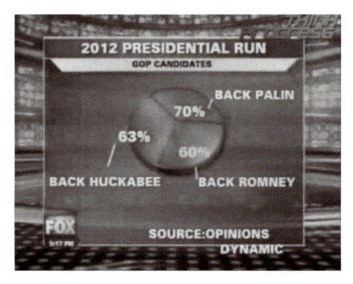

Figure 8.10 Pie chart of support for 2012 Republican presidential candidates

Source: ThinkProgress

Line charts

What are they used for

Line charts are generally used to show how some quantity has **changed over time**. The bottom axis (the x-axis) is therefore almost always some measure of time – seconds, hours, days, years, etc. The vertical (*y*) axis can indicate any quantity that can be measured on a continuous scale (exactly like a bar chart): stock prices, temperature, crimes, sales, whatever. The quantity at each time interval is plotted as a point (rather than a bar), and these points are joined together to make a line.

One of the most famous charts of all time, the so-called 'hockey-stick' graph of climate change, is a line chart. This chart first appeared in a 1999 paper by American climate scientists Michael Mann, Raymond Bradley, and Malcolm Hughes.[4] Using data collected from tree rings, ice cores, and other sources, it showed estimates of average temperatures in the Northern hemisphere over the previous 1,000 years. Some of the data behind the graph is reproduced in Table 8.1 (I've left big chunks out because otherwise it would take up the whole rest of the chapter).* You should note that temperature is not measured in straightforward degrees Celsius. It is instead given as the departure from a baseline average, which in this case is the average temperature between 1900 and 1998. A positive number means that a given year was hotter than this baseline average and a negative number means it was colder.

---

* The data is publicly available at: ftp://ftp.ncdc.noaa.gov/pub/data/paleo/contributions_by_author/mann1999/

Table 8.1 Global temperatures by year

YEAR	TEMPERATURE ANOMALY (°C)
1000	0.07
1100	−0.02
1200	−0.20
1300	−0.03
1400	−0.31
1500	−0.19
1600	−0.13
1700	−0.39
1800	−0.08
1825	−0.21
1850	−0.25
1875	−0.24
1900	−0.13
1925	−0.03
1950	−0.01
1975	0.02
1998	0.78

Source: Mann et al. (1999)

In Figure 8.11, this data is plotted as a line graph. The lighter section represents temperatures estimated from tree rings, ice cores, and other indirect sources. The darker section represents temperatures directly recorded from thermometers.

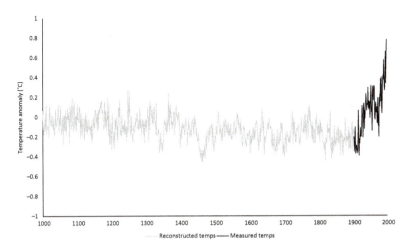

Figure 8.11 Line chart showing global temperatures by year

Source: Data from Mann et al. (1999)

The advantage of the chart in telling the 'story' of the data is clear. From reading the figures in the table, we can get some idea of what's going on. For example, we can see that the temperature in 1800 was hotter than 1900, and that the temperatures at the end of the millennium tend to be hotter than those at the beginning (bear in mind that this process would be much more difficult if we were looking at all 1,000 lines of numbers). However, by looking at the graph the message comes across much more powerfully. Global temperatures vary a lot year to year (that's why the graph is so spiky). However, up to 1900 they are generally pootling along in a straight line. Then, in the 20th century, as we built more factories, more power plants, and more cars, temperatures shot up dramatically. This is how the graph got the 'hockey stick' name. The period up to the beginning of the 19th century is the handle (if that's what it's called?) and the period afterwards is the … bit you hit the ball with (I don't know anything about hockey).

The stark, simple message of this graph made it immediately popular with organisations who needed to explain the importance of climate change to politicians and the general public. In 2001, the Intergovernmental Panel on Climate Change (IPCC) were due to publish an important report on the current state of knowledge about climate change. In the debate around what would go in the report the hockey stick graph was identified as 'a clear favourite for the policy makers' summary'.[5] It duly appeared in the report and spread yet more widely after that. As clear visual proof of climate change, it became a powerful weapon in the arsenal of environmentalists the world over. It is probably not an exaggeration to say that the hockey stick graph was instrumental in helping to shift public attitudes on the reality of human-caused climate change.

The graph also became the focus of attempts by sceptics to debunk the science behind global warming. Estimating global temperatures over a period of hundreds of years is a tricky business. It requires assembling and interpreting evidence from many different sources, and there is a lot of room for error. Even some fellow climate scientists felt that the graph was potentially misleading. For sceptics, the issues with the data were enough to declare the graph an outright hoax.

I'm not a climate scientist, so I'm not here to adjudicate on whether the hockey stick graph is an accurate representation of climate change (though it's worth noting that many subsequent studies have confirmed the story of a sharp increase in temperatures beginning in the 20th century). Instead the point is to illustrate the power numbers can have when they are represented visually. This is a lesson that people who want to mislead you about numbers know by heart.

What makes a line chart misleading?

Just as with a bar chart, the message of a line chart comes through comparing the height of the line at different points in time. Therefore, as with bar charts, the easiest way to produce a misleading line chart is to mess with the scale of the *y*-axis – thereby either exaggerating small differences or minimising large ones. Here, for example, is a tweet from leading US conservative news magazine *National Review* (Figure 8.12):*

The only #climatechange chart you need to see. natl.re/wPKpro

(h/t @powerlineUS)

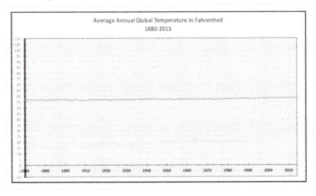

10:36 pm - 14 Dec 2015

Figure 8.12 Screenshot captured from @NRO Twitter feed

This graph purports to show the trend in global temperatures over time. Unlike the hockey stick graph, it only shows changes from 1880 onwards. However, this covers most of the 'blade' (I looked it up) of the hockey stick. Why aren't we seeing a dramatic rise in temperatures here?

The fact is that we are. The numbers being plotted here show that between 1880 and 2015, global temperatures rose by about 1.5°F. It may not seem like it, but in climate terms that is a lot. Only a few degrees of warming is enough to make substantial changes to conditions on earth, including sea-level rises, extreme weather, and effects on animal species. But the creator of this graph has made this change look very small by starting the *y*-axis at zero. Global average temperatures have never been and never will be zero, or anywhere near zero. They weren't even close to zero during the last ice age! The same goes for extending the axis up to 110°F (which would only happen if the entire earth was as hot as the Sahara desert in summer). If you are making a genuine attempt to show how much global temperatures have changed over time, it would make sense to use a much more restricted scale – say between 50°F and 60°F.

---

*   Hat tip to *Quartz* magazine's 'Most misleading charts of 2015', where I found this.

This might strike a lot of people as wrong. Didn't I just criticise Fox News for using a restricted scale to exaggerate differences? Shouldn't the *y*-axis always start at zero? The answer to the first question is yes, but the answer to the second one is no. To see why, let's switch to a more everyday example. Say you are trying to lose weight. To keep track of your progress, you weigh yourself on the last day of every month over the course of a year. You start the year at 70 kg (154 lb). For an adult woman of average height, this would put you just into the overweight category according to your BMI. By the end of the year you are down to 64 kg (141 lb) – putting you squarely in the 'healthy weight' category. Figure 8.13 is what these results might look like plotted on a line graph, starting at 0.

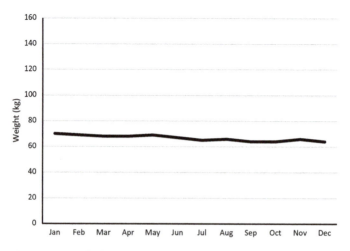

Figure 8.13 Line graph showing hypothetical changes in weight over time

Doesn't look like much has changed does it?

The purpose of a chart is to tell a visual story that is *true to the message of the data*. The story of this data is that your weight has changed by a meaningful amount, just as the story of the climate data is that global temperatures have changed by a meaningful amount. This is not the message that comes across in the graphs. Making sure the graph tells the true story of the data means selecting your scale carefully. Choose a range of values that are realistic to the thing you are measuring. Global temperatures are not going to fall to zero, or rise to 110°F – so don't choose these as the limits of your scale. You are never going to weigh zero kilograms, so don't start your scale at zero.

If you're keen on creating misleading line graphs, but you're bored of simply exaggerating or hiding differences, why not do both at the same time – as the intrepid designers of the graph in Figure 8.14 seem to have done?*

---

* This chart is also featured in *Quartz's* Most Misleading Charts of 2015, though I became aware of it at the time through a PolitiFact article.

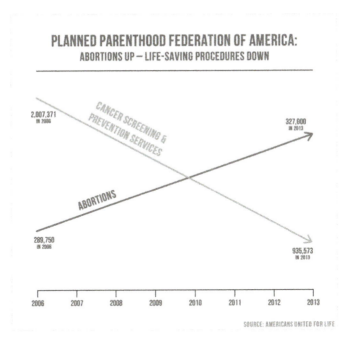

Figure 8.14 Line graph showing changes in Planned Parenthood procedures between 2006 and 2013

Source: Americans United for Life

This is a graph produced by an American anti-abortion organisation called 'Americans United for Life'. Planned Parenthood is an American non-profit which provides reproductive health services, including breast cancer screening, STD testing, and abortions. The lines on this graph convey three visual messages:

1. From 2006 to 2013 the number of 'life-saving procedures' – such as cancer screenings and preventative services – Planned Parenthood carried out decreased substantially (the lighter grey line, which is pink in the original image).

2. Over the same period, the number of abortions they carried out increased by the same amount (the darker line, red in the original).

3. After 2010, Planned Parenthood carried out more abortions than 'life-saving procedures' (the dark line crosses the light line).

Only the first of these three messages is remotely accurate. The key to understanding why is to note that the two lines – the light grey one and the dark grey one – are plotted on *different scales*. You can see this if you look closely at the numbers. Cancer screenings and preventative services drop from around 2 million to around 1 million; whereas abortions rise from about 290,000 to 330,000. What Americans United for Life have done

173

is essentially create two different graphs, with two different scales, then lay them on top of each other. By doing this they have made an increase of 40,000 abortions look the same size as a decrease of 1 million preventative services. Crucially, they have also managed to make it look like Planned Parenthood carry out more abortions than they do 'life-saving procedures', when in fact the opposite is true (to the tune of around 700,000 more of the latter than the former).

You might argue that Americans United for Life are not lying. The real numbers are there on the chart if you care to look. But this ignores the fact that the graph itself tells a story. And that visual story is all many people will take away. As we've covered numerous times already, *the whole point of a graph is to accurately convey the story of the numbers in a visual form.* This becomes even more important if the graph is presented in a setting which precludes close analysis, for example on TV or in a US congressional hearing. I mention the latter because this graph was indeed held up by US Congressman Jason Chaffetz during a congressional inquiry into whether the government should continue to give money to Planned Parenthood. Pointing to the graph, he said 'In pink, that's the reduction in the breast exams, and the red is the increase in the abortions. That's what's going on in your organization.'[6] He did not read out the numbers.

Scatter plots

What are they used for?

Scatter plots are used to show the nature of the relationship between two things that are both measured on a continuous scale, such as height and IQ score, or age and salary. But these are boring examples, so let's look at something a bit more interesting from the world of social science.

In 2009 a pair of British sociologists, Kate Pickett and Richard Wilkinson, published a book called *The Spirit Level: Why Equality Is Better for Everyone.*[7] In this book, they argue that there is something inherently damaging about living in an unequal society (a society with big gaps between rich and poor). In unequal countries like the USA and the UK, you are constantly comparing your wealth and status with others. You are always looking around to see that John has a much more expensive car than you, or that Serena can afford a nice flat, while you're living in a bedsit that is 70% cockroaches. If you were living in a more equal country (like Sweden or Japan), then you might not be better off in absolute terms – you might be driving the same crummy car and living in the same infested bedsit – but there wouldn't be as many opportunities to have your nose rubbed in just how much better other people are doing than you. Wilkinson and Pickett argue that inequality therefore causes all sorts of social problems –

including higher rates of violent crime, more drug addiction, more teenage pregnancies, more mental illness, and even shorter life expectancy.

For now, let's focus specifically on violent crime. Wilkinson and Pickett's theory would predict that countries with higher levels of economic inequality would have higher rates of violent crime. So is this true? I've produced Table 8.2 which gives the homicide rate and level of income inequality for a set of rich countries, using data from the World Bank's World Development Indicators database:*

Table 8.2 Income inequality and homicide rates in a selection of economically developed countries

	HOMICIDES PER 100,000 PEOPLE (2010)	GINI INDEX OF INEQUALITY (2010)
AUSTRALIA	1.0	34.94
AUSTRIA	0.7	30.25
BELGIUM	1.7	28.53
CANADA	1.6	33.68
CZECH REPUBLIC	1.0	26.63
DENMARK	0.8	29.02
FINLAND	2.2	27.74
FRANCE	1.3	33.78
GERMANY	1.0	31.14
GREECE	1.6	34.48
IRELAND	1.1	32.3
ISRAEL	2.0	42.78
ITALY	0.9	34.41
NETHERLANDS	0.9	28.73
NORWAY	0.6	25.86
POLAND	1.1	33.25
PORTUGAL	1.2	35.84
SLOVAK REPUBLIC	1.6	27.32
SPAIN	0.9	35.79
SWEDEN	1.0	26.81
SWITZERLAND	0.7	32.72
UK	1.2	34.81
USA	4.8	40.46

Source: World Bank World Development Indicators

Note: The Gini index is a way of measuring how unequally income is distributed in a given population. It ranges from 0 (every member of the population has exactly the same income) to 100 (all the income goes to a single person and everyone else gets nothing). Higher numbers therefore mean more inequality.

---

*   I'm focusing on rich countries because Wilkinson and Pickett argue that the psychological effect of inequality matters more after people's basic needs have been met.

It's not particularly easy to answer our question just by looking at this table. We can sort of see that some of the most unequal countries, such as Israel and the USA, have high homicide rates, but we can't get a sense for the overall relationship. As we've discussed a few times already, this is why visual representations can be so useful. One way to represent this data visually would be to plot all the homicide data on a bar graph, as in Figure 8.15.

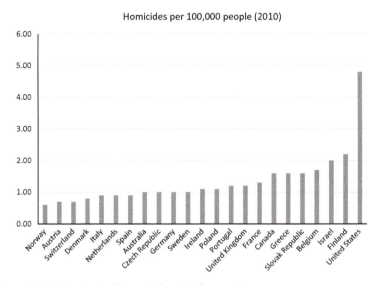

Figure 8.15 Bar chart of homicide rates by country

Source: Data from World Development Indicators

That gives us a visual sense for how big the differences are between, say, the USA and other countries. But the question we are interested in involves comparing two pieces of information (two variables) – inequality and the homicide rate. In this plot we are only presenting one.

Another approach we could take is to split the countries into categories according to their level of inequality. Let's say we group all the countries with Gini coefficients less than 33 together (low inequality), and all the countries with Ginis of 34 or above together (high inequality). Then we could compare the average homicide rate in these groups of countries using a bar chart (Figure 8.16).

This chart contains both of the variables we are interested in, so it does help us answer our question. But in order to create this chart we've had to lump groups of countries together. We've therefore lost any information about differences within these groups (for example, between the USA and the UK).

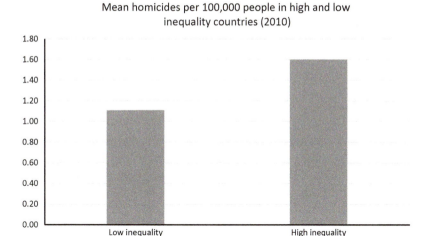

Figure 8.16 Bar chart of average homicide rates for high (Gini index ≥34) and low (Gini index <34) inequality countries

Source: Data from World Development Indicators

Scatter plots help solve this problem. They allow you to plot all the data on the graph at the same time. Figure 8.17 is a scatter plot of the data from the table.

Each dot on the graph is a country. The dot's position on the *x*-axis tells us how unequal that country is. The dot's position on the *y*-axis tells

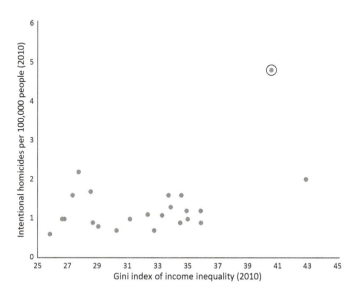

Figure 8.17 Scatter plot of inequality and homicide rates

Source: Data from World Development Indicators

us how many homicides they have per 100,000 people. For example, the country with the circle around it has a Gini index of about 40 and has 5 homicides per 100,000 people. In case you hadn't guessed, this is the USA.

By looking at the overall pattern of the dots we get a visual idea of how inequality and the homicide rate are related. The relationship is not completely clear, but it does seem like the more unequal countries (towards the right of the plot) tend to have more homicides.

One thing we can do to make this relationship clearer is add a line-of-best-fit. This is a line we draw through the data to illustrate the direction and strength of the relationship. The line-of-best-fit should be drawn such that it minimises the distance of all the dots away from the line (that's what 'best fit' means). This could be a very tedious process. First you would draw the line somewhere and add up all the distances of the dots away from the line. Then you would move the line and repeat the process. You would keep doing this until you found the position where the sum of all the distances was the smallest. Luckily, the computer will do all the grunt work for you. Figure 8.18 is what our plot looks like with a line-of-best-fit (here I have also replaced the dots with the abbreviated country names so you can identify which countries are which).

The line-of-best-fit helps clarify that there is a positive relationship between inequality and homicide. Though we can see that the relationship is by no means perfect. For example, there is a group of three low

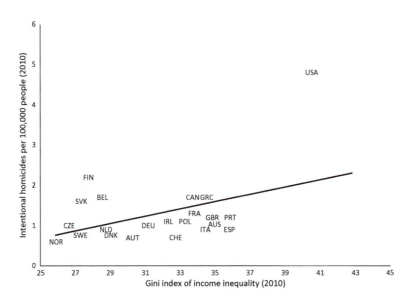

Figure 8.18 Scatter plot of inequality and homicide rates, with line-of-best-fit

Source: Compiled from World Development Indicators

inequality countries (Finland, Belgium, and Slovakia) on the far left of the plot that have higher homicide rates than countries further to the right. But in social science, no relationship is ever perfect. Social outcomes like the homicide rate result from a complicated mess of interacting causes. We would never expect to be able to perfectly predict the number of murders that are going to take place from just one variable like inequality.

In *The Spirit Level*, Wilkinson and Pickett use a lot of scatter plots like this to make their case that income inequality is bad for society. For example, they show that people living in more unequal countries trust each other less, are more likely to be addicted to drugs, are more likely to be obese, are more likely to go to prison, and are more likely to die young. On its release, the book sparked big political debates, both in Britain and elsewhere. It was one of those books, like Thomas Piketty's *Capital in the 21st Century* or Sheryl Sandberg's *Lean In*, that it seemed like every journalist and politician was reading. And, like Piketty's bestseller, it helped to put economic inequality right at the top of the political agenda. Senior politicians around the world (including the leaders of both of Britain's major political parties) were mentioning *The Spirit Level*'s findings in their speeches, and promising to do something about the scourge of economic inequality.

It is extremely unlikely that *The Spirit Level* would have had such a big impact without the visual message conveyed by the scatter plots. Tables of numbers and explanatory text would have contained exactly the same data, and would have told exactly the same story to those able and willing to listen. But the scatter plots convey the story so much more clearly and powerfully. They give a non-statistical audience (politicians and the general public) a way to understand the evidence – a way to directly *see* how much better or worse their country was doing in comparison to others.

Of course, as we've seen, this power to tell a convincing story also comes with substantial risks. Just like other visualisations, scatter plots are vulnerable to being manipulated in service of a particular message. A nip here, a tuck there, and what looks like a random collection of dots can start to seem like proof of a deep underlying relationship.

What makes a scatter plot misleading?

Visually, a scatter plot can either convey the message that two things are positively related, that they are negatively related, or that they are not related at all. Most of the time, if someone wants to mislead you using a scatter plot, it's one of the first two messages they want to sell: they want to give you the idea that there *is* a relationship, not that there isn't one. One of the simplest, and therefore most popular, ways to do this is to exploit the line-of-best-fit.

As we've already discussed, drawing a line of best fit is a perfectly sensible thing to do. It helps clarify the nature of the relationship underpinning the dots on the plot. However, in doing so it can draw the eye in such a way that it completely dominates our perception of the plot. For example, Figure 8.19 is a graph from *The Spirit Level* showing the relationship between income inequality and life expectancy in a group of rich countries.

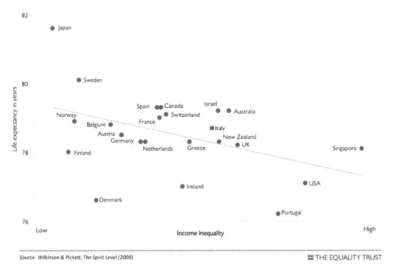

Figure 8.19 Scatter plot of inequality and life expectancy, with line-of-best-fit

Source: The Equality Trust

And Figure 8.20 is the same plot without the line-of-best-fit.

The dots are all in the same place, but without the line guiding your eye, the relationship suddenly looks a lot weaker. This is not to say that the graph is completely misleading. The underlying figures show that there is indeed a negative relationship between inequality and life expectancy. However, the powerful visual impact of the fit line can be exploited by unscrupulous people to make even a random collection of dots seem like evidence of a strong relationship. That's why, whenever you see a scatter plot with a bold line-of-best-fit, you should always try to imagine what the relationship would look like without the line.*

Another way to make a scatter plot tell the story you want is to simply add or remove points until the pattern is more agreeable. For example, in the life expectancy graph, Denmark is not really helping make Wilkinson and Pickett's case. It is a country with low levels of inequality in which people nevertheless die relatively young. If we removed Denmark from

---

*   If you want to do more than imagine, you can always copy the graph into some image-editing software and just rub out the line.

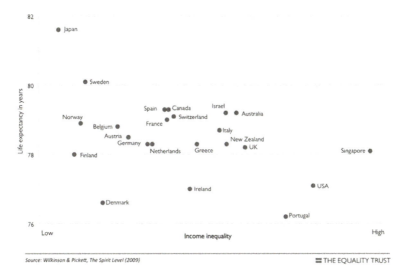

Figure 8.20 Scatter plot of inequality and life expectancy, without line-of-best-fit

Source: The Equality Trust

the plot, the relationship between inequality and life expectancy would look a lot stronger (you can see this if you just put your thumb over it in the graph).

On the other side of the coin, Japan (an equal country where people live a long time) and the USA (an unequal country where people tend to die relatively young) are both countries that make the relationship a lot stronger. Remove them from the plot (you're going to need both thumbs) and the relationship between inequality and life expectancy almost disappears.

In this kind of research, there are no hard and fast rules about which data points should go in the plot and which shouldn't. Maybe, in your opinion, the quality of the data from Singapore is not very good, so it should be excluded. Or maybe you think that, in the homicide graph, the USA is just too much of an outlier (they have *a lot* of murders) to include. These are all perfectly sensible judgements. However, even without meaning to, it's easy to start biasing these decisions in the direction of the answer you want. For example, maybe you're a little stricter about data quality with the countries that don't fit the pattern than with the ones that do. And of course, if your intent is to mislead people, then you can just exclude whatever data points you want and come up with a defensible reason later. This is actually something that critics of *The Spirit Level* accused Wilkinson and Pickett of doing in their scatter plots. You can read more about these criticisms, and Wilkinson and Pickett's detailed response, on their website at the Equality Trust (search for 'equality trust spirit level faq').

One final way in which scatter plots can mislead is if they are presented as evidence of causation. This has nothing to do with the visual presentation of the plots themselves, but with how they are interpreted. As we discussed in the previous chapter, people are very quick to interpret a relationship between two things as evidence that thing X *causes* thing Y. Being able to *see* the relationship through a scatter plot can worsen this tendency. People who are trying to tell a causal story will therefore often rely on scatter plots to sell their argument. Needless to say, representing a relationship visually does not make it any better evidence of causation.

Nonsense graphs

"Never attribute to malice that which can be adequately explained by stupidity" – Hanlon's Razor

At a few points in this chapter, I've implied that people may manipulate graphs intentionally for deceitful purposes. People want to sell a story that is not supported by the data, so they torture a graph until it complies. This does certainly happen. However, in the mainstream media landscape, intentionally misleading graphs are vastly outnumbered by graphs which are simply nonsense. Newspapers, magazines, and the internet are positively awash in graphs, charts, diagrams, and 'infographics' that were not created by evil geniuses trying to pull the wool over our eyes, but instead by well-meaning graphic designers whose eye for good colour combinations is sadly yoked to the statistical insight of a Yorkshire terrier.

Good data visualisation is hard. You have to really understand the message of the underlying data, and make sure your graph or chart conveys that message faithfully and intuitively. Unfortunately, the motivation of many media outlets appears only to be: 'make the numbers look pretty.' Established, helpful plots like bar and line charts are therefore ignored or distorted beyond recognition – replaced by big, colourful illustrations which, at best, add nothing to the actual numbers, and at worst are actively confusing and misleading.

I couldn't end this chapter without sharing a few of my absolute favourites with you:

Why have one pie when you can have six?*

The graph in Figure 8.21 is from a 2016 *VICE* news article titled 'Exclusive: New Conviction Data Tells Us How the UK Sells Drugs'.[8] The story is based on unpublished figures *VICE* obtained from the British Ministry of Justice, showing the breakdown of drug convictions by ethnicity. The graph is supposed to show how many people in each ethnic

---

*   Hat tip to the Junk Charts blog (junkcharts.typepad.com) for finding this one.

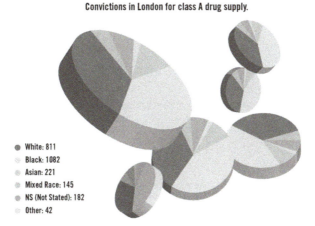

Convictions in London for class A drug supply.

White: 811
Black: 1082
Asian: 221
Mixed Race: 145
NS (Not Stated): 182
Other: 42

Figure 8.21 Pie chart(s) showing the breakdown of convictions for class A drug supply by ethnic group

Source: VICE Media

group were convicted of selling Class A drugs (this includes cocaine, heroin, and ecstasy) in London.

This seems like important information. And a pie chart is arguably a good way of representing the proportion of people convicted from each ethnic group. In the original colour image, the wedges are also easy to differentiate, and line up correctly with the legend. All the makings of a perfectly serviceable pie chart (though it would have been helpful to have printed the percentages in the legend too, rather than just the raw counts). It's at this point that *VICE* have decided to add some graphic design 'flare'. Rather than provide a single readable 2D pie chart, they have decided to go with six identical 3D versions, rotated at random angles and strewn across the page.

As some commenters subsequently noted, the idea here may have been to evoke a collection of round pills (get it? Drugs!). A classic example of a 'clever' graphic design idea getting in the way of clearly presenting some important data.

Obama's legacy in nine unreadable charts

Donald Trump tweeted the chart in Figure 8.22 in June 2016, with the caption ' … THIS IS @POTUS'S LEGACY! AN ABSOLUTE DISASTER!!! WE NEED @realDonaldTRump NOW!! #MAGA #TRUMP2016'.*

---

*   I originally spotted this chart on viz.wtf, an excellent crowdsourced repository of nonsensical graphs. The original tweet can be seen here: https://twitter.com/realDonaldTrump/status/738495529005420544.

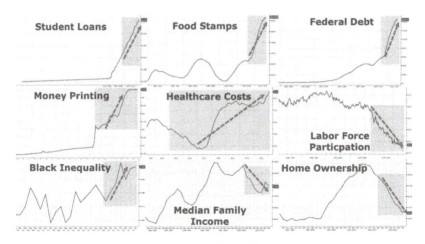

Figure 8.22 Image captured from @realDonaldTrump Twitter account

This set of nine line charts purports to show trends in various different factors over time, with Obama's period in office shaded in grey (pink in the original colour image). The clear implication is that, over the course of Obama's presidency, all of the things measured in the graphs have gotten much worse: student loans are way up, the national debt has skyrocketed, home ownership has plummeted, and so on.

There is only one small problem with these charts – and that is the complete inability of any reader to interpret what they are actually showing. Even if the text were large enough to read (which it isn't, even in the original image), there are no titles on the *y*-axes, meaning we have no idea how any of these factors are being measured. Does 'Black Inequality' refer to differences in average wages, differences in employment rates, or something else? What does 'Money Printing' mean? Does 'Student Loans' mean the number of people with loans, or the average amount of money they borrow? Or maybe it's the average length of time loans take to repay? For that matter, why do the *x*-axis labels for this particular chart only start four-fifths of the way across the axis?

At the risk of repeating myself, charts are a way of trying to communicate data more clearly and intuitively. The only message cramming nine tiny unreadable charts into a tweet communicates is that you don't really understand what charts are for.

The worst graph in the world

This next example (Figure 8.23) was statistician Andrew Gelman's 'Worst Graph of the Year' in 2011.[9] It is from a PowerPoint presentation used as part of counterterrorism training for FBI agents.* It is a line graph which apparently shows that, while devout Christians and Jews

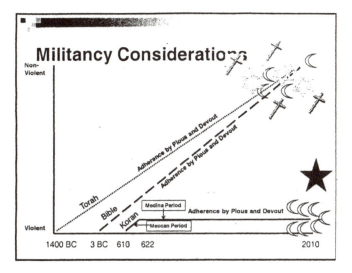

Figure 8.23 Line graph (apparently) of violence over time by three religious groups

Source: andrewgelman.com

have become steadily less violent over time, devout Muslims are about as violent as they were in the 7th century.

There are so many problems with this chart that it's hard to know where to begin. The point of a line graph is to indicate levels of some measured quantity at a series of points in time. 'Violence' is supposedly what is being quantified here, but there is absolutely no indication of how this is being measured. Could it be the number of deaths attributed to 'devout' members of each faith? In which case you might think the Crusades would cause the 'Bible' line to dip a bit in the middle. But instead the Bible and Torah lines describe a perfectly straight trajectory from maximally violent beginnings to peaceful modernity.**

The most likely scenario here is of course that no measurement for violence is given because nothing has, in fact, been measured. These lines are just the designer's intuition about historical trends in these three religions. Rather than simply saying what he thinks, he has used a graph, which helpfully lends his speculations the illusion of scientific credibility. Needless to say, this is not what graphs are for. Graphs are a way of presenting numbers in an intuitive way. Perhaps the simplest lesson of data visualisation is therefore: *if you don't have any numbers, don't draw a graph!*

---

* The chart comes from a presentation by an FBI trainer named William Gawthrop. His presentation included the following disclaimer: 'the views expressed in this presentation are those of the author and do not necessarily reflect the views of the agency of the United States Government.'

** As Gelman notes, this suggests that early Christians were extremely violent. As he puts it: 'I thought Christ was supposed to be a nonviolent, mellow dude. The line starts at 3 B.C., implying that *baby Jesus* was at the extreme of violence.'

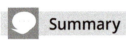

Summary

Graphs and charts are a way of portraying numbers visually. A graph or chart comprises a set of visual elements (such as the length, width, colour, and form of shapes). Each of these elements can be used to convey numerical information. For example, in a bar chart, the length of the different bars is used to convey the magnitude of a measured quantity (e.g. average income) for different groups (e.g. people in different types of jobs).

There are a small number of commonly used chart types. The most commonly used types are bar charts, line charts, pie charts, and scatter plots (see 'Terminology used in this chapter' below). Most charts you will encounter in the media or in science will be variations of one of these core types.

Charts are great at making data easier to understand. For example, it's much easier to understand how something has changed over time by looking at a line chart than it is by looking at a long column of numbers.

Charts can be misleading. Changing elements of the design of a chart can fundamentally change the message it appears to convey – for example by exaggerating differences, or making two things seem to be more closely related than they actually are. Great care needs to be taken both when creating and interpreting charts to make sure this doesn't happen.

Terminology used in this chapter

<u>Visual metaphor</u>: In a chart, a visual metaphor is a visual element that carries information about a quantity. For example, in a pie chart breaking down a person's income from different sources (jobs, investments, welfare, etc.) the size of each slice is a visual metaphor for the proportion of that person's income coming from each source.

<u>x-axis</u>: The horizontal (flat) axis on a chart.

<u>y-axis</u>: The vertical (upright) axis on a chart.

<u>Bar chart</u>: A chart in which a given quantity is represented by the height or length of a 'bar'. The heights or lengths of bars can be compared between groups or categories.

As well as being a generic term for charts of this type, a bar chart can also specifically mean a chart in which the bars lie horizontally. This can be distinguished from a column chart, in which the bars are arranged vertically.

<u>Pie chart</u>: A chart representing proportions of a single whole. For example, a pie chart might be used to show what proportion of total government spending is allocated to different areas (education, welfare, defence, etc.). Proportions in a pie chart should not add up to more than 100%.

Line chart: A chart representing levels of a quantity over time. For example, a line chart might be used to illustrate changes in the US homicide rate from 1950 to today.

Scatter plot: A chart representing the relationship between two continuous quantities. Markers (most commonly dots) represent the value of each data point in terms of the two quantities being measured. For example, a scatter plot might be used to represent the relationship between the number of hours of homework a student does per week (on the *x*-axis) and their final score on an exam (on the *y*-axis). In this case, each dot would represent a single student. The position of the dot along the *x*-axis would show the amount of time this student had invested in homework, and the dot's position on the *y*-axis would show their score on the exam.

 ## Seeing beyond the headlines

Graphs and charts can be tricky. Done well, they can give you a deeper intuitive understanding of the data than you could ever get from just looking at the numbers. Done poorly, however, they can easily send entirely the wrong message. Here are four questions to ask of any data visualisation:

1. WHAT TYPE OF CHART AM I LOOKING AT?

In theory, the chart in front of you could be an entirely novel invention of the author – sprung forth from the computer of a modern-day William Playfair. More likely, you'll be looking at some version of a bar, pie, line, or scatter chart. Sometimes it will be straightforward to work out which. Other times you will have to see through some fancy graphic design work: bars replaced by rockets or sacks of money, pie charts rendered as eyeballs or hearts or people.

2. WHICH VISUAL ELEMENTS ARE CARRYING INFORMATION?

If the chart is one of the four basic types, this should be easy to work out. For example, if it's a bar chart, then the primary information-carrying element is the height of the bars. In a clustered or stacked bar chart, the colour of the bars might also carry information.

In more complex charts, or in charts upon which too much graphic design has been perpetrated, you might have to do a bit more work. Look at the visual differences – colour, shape, height, area, etc. Which of these differences seem like they are supposed to carry information, and which are just distractions ('chartjunk')?

3. WHAT QUANTITY DOES EACH VISUAL ELEMENT REPRESENT, AND HOW?

There should be some text on the graph to tell you what each visual element represents. For example, in a simple bar chart, a title (either printed above the graph or next to the y-axis) should tell you what the height of the bars represents. In a pie chart, the labels printed on the wedges (or in a legend next to the chart) should tell you what the area of each wedge represents.

If there is a visual element that is supposed to be carrying information, but there is no text to explain what that information is – for example, if a bar chart does not explain what the y-axis is measuring – then you are looking at a bad chart.

4. DOES THE CHART ACCURATELY CONVEY THE STORY OF THE DATA?

Once you have identified the information each visual element is supposed to be carrying, you can read that information off to understand the story of the underlying data. Does this story match up to the visual impression given by the chart, or is there some distortion going on? For example, as in the Bush tax cuts graph, do the visuals give the impression of a bigger difference than a straightforward reading of the data would suggest?

Examples

CLAIM	TYPE OF CHART	RELEVANT/ IRRELEVANT VISUAL ELEMENTS	WHAT QUANTITIES REPRESENTED?	VERDICT: ACCURATE CHART?
Bush tax cuts chart (Figure 8.6)	Bar chart	Bars carry information. No other visual elements present	Height of bars represents top rate of tax	NO. Difference between bar heights suggests larger difference than present in the data.
FBI training graph (Figure 8.23)	Line chart	Lines carry information. Religious symbols do not carry information	Height of line indicates extent of non-violence (but no details of measurement given)	NO. Chart does not appear to be based on any actual measurement

Exercises for Chapter 8

Exercise 1a

The Gapminder Foundation is an organisation founded for the purpose of combating widespread misperceptions relating to global development, for example that the world population is growing out of control, or that there is an unbridgeable divide between the 'First World' and the 'Third World' in terms of human health.

You can watch Gapminder's founder, the late Hans Rosling, discussing these issues in his inimitable style: just search YouTube for 'Hans Rosling the best stats you've ever seen' (the link to the video is also on this book's companion website).

As you can see from the video, graphics are one of the main tools Rosling used to make his case. In the first section of the video, he uses a modified version of a scatter plot to show how fertility and life expectancy around the world have changed over time.

1. **In this first plot, what does each circle's position on the *x*-axis represent?**
2. **What does its position on the *y*-axis represent?**
3. **What does its size represent?**
4. **What does its colour represent?**

Exercise 1b

The Gapminder website allows you to easily recreate the graphs from Rosling's video with more recent data. Just visit the gapminder.org website and click 'Gapminder Tools' (the link can also be found on this book's companion website).

A neat feature of the 'bubble chart' tool is that it allows you to directly manipulate all of the chart's visual metaphors – including what is plotted on the *x* and *y* axes, and what the colour and size of the bubbles represent.

Using these tools, produce a bubble chart that allows you to answer the following questions:

1. Do countries that spend more on healthcare, per person (in total – that is, including both government and private spending) tend to have better average life expectancy?

   NOTE: You might have to fiddle with the x or y axis minimum values to get a sensible-looking chart.

2. Can you identify some rich countries that spend relatively little on healthcare? What do these countries have in common?

NOTE: To do this you will have to make the size or colour of the bubbles represent a county's wealth (e.g. its GDP or GNI per capita).

3. The USA is among the top three healthcare spenders. Can you identify any countries that spend much less, but nevertheless have a similar average life expectancy?

4. Find your country of origin. How many countries are spending the same amount or less than your country on healthcare but are nevertheless doing better in terms of life expectancy?

Exercise 1c

The Gapminder bubble chart tool includes data on a wide variety of topics, including health, murder rates, poverty, inequality, education, energy use, and carbon emissions.

Examine the variables on offer. Think of a research question you could answer with this data, and put together a bubble chart to answer this question.

NOTE: Be sure to make use of the 'data doubts' feature on the Gapminder website. As we've discussed throughout this book (especially in Chapter 4), some things are hard to count. 'Data doubts' explains any issues there might be with the variables you have chosen for your chart.

Exercise 2

In December 2015 the Obama White House tweeted the image in Figure E8.1 advertising improvements in high-school graduation rates under the Obama administration.

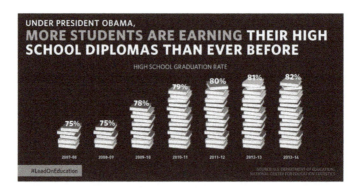

Figure E8.1 US high school graduation rate from 2007/8 to 2013/14

Source: @ObamaWhiteHouse Twitter archive

1. What type of chart is this?

2. Is this the most suitable type of chart for representing this data? If not, which type of chart would be more suitable?

3. Do this chart's visuals appear to accurately represent the data? If not, why not?

4. Using the numbers provided, plot your own chart. Does your chart convey the same message as the image above?

NOTE: Instructions on how to produce the relevant chart in Excel are provided on this book's companion website.

---

www.macmillanihe.com/devries-critical-statistics

Go to the book's companion website for further examples, data, links, and other useful resources.

ONLINE RESOURCES AVAILABLE

---

9 CONTEXT IS EVERYTHING

On 3 June 2017 three men drove a van into a crowd on London Bridge, killing three people. The men emerged with knives and continued their attack on nearby streets, killing a further five people and injuring 48. Because the attackers were motivated by Islamist extremism, the attack received worldwide attention. US President Donald Trump took to Twitter to express his dissatisfaction with the response of London Mayor Sadiq Khan:

> *"We must stop being politically correct and get down to the business of security for our people. If we don't get smart it will only get worse ... At least 7 dead and 48 wounded in terror attack and Mayor of London says there is 'no reason to be alarmed'."* – Tweets by Donald Trump on 4 June 2017

The facts in Trump's tweets are all accurate. The numbers were correct at the time he was writing, and in a statement the morning after the attack, Kahn did indeed tell Londoners that there 'was no reason to be alarmed':

> *"I'm appalled and furious that these cowardly terrorists would deliberately target innocent Londoners. There can be no justification for the acts of these terrorists and I am quite clear that we will never let them win. My message to Londoners and visitors to our great city is to be calm and vigilant today. You will see an increased police presence today, including armed officers and uniformed officers.* **There is no reason to be alarmed by this** *... "* – Sadiq Khan in a televised interview on 4 June 2017 (my emphasis)

You can see the problem here. By taking his words out of context, Trump has made it appear as if Khan was telling Londoners that they should not be alarmed *by the terrorist attack itself.** Placed in the context of his full statement, it is clear that Khan is actually referring specifically to the increased police presence (including the presence of armed police).

---

* Responding to Trump's tweet, many people speculated that Khan wanted to downplay the significance of the attack because he is Muslim himself.

In the era of fake news, we are used to talking about the importance of facts. We need to make sure we have all the facts. We need to get our facts straight. Facts, unlike opinions, are sacred. But facts are meaningless without context. That Khan said 'there is no reason to be alarmed' is an indisputable fact: there is recorded video evidence of him saying those exact words. But what those words *mean* depends entirely on the context in which they were uttered. If I tell you that your friend used the n-word, this fact means something entirely different if your friend is white and she shouted it at someone on a bus than if your friend is black and she used it in a blog post describing her experience of racism.

Statistics are a kind of fact. And just like all facts, their meaning can change dramatically depending on the context in which they are placed. Strip away all contextual information and a statistic becomes meaningless. Selectively add and take away context and you can make a number appear to mean almost anything you want.

A concrete example: in 2016 the UK government spent roughly £2.2 billion on direct welfare payments to able-bodied people who were unemployed.* In the context of most people's everyday experience, £2.2 billion is a lot of money. So we could translate this statistic as meaning 'the government spends a lot of money on unemployment benefits'.

However, people's everyday experience is probably not a very helpful guide here, so let's try placing the number in a different context by comparing it to other areas of government spending. For example, we could compare the £2.2 billion spent on unemployment benefits to the £37 billion spent on defence, or the £111 billion spent on old-age pensions, or even the £3.1 billion spent in the same year on 'recreational and sporting services'. All of a sudden, the £2.2 billion figure looks much smaller. In fact, given this context, we might be tempted to translate the statistic as meaning 'the government spends only a small amount of money on unemployment benefits'.

You can see that by changing the context we can change the meaning of a statistic dramatically. If you were a left-wing politician interested in making welfare more generous, which context would you choose? What if you were a right-wing journalist in favour of cutting benefit spending?

This issue is a little different from those we've discussed in previous chapters. Up to now, our focus has primarily been on whether a number accurately reflects what's happening in the real world. For example, a number might be bad because it's from a sample that doesn't represent the population, or it might be bad because of a poorly worded survey

---

*   I'm specifying direct payments here because unemployed people, along with people on very low incomes, are also often entitled to receive help with housing costs ('Housing Benefit'). The proportion of Housing Benefit spending which goes on people who are out of work is not clear from government statistics. However, it is likely to be in the region of £2 billion to £4 billion.

question. In this chapter, we'll see that the manipulation of context can make even good numbers misleading.

'Is that a big number?'

The welfare spending example shows that the detailed context around any particular statistic can be complex. However, in this and almost all other cases, the *role* of context is actually quite simple. Fundamentally, context tells us whether a number is big or small.

This might sound absurdly simplistic, but it cuts right to the heart of how we use statistics. As statistician Andrew Dilnot writes in his seminal book *The Tiger That Isn't*, the question 'is that a big number?' 'may sound trivial, but it captures the most underrated and entrenched problem with the way numbers are produced and consumed'.

On the surface, there are countless stories you can tell with numbers. You can tell stories about terrorism, or contraception, or poverty, or police racism, or any of the other topics we've discussed in this book so far. You can use numbers to talk about any subject you want. However, at bottom, almost all stories about numbers fit into just two basic moulds: they are either telling you that there is a lot of something, or that there is not a lot of something.

When a newspaper tells us that 600 women got pregnant despite having contraceptive implants, they are telling us that 600 is a big number. When a campaign group says that the government is only spending 50 pence per child on school dinners, they are telling you that 50 pence is a small number. In both of these cases, what tells us whether the number is big or small is not the number itself, but the context around it. As we discussed in Chapter 1, set in the context of other contraceptive methods, 600 pregnant women is actually a small number. And, depending on what it buys when you factor in economies of scale, 50 pence might actually be a big number.

Four questions

Because the context in which a number is placed can change its apparent meaning so dramatically, 'context tricks' are a particularly powerful weapon in the arsenal of the statistical bullshit artist. These tricks can be quite difficult to spot – for the same reason that you're more likely to notice problems with the content of a photo than you are to spot that the framing is off. However, when approaching a statistical claim, there are four questions we can ask to help focus our attention on potential context tricks:

1. Is the author trying to say that the number is big, or that it is small?

2. What contextual information does the author include?

3. What potentially relevant information does the author *exclude*?

4. Does the excluded information make the number seem bigger or smaller?

In the rest of this chapter I'm going to use these questions to interrogate some real claims from journalists and politicians, starting with a topic we first discussed in Chapter 6: police shootings in the USA.

'There is no epidemic of police killing black people ... '

In September 2016 *Breitbart* published a story under the headline 'Five Facts About "black Oppression" Colin Kaepernick Needs to Know'.[1] Colin Kaepernick is an African American football player who refused to stand for the national anthem in protest against police brutality. The *Breitbart* article lists five facts that supposedly demolish the rationale behind his protest. Here are two of them:

> **"FACT 2: It would take cops 40 years to kill as many black men as have died at the hands of other black men in 2012 alone:**
>
> University of Toledo criminologist Dr. Richard R. Johnson ... found that an average of 4,472 black men were killed by other black men annually between January 1, 2009, and December 31, 2012. Professor Johnson's research further concluded that 112 black men died from both justified and unjustified police killings annually during this same period.
>
> **FACT 3: From 1980 through 2008, 93 percent of black victims were killed by blacks (*sic*) killers – not police:**
>
> There is no epidemic of police killing black people in America. It simply is not true. And according to the FBI's latest annual 'Crime in the United States' report, 90 percent of black Americans killed in 2009, 2010, 2011, 2012, and 2013 were killed by blacks"
>
> – Jerome Hudson, Breitbart.com, 2 September 2016

The central number in this story is the number of black people killed by police. The story cites criminologist Dr Richard R. Johnson, who puts the number of black men* killed by police from 2009 to 2012 at 112. If we compare this to figures from the *Washington Post*'s database of police shootings, we could argue that this figure is probably a bit low. However, it is at least in the right ballpark.

---

* Across all ethnicities, around 95% of people shot by police are men.

Is the author trying to say that the number is big, or that it is small?

This one is easy. Both of the facts in the story are given in support of the idea that 'there is no epidemic of police killing black people'. The writer, Jerome Hudson, is saying that the number of black people killed by police is a **small number**.

What contextual information does the author include?

To support his argument, Hudson places **the number of black people killed by police** in the context of the **number of black people killed by black civilians**. He does this in two different ways: (1) by comparing the 112 black men killed by police from 2009 through 2012 to the 4,472 black men killed by other black men over the same period, and (2) by citing the high proportion of black Americans killed by other black Americans from 2009 to 2013.

Again, while there are some questions as to the accuracy of the numbers calculated by Dr Johnson, the 90% figure given as the proportion of black people killed by other black people is accurate. Table 9.1 gives the FBI's most recent figures for the proportion of black murder victims killed by assailants of different races.

Table 9.1 Percentage of black murder victims killed by assailants of different races

White assailant	8.5%
Black assailant	90.0%
Assailant of other race	0.6%
Assailant of unknown race	1.4%

Source: 2017 FBI Uniform Crime Reports

These figures are relatively consistent from year to year. The overwhelming majority of black murder victims are killed by a black assailant. However, is the proportion of black people killed by black civilians an appropriate comparison for the number of black people killed by police? You will have your own view, but personally, I don't think it is. To give you an idea of why, Table 9.2 presents a broader view of the FBI statistics.

As you can see, the story of these figures is not that black people specifically are mostly killed by other black people, it's that **murder victims both white and black are most often killed by members of their own race**. In a racially segregated society like the USA, people predominantly work, marry, and socialise with people of the same race. Most killers kill people they know. The natural consequence of this is that murderers tend to kill people of their own ethnic group.

Table 9.2 Percentage of murder victims of each race killed by assailants of each race

Race of victim	Race of assailant			
	White	Black	Other race	Unknown race
White	81.6%	15.2%	1.1%	2.1%
Black	8.5%	89.5%	0.6%	1.4%
Other race	25.3%	16.7%	55.7%	2.3%
Unknown race	50.0%	18.6%	4.7%	26.7%

Source: 2017 FBI Uniform Crime Reports

This is why the proportion of black people killed by other black people is not an appropriate comparator for the number of black people killed by police. There is no country on earth in which the proportion of citizens killed by police even approaches the proportion killed by other citizens. Using this comparison to say that police killings are not a problem is like saying that drunk driving is not a problem because most car accidents involve drivers who are sober.

What potentially relevant information does the author exclude?

We have established that the context the author has chosen is inappropriate. So what contextual information would be more appropriate? This is always the trickiest question to answer, because it requires us to think outside of the story in front of us. However, in this case, there is an obvious choice. The most straightforward way to determine whether the number of black people killed by police is a big number is to compare it to the number of white people killed by police. As we discovered in Chapter 6, in 2015 the death rate of black Americans from police shootings was 0.6 per 100,000 people. The corresponding rate for white Americans was 0.25 per 100,000 people. In other words, black Americans are more than twice as likely as white Americans to be shot and killed by a police officer.

Another potentially informative piece of context would be the record of other countries on the same issue. Do American police officers kill people more often than officers in other developed countries? (Yes.) Are the ethnic disparities in who is killed more pronounced in the USA than elsewhere? (More difficult to answer, but likely yes.)

Does the excluded information make the number seem bigger or smaller?

The answer to this final question is now quite obvious. The inappropriate context offered in the original article suggested that the number of black people killed by police in the USA was small. Additional (and more appropriate) contextual information suggested that the number is actually quite large.

Despite the controversial nature of the topic, this has proved to be quite a straightforward case. A clearly superior piece of contextual information has led us towards a more accurate reading of the statistics. However, this process is not always as clear-cut, as we'll see from the next two examples.

Emotive statistics

Statistics on emotive issues like race can be difficult to deal with. If a statistic seems to lead to a racist conclusion, a natural reaction – if you're socially liberal – is just to push it away. Safest simply to label it as racist and move on. On the contrary, if you're sceptical of liberal 'political correctness', the fact that this statistic is causing so much fuss might make you more likely to believe that it's true.

Neither of these reactions is particularly helpful. Statistics are a tool we use to help us better understand what's going on in the world. If that's your goal – rather than scoring points for your team – the best reaction is not to push a statistic away because it makes you uncomfortable, nor to draw it close because it makes the other side squirm. Instead, pick it up and really have a look at it. Sometimes it will fall apart immediately. Other times it won't. In which case you'll need to do some real thinking. Is it a hard truth you're going to have to grapple with? Or, like the *Breitbart* statistics, is it more like a trick of the light?

American carnage

In September 2016 the FBI released its annual crime statistics for the USA. Among other things, their figures showed that the number of homicides recorded by police had increased from 4.5 per 100,000 people in 2014 to 4.99 per 100,000 people in 2015 – an increase of 10.8%. For then presidential hopeful Donald Trump, this was grist to the mill of his narrative of 'American carnage':

> *"On Crime, the murder rate has experienced its largest increase in 45 years"* – Donald Trump in a speech in Fayetteville, North Carolina, 6 December 2016

Before you say anything – yes, we're going back to the Trump well again. I should say that this is not because I'm a middle-class leftie academic who thinks only right-wing people lie with statistics. Despite being a middle-class leftie academic, I know that the left is often just as guilty of flagrant number abuse as the right. Critical thinking does not just mean pointing out the dodgy numbers used by people we already disagree with. We need to be just as sceptical and critical of the statistics coming from our own side. However, with that said, it's difficult for me to write a book about statistics in 2018 without acknowledging the fact that the current occupant of the world's most powerful office is a veritable human firehose of misleading numbers.

Is the story trying to say that the number is big, or that it is small?

As was the case for the previous example, this is a pretty easy question to answer. Trump's message in the debate is clear: the 11% increase from 4.5 per 100,000 to 5 per 100,000 is a big (and scary) number.

What contextual information does the author include?

This is a short quote, so there's not much to go on. However, Trump does place the 11% increase in a historical context, describing it as the 'biggest in 45 years'. In this he is correct. Before 2015 the last time the homicide rate jumped by as much as 11% in a single year was between 1970 and 1971 (when it rose by 11.1%).*

What potentially relevant information does the author exclude?

To answer this question, let's consider a hypothetical situation. At the age of 11, you were receiving £15 a week in pocket money. Your parents raised this by £1 every year, until, at the age of 16, you were getting £20 a week. However, after your mum's credit card is somehow used to buy £200 of gold bars in *Battle of the Magic War Men* for the iPad, your allowance is halved, to £10. After a few months, your parents soften and raise your allowance by £2, up to £12.

One way of describing this change would be to call it 'the largest ever increase in your allowance'. This is true: your allowance has never gone up by as much as £2 in one go before. However, we would be missing a very important part of the story – that your allowance is still much lower now than it used to be.

What has this got to do with Donald Trump and the homicide rate? Well, the graph in Figure 9.1 gives the police reported homicide rate from 1971 to 2015 (as reported in the FBI's Uniform Crime Reports).

The two dots at the end of the line show the 11% increase we have been talking about. It's tricky to see, but by comparing this uptick in

---

* Later, Trump switched from claiming that the USA had seen the biggest *rise* in homicide for 45 years to claiming that the *murder rate itself* was the highest it had been in 45 years. The former claim is factually accurate. The latter is utterly false, as you'll see.

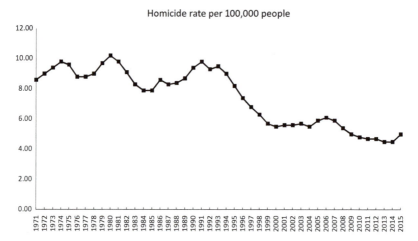

Figure 9.1 US national homicide rate over time

Source: FBI Uniform Crime Reports

homicides with previous single-year changes, you can see that it is quite large. However, it is dwarfed by the steep decline beginning around 1994. Between 1993 and 2014 the homicide rate in the USA almost halved, from 9.5 per 100,000 to 4.5 per 100,000. This is a vital piece of context when we are trying to interpret the 11% increase from 2014 to 2015 – and it is the context most criticisms of Trump's statement focused on.

However, this is not the only context we could draw on. In addition to past figures in the USA we could also compare US homicide rates to those in other countries. For example, in France the police recorded homicide rate is 1.58 per 100,000. In Britain it is 0.92. In Germany it is 0.85. In Japan it is 0.31. We could also consider the raw figures in a more personal context. As Leon Neyfakh of *Slate* magazine pointed out in response to criticism of Trump's claim, approximately 1,500 more people were killed in 2015 than in 2014. On a basic, human level, that's a lot of people – a lot of a grieving families, a lot of lives tragically cut short.[2]

Does the excluded information make the number seem bigger or smaller?

There is no question that Trump's original statement was precisely cali-brated to make the increase in the homicide rate seem large. 'The biggest rise in the murder rate 45 years' sounds like a very big number indeed. It sounds like Americans should be locking their doors and barring their windows to ward off a surge of deadly violence. However, the addi-tion of further historical context shrinks the number substantially. The

10.8% increase Trump is describing is a substantial one, but it still leaves America much safer than it was even in the mid-2000s.

The other pieces of contextual information we discussed serve to re-inflate the figure a little, though. For example, the 1,500 additional deaths recorded in the USA in 2015 represent a larger number of murders per capita than Japan's *total* murder rate.

This case is therefore less straightforward than the *Breitbart* example. There are legitimate pieces of context which make the statistic look bigger or smaller. This illustrates a deeper point – that numbers can

The lens of history

As the homicide example shows, history is a vitally important piece of context when you are trying to understand a statistic. To understand whether you're looking at a big number, a good place to start is to see what the same number was last year, and the year before that. Is 2017's global average temperature of 14.8°C high? In historical terms it certainly is. Is the figure of 1.3 million asylum seekers arriving in Europe in 2015 a big number? In the context of the last 50 years, yes it is.

Historical context is invaluable. However, historical comparisons are also fraught with peril. If you're not paying attention, you can easily arrive at faulty conclusions. One of the most important things to bear in mind when making historical comparisons is that the *meaning* of the thing you are comparing may have changed dramatically over time. We encountered this issue in Chapter 4 when we discussed sexual assault statistics in Sweden. Between 2004 and 2005, the number of rapes recorded by police in Sweden almost doubled – not because many more crimes were occurring, but because, in 2005, Swedish police adopted a broader definition of rape. If we were trying to set sexual assault in Sweden into some kind of historical context, we need to account for the fact that what is meant by the 'rape rate' has changed over time.

A similar issue arose in the UK in 2015. From 2014 to 2015 the overall crime rate recorded by the British Office for National Statistics (ONS) more than doubled, from just under 7 million to a little over 14 million. This is not because a fraction of the British public woke up on 1 January 2015 and decided that this was the year they were finally going to do some crime. It was because in 2015 the ONS started including cybercrime in their official overall crime figures.*

These two examples are based on clear-cut changes in definitions, explicitly announced by the relevant statistical bodies. But historical comparisons can also run afoul of more subtle changes in the meaning of a statistic. This is a common problem when trying to understand changes in the prevalence of diseases. For example, the number of children diagnosed with autism has increased substantially over the last 40 years. Is that because more children have the condition? Or is it because doctors have gotten better at detecting and diagnosing it?

I recently came across a novel example of this sort of problem while I was researching the statistical arguments of prominent 'race realists'. 'Race realists' advocate for the acceptance of what they call 'human biodiversity'. This is a fancy way of saying that they want society to accept that black people are biologically inferior to white people. One of the things race realists propose is that black people are naturally more aggressive and therefore prone to criminality. The statistical argument I saw in favour of this rested on the fact that the number of black people sent to prison each year in Southern states was substantially higher after slavery was abolished than it was while slavery was still in force. The author's argument was that the 'strong social control' of slavery restrained black people's natural criminality. This criminality was unleashed after this control was removed.

You may have already noticed the problem with this argument (aside from it being spectacularly racist), but I'll spell it out anyway. The author is using the number of black people sent to prison as a measure of black criminality. But the *meaning* of the black incarceration rate is clearly very different before and after the end of slavery. Before the end of slavery, the vast majority of black people in the states in question were held as slaves – *and were therefore already effectively imprisoned*. It should not be surprising that the police were not arresting and imprisoning black people in large numbers when most were already held captive by white slave-owners (who often administered their own summary 'justice' for perceived infractions). This is before we even consider the fact that, in order to use the incarceration rate as a measure of black behaviour, you have to assume that police *in the late 18th and early 19th centuries* were completely fair-minded in their selection of whom to arrest and prosecute.**

---

*   I happened to be having a drink with someone from FullFact (Britain's premier fact-checking outfit) a few weeks before these statistics were released. He mentioned that his colleagues were on high alert in anticipation of a stream of misleading 'crime doubles in a year' headlines. In the end (somewhat to my surprise I must admit) most of the British press handled the situation quite responsibly. Though there were some notable exceptions. The *Daily Telegraph* for example, ran the story under the headline "Violence surges as crime totals double" (helpfully illustrated with a large photo of a hooded youth brandishing a knife).

** When thinking about crime and incarceration rates in the antebellum South, you might also consider the fact that 'participation in the institution of slavery' would not count towards the statistics on crimes perpetrated by white people. Strangely, this is not a point often raised by the 'race-realists'.

(and often do) have more than one legitimate interpretation. Whether a 10.8% jump in the homicide rate is a big number depends on your point of view. If you are an American wondering how worried you should be about your personal safety, then maybe the historical comparison is helpful: you are still safer now than you were 10 years ago. If you are the president, then the historical comparison is also useful, but so is the comparison with other countries: What are they doing right that America is doing wrong? The purpose of thinking about the context for a number is not only to decide whether it is 'bullshit' or not, but to grapple with what a number actually means in the real world.

Competing contexts: What is the Queen of England worth?

In 2017 the UK government announced that the Queen was getting a pay rise. The Queen technically owns a lot of very expensive land and property around the country. However, she doesn't receive the profits from these estates directly. Instead the money goes to the British government, who then give a proportion to the Queen as a sort of salary, called the Sovereign Grant. The rest of the money goes into the general pot for the government to spend on the things governments normally spend money on – building hospitals, maintaining roads, hiring school teachers, and so on. Since 2011 the Sovereign Grant has been set at 15% of Crown Estate profits. In 2016 this amounted to around £43 million. The government's announcement was that in 2018 the Queen's share of Crown Estate profits would rise to 25%, taking her 'salary' somewhere closer to £82 million.*

The left-wing *The Guardian* newspaper covered this story in detail, and their coverage is useful in that it features two contrasting frames: *The Guardian*'s own, and that of a representative of the Royal Family. Here is *The Guardian*'s headline, along with a relevant passage from their story:[3]

"Queen's income rises to £82m to cover cost of Buckingham Palace works

Crown Estate increases profits as royal accounts reveal Prince Philip spent £18,690 on a train trip to Plymouth

The Queen is set for a near doubling of her income to more than £82m due to a government decision to increase her funding to cover 'essential works' to Buckingham Palace.

The Crown Estate, which owns most of Regent Street and swaths of St James's as well as thousands of acres of farmland, forests, and coastline, made £328.8m profit in the year to the end of March 2017, an 8% increase on the previous year.

---

* The stated purpose of this rise was to cover the cost of renovating Buckingham Palace.

> The Queen's sovereign grant, the amount she receives from tax-payers is calculated as a percentage of Crown Estate profits. In November, it was announced that the percentage would rise for 19 years from 15% to 25%.
>
> Details of the increase were released as Buckingham Palace accounts reveal the royal family last year spent £4.5m on travel ... the accounts show it cost an estimated £154,000 for Prince Charles and the Duchess of Cornwall to hire [the Voyager state jet] for a week-long trip to Romania, Italy and Austria."

And, here is the response (quoted in the same story) from a Palace representative, the splendidly titled Keeper of the Privy Purse, Sir Alan Reid: '[the cost of the queen] accounts for 65p per person per annum in the UK; that's the price of a first-class stamp.'*

Is the story trying to say that the number is big, or that it is small?

As with the previous two examples, the answer to this one is pretty obvious. *The Guardian*, not known to be a cheerleader for the monarchy, are trying to say that £82m is a very big number. Sir Alan Reid, in gallant defence of Her Majesty, is making the seemingly more difficult case that £82m is actually quite a small number.

What contextual information does the author include?

On first glance, it may seem like *Guardian* are much in the way of context at all. However, they are taking advantage of the fact that most readers will bring their own context to the story. Confronted with any story about money, most people will instinctively set the amounts in the context of their own lives. And given that most people live in a world of tens and hundreds and thousands, £82 million is going to seem like a very big number indeed. *The Guardian* have further encouraged this reading by peppering their coverage with references to commonplace things on which the royals spent seemingly unfeasible amounts of money. These included an £18,690 train journey taken by Prince Philip, and flights around Europe which set Prince Charles and the Duchess of Cornwall back £154,000.

This is a classic technique used by journalists, politicians, and campaign groups when they are attempting to sell the public on the idea that too much money is being spent on something. Whether you're a right-wing journalist decrying sums wasted on poor people and public

---

* Here Sir Alan is talking about 2016's £42.8m figure. The increased figure of £82 million would be more like £1.26 per person – so two first-class stamps.

broadcasting, a left-wing campaigner blasting the amount being thrown at the latest military gadget, or a politician announcing the good their new 'multimillion pound' apprenticeship programme is going to achieve, a good tactic is just to throw the total out there without explanation – trusting to the fact that anything in the millions or billions is always going to sound like a big number.

On the other side, Sir Alan employs an equally well-worn tactic for making a number look small: divide it up into bits. You can see this approach in action anytime someone wants to minimise how much something will cost. Want to sell someone a new Toyota? Why not break down the £16,000 asking price to a more appealing-sounding £165 a month. Want to get people on board with your new tax increase? Rather than focusing on the overall figure, better to describe how much it's going to cost per person. Almost any amount of money will seem small if you divide it by the entire population of a country. Then you can compare this shrunken figure to something commonplace and inexpensive, like a cup of coffee (this is a popular choice), a Netflix subscription, or, indeed, a first-class stamp.

What potentially relevant information does the author exclude?

There are two pieces of context we've noted before that neither Sir Alan nor *The Guardian* include – a comparison over time, and a comparison with other countries (for example, how much do Belgium, Denmark, and Spain spend on their royal families?). However, I'm not going to dwell on these here because there is another, more obvious comparison to be made.

Both *The Guardian* and Sir Alan treat the Queen's income as an item of public expenditure. *The Guardian* explicitly notes that the £82m ultimately comes from taxpayers, and Sir Alan implicitly does the same when he expresses it as a contribution per head. Given this, it would make sense to compare the money spent on the Queen to other things the government spends money on. For example, Table 9.3 sets the Queen's £82m next to a few other items of government expenditure.

As you can see, the Queen is considerably less expensive than the entire country's street lighting, but considerably more expensive than a new MRI machine.

Does the excluded information make the number seem bigger or smaller?

As in the homicide example, there are multiple legitimate perspectives we could take on whether the Queen's £82m income is a big number. Even the 'personal' context, which can sometimes lead us astray when

Table 9.3 Selected items of UK government spending

State pension	£111,341 million	(Per Year)
Unemployment benefits	£2,227 million	(Per Year)
Street lighting	£850 million	(Per Year)
Protection of biodiversity and landscape	£460 million	(Per Year)
F35-C Lightning fighter jet*	£95 million	
Cramlington Emergency Care Hospital**	£90 million	
Queen's Sovereign Grant	£82 million	(Per Year)
MRI scanner***	£0.9 million	

Source: 2017 UK HMRC Public Expenditure and Statistical Analyses report, unless otherwise specified

it comes to interpreting large sums of money, could be legitimate here. The Royal Family are just a family after all. Why should their income so vastly outstrip that of most of their subjects? They have expenses that no regular family does, such as the cost of state visits around the world, and the upkeep of massive historic buildings like Buckingham Palace. However, they also get the benefit of the pomp and circumstance that attends their role, and, of course, of actually *living* in those massive historic buildings.

However, in addition to this, the comparison with other items of government spending gives us an anchoring point for how much money £82m actually is. It restrains any wild ideas about what we could do with the money if we stopped paying the Queen's salary. We're not going to be using it to give everyone free university tuition (estimated cost: around £1,000 million a year) or to plug up the gaps in the NHS. That said, it also shows that £82m is not a mere piffling trifle, barely worth considering. It could come close to paying for a new hospital building (every year).

Camera tricks

Tom Cruise is famously shorter in real life than he looks in a lot of his movies. He is about 5'7", but if you watch *Jack Reacher*, or *Mission Impossible*, you would be forgiven for thinking he's at least six feet. Film-makers use

---

* Figure reported on Lockheed Martin's website.
** Figure reported on the NHS website.
*** Figure reported on the website of the UK National Audit Office.

a few different tricks to make Cruise look tall. For example, they might pair him with a shorter leading actress, or they might shoot him from lower angles, or make him stand closer to the camera.*

Statistics are a bit like Tom Cruise – how big they look depends on what they are standing next to and where you put the camera. In the first example in this chapter, a *Breitbart* journalist made the number of black men shot by police look small by standing it next to an unfeasibly large number. Our next example saw Donald Trump fix the camera in such a way as to make it seem like America was in the grip of an unprecedented crime wave. Finally, we saw *The Guardian* and Sir Alan Reid offer contrasting shots of the Queen's £82m pay packet.

The four questions we went through in each case helped us do two things. First, they made us think about how the author had positioned the camera. What effect were they trying to achieve? How had they composed the shot in order to achieve that effect? Second, they encouraged us to reach in, pick up the camera, and move it around ourselves – to take in the other actors standing out of shot, who, for example, make the homicide rate look small and the police shootings figure look big.

The numbers we see in the media are rarely provided with enough context. More often than not, the journalist, politician, or salesman behind the numbers has a specific agenda. They have a particular message they want you to come away with, and they will provide you with only the context that helps sell that message. They will fix the camera in place so that you only see what they want you to see. If we want to know what's really going on behind the headlines, we should not settle for the frame we are given. We need to pick up the camera for ourselves and compose our own shots. In many cases, moving the camera will reveal that we've been tricked – that we've been fooled by forced perspective into thinking that a number is much bigger or smaller than it really is. The equivalent of thinking that Tom Cruise is as tall as Morgan Freeman, when he's actually the same height as Elijah Wood. Other times, the original shot will have been reasonable and defensible, but a different framing will still leave us better informed. When it comes to understanding what a number really means, there's no such thing as too much context.

---

* If you watch his films carefully, you can see this in action. For example, there's a campfire scene in the otherwise forgettable *Knight and Day* in which Cruise looms over co-star Cameron Diaz, despite her being 5'9" to his 5'7".

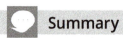

Summary

Is that a big number? As simplistic as it seems, the message of most statistical claims is either that a number is big, or that it is small.

Determining whether a number is big or small requires an understanding of the context. In the context of your life, a million dollars is a big number, but in the context of total government spending, or of a large company's sales, a million dollars is a small number. A hundred burglaries is a lot if they all happen in your neighbourhood in one week. It is not a lot if we are talking about the whole country over the space of a year.

Missing context. Purveyors of statistical claims often fail to provide vital contextual information. Often this is accidental. However, sometimes it is done purposefully to make a particular number appear larger or smaller. It's always worth considering what contextual information might be missing from a claim, and how this missing context might affect your perception of the number.

Seeing beyond the headlines

Context can fundamentally change the meaning of a number. In this chapter, I proposed four questions to help clarify what a number really means. Here are those questions again in the form of a table, with one of the examples from the chapter filled in:

CLAIM	AUTHOR IS SAYING NUMBER IS BIG OR SMALL?	CONTEXT INCLUDED	CONTEXT EXCLUDED	VERDICT: EFFECT OF CONTEXT
Biggest increase in homicide rates in 45 years	Big	Size of the increase relative to previous increases	Larger change in the absolute homicide rate over time	Excluding the historical context has made the number appear much bigger

Exercises for Chapter 9

Exercise 1

The following is a hypothetical claim from an Australian newspaper:

> *"Epidemic of female violence sweeps nation. Is a resurgence in 'ladette'*
> *culture to blame? ... The number of women committing assaults has*
> *hit record highs this year: police statistics show that in 2015–16 more*
> *than 16,000 women have committed assaults 'intended to cause*
> *injury'."*

This claim is based on publicly available data from the Australian Bureau of Statistics. The best way to find this data is to google 'Australian bureau of statistics recorded crime offenders' (the link to this data is also provided on this book's companion website).

Download the data on offenders. Are the newspaper's claims reasonable?

Exercise 2

As we discussed in the chapter, announcements about government spending are often difficult to interpret due to a lack of context. Is £300 million for more schoolteachers a lot of money? Is an extra $4 billion for road repair a gross extravagance, or nowhere near enough?

Pick an online newspaper or magazine. Scroll through the news stories until you find one announcing some new item of public spending.

Examine the number with the aid of the toolbox provided at the end of the chapter. What would be the most appropriate context (or contexts) in which to place this number? Does placing the number in this context change your perception of whether it is a small or a large amount of money?

HINT: Examples of the kind of story I'm talking about are (1) predictions of the total amount of money Britain will have to pay as a penalty for leaving the EU (around £15.4bn), or (2) the $2m Trump is reportedly spending on redecorating the White House.

---

www.macmillanihe.com/devries-critical-statistics

Go to the book's companion website for further examples, data, links, and other useful resources.

ONLINE
RESOURCES
AVAILABLE

10 DO IT YOURSELF

In April 2013 *PolitiFact* journalist Louis Jacobson wanted to know if it was true that almost all American felons had grown up in households without a father.[1] To answer this question he looked at data from two nationally representative surveys conducted by the US Justice Department: the Survey of Inmates in Local Jails and the Survey of Inmates in State and Federal Correctional Facilities (prisons in other words). He found that in both of these surveys just under half of the inmates had grown up with both parents. Felons were more likely than the general population to grow up in single-parent households, but it was not true that almost all of them grew up without a father.

In the olden days, if you wanted answers to questions like this, your only option was to look at the work of professional scientists. 'Data', for example from government surveys, meant paper files locked in dusty filing cabinets in the basements of government departments. If you weren't drawing a salary as an economist, a sociologist, or a political scientist, you weren't getting at those files. And even if you could, you would need months of free time (and probably a staff of paid research assistants) to turn these files into usable data. On top of that, any statistics you wanted to produce would need to be calculated by hand, with pen and paper (or, at best, a digital calculator). Even relatively simple analyses might require pages and pages of handwritten numbers and calculations.

Nowadays, a lot of the same data professional social scientists use for their research is freely available online for anyone to peruse. Data on crimes recorded by the police, on government welfare programmes, from national censuses, from big social surveys – it's all there. And, you don't need to master complex equations to use it – computers can do the mathematical heavy lifting for you. To do the sort of data-driven research that was once the exclusive province of professional academics, all you need is an internet connection and some basic spreadsheet software. Of course you also need to understand what the numbers you're looking at actually *mean*. But (as I hope this book has shown) this has less to do with complicated maths than it does with understanding a few of the basic principles that lie behind common statistics.

The upshot of all this is that, when it comes to the big debates in society – about race, about gender, about crime, about politics, about economics – you don't always have to rely on someone else to do the work for you. If you've read an article you are worried is biased towards one side or the other, you can check the numbers for yourself. If you have a question that it seems like no one else has answered, you can find some data and try to answer it yourself.

That's what this final chapter is about. A lot of the examples I've used in previous chapters have focused on statistical mistakes and misunderstandings – on the principle that the best way to understand how something works often is to see how it breaks. As such, much of the book up to now could be read as a sort of 'how-not-to' of statistics. In this chapter we're going to switch gears and focus more on 'how-to'. Specifically, we're going to use publicly available data to try to get to grips with one of the big questions of our time: How big is the pay difference between men and women?

The gender pay gap

Women generally earn less money than men. As far as we can tell with the data we have, this is true in every country on earth. The gender difference in pay is bigger in some places than others, but even in European countries it is substantial.

From a feminist perspective, this is clearly a problem that needs solving. Every year, left-wing and feminist organisations produce a steady stream of articles, infographics, videos, and reports highlighting the ongoing issue of gender pay inequality. They argue it is a gross injustice that the gap is still as big as it is. It is evidence that, far from being a thing of the past, sexism and discrimination continue to be a significant barrier to women's opportunities.

One of the clearest demonstrations of the scale of the gender pay gap is 'Equal Pay Day'. This marks the point in the calendar by which the average man has earned what the average woman will earn in a whole year. In the UK, the Fawcett Society* calculate that the average woman earns around 86% as much as the average man, making Equal Pay Day 10 November. In France, Equal Pay Day is three days earlier, on 7 November. In Australia, the Workplace Gender Equality Agency celebrates Equal Pay Day on 4 September (though celebrates is probably not the right word).

For many feminist campaigners, Equal Pay Day is an opportunity to argue for changes that would help fix the pay gap. For example, bosses could be required to tell their employees what everyone else at the company is being paid – to allow women to see where male colleagues are receiving more for equivalent work. Or jobs could be offered at a fixed salary, so behind-the-scenes pay negotiations don't yield higher pay for male hires.

---

*   A feminist campaign organisation named for suffragette Millicent Fawcett.

However, not everyone agrees that the gender pay gap represents a problem that needs to be fixed. In fact, some critics have gone as far as to label it a myth:

"How common sense shows the gender pay gap is a myth" – News. com.au, 8 September 2016

"The Gender Wage Gap Myth and 5 Other Feminist Fantasies" – Time, 17 June 2016

"Don't Buy Into the Gender Pay Gap Myth" – Forbes, 12 April 2016

Articles like these accuse wage gap campaigners of making statistical mistakes which have led them to overestimate gender differences in pay. They also argue that most of the gap is not caused by women being paid less for equal work, but by women opting for lower paid careers or choosing to take time out to have children. In 2017 a widely read article in *The Economist* magazine cited figures showing that, if you compare men and women doing the same job at the same level for the same company, the gender pay gap almost completely disappears.[2] Similarly, British bank TSB initially found that, on average, women at the company were paid 31% less than their male colleagues. However, they found that just 1% of this difference came from unequal pay. The rest was the result of women doing different kinds of work.

This is not a trivial difference of opinion. If the feminists are correct, persistent sexism is causing women to lose out in a big way. As the Fawcett Society puts it, women are effectively 'working for free' for a large proportion of the year. However, if the critics are right and the gender pay gap is a myth, then women (and policymakers) should stop worrying. There is no need to demand more robust equal pay laws, or to force companies to make their pay data public, because there's no real problem.

Faced with this debate, one option is of course just to stick with our 'side'. If we are liberal and progressive, then most people on our side hold that the gender pay gap is a problem. Therefore, we should think it is a problem too. The next time Equal Pay Day rolls around we should probably post something on Twitter or Facebook about the ongoing evil of sexist discrimination. If we are conservative on the other hand, then many of the people we follow say the gender pay gap is a myth. Next Equal Pay Day we should probably post something about how those deluded liberals are at it again.

There are, however, better available alternatives to simply going along with prevailing opinion. Most of the data which inform the pay gap debate are freely available online. We don't have to take anyone's word on whether the pay gap is a myth – we can look at the data ourselves.

That's what we're going to do in the rest of this chapter (focusing on the situation in the UK because that's where I live, and consequently where I know the data the best – nevertheless, the principles are the same wherever you are in the world).

The data

The first step we need to take in investigating the gender pay gap is to look for relevant data. Ideally, we need information on what men and women are paid in different types of jobs.

If you think back to Chapter 3, you'll remember that there are only really three places this sort of information can come from:

1. A big government database recording everyone's payslips, along with their gender.

2. Payroll data held by private companies.

3. A sample survey.

In Britain at least, there is no big government database. And private companies are not in the habit of sharing their payroll data publicly. We're therefore going to have to get our information from a sample survey. In the UK the most relevant source is the Annual Survey of Hours and Earnings (or ASHE for short). This survey, carried out by the Office for National Statistics (ONS), is the source the government themselves use to produce official pay statistics. The ONS speak to a nationally representative sample of employers every year to get data on between 140,000 and 180,000 employees.

How did I work out what was the best source of data to use? I read a bunch of articles about the gender pay gap in the UK and noted where they got *their* data from. Almost all of these articles mentioned the ASHE, so this was the obvious choice. For most topics there are only a few good sources of data, so almost everyone ends up getting their information from the same place. This approach is a lot easier than spending hours wading through labyrinthine government websites looking for relevant data.*

The raw data from the ASHE (details on each individual employee) is not available to the public without a special licence. Instead, what we've got to work with are the statistical breakdowns the ONS release every

---

* If you want to see a quantitative social scientist go red in the face, just ask them about their country's official statistics website. I think the design philosophy behind these sites is best captured by the scene from *The Hitchhiker's Guide to the Galaxy* in which Arthur Dent attempts to find a council notice about plans to demolish his house: '"But look, you found the notice, didn't you?""Yes," said Arthur, "yes I did. It was on display in the bottom of a locked filing cabinet stuck in a disused lavatory with a sign on the door saying 'Beware of the Leopard'."'

October. However, these are extremely detailed so they should be sufficient for our purposes. These spreadsheets are available from the ONS website. If you want to follow along and conduct this analysis yourself, you can find specific instructions on this book's companion website.

The details here are obviously specific to this particular survey. However, the general approach is similar whatever subject you are researching. First figure out the most appropriate source of data, then keep digging until you hit spreadsheets.

How big is the gender pay gap overall?

When we're comparing what people earn in everyday life, we tend to use annual figures. Our teacher friend Sally earns £28,000 a year, whereas our banker friend Nigel earns £150,000 a year. This would therefore seem like a good place to start.

If we look up the relevant figures in the ASHE spreadsheets, we can see that the average woman in the UK earns £21,671 a year, whereas the average man earns £34,845 a year. This is an absolute difference of £13,174. If we express women's earnings relative to men's we can see that the average woman earns just 62% of what the average man earns.

Whichever way you slice it, this is a big difference. However, there is a problem with this comparison. Actually there are several. The first is that women, for a variety of reasons, are more likely than men to work part-time. People who work part-time obviously tend to earn a lot less than people who work full-time. So if we lump full- and part-time workers together into a single average, the figure for women's earnings will always be lower. The solution to this problem is to look at hourly pay rather than annual pay. We should also focus just on full-time workers because, even when compared hour-by-hour, part-time jobs still tend to pay less than full-time ones do.

According to the ASHE data, the (mean) average pay for a woman working full-time is £14.94 per hour (working 37.5 hours a week for 52 weeks a year this would come to £29,133). The same figure for men is £17.34 (£33,813). In other words, the average woman working full-time earns 86% as much as the average man. This is the exact method the Fawcett Society use to pinpoint 10 November as Equal Pay Day in the UK.

But here's where we come to the second problem (which, if you remember Chapter 5, you may have already twigged). As we discussed in Chapter 5, averages, and particularly the mean average, do not necessarily represent what's 'normal' for a given group of people. Remember the people in the bar in the Bill Gates joke. The 'average person' in that bar went from earning something like £10 an hour to earning several *thousand* pounds an hour, all without getting up from their seats. Without anyone else being paid an extra penny, adding Bill Gates' epic pay packet to the mix pushed the mean average up dramatically.

Imagine a world that looks a lot like ours, in which there are substantial gender differences in pay among the richest 0.1% of the population. At the very top of the scale – among the hedge-fund managers, CEOs, tech barons, and the like – men significantly outnumber and out-earn women. In the rest of the population, however, *men and women are paid exactly the same.* If we compared the mean average pay for men and women in this imaginary society, we would still find that 'the average man' earned substantially more than 'the average woman'. 99.9% of women are paid the same as 99.9% of men, but because we are comparing mean averages, there would still appear to be a 'gender pay gap'.

To make sure this isn't what's happening in the real world, we should use the median instead of the mean.* If you remember from Chapter 5, the median is the exact middle value in a set of numbers. If you lined up all the men in society according to their earnings, the median pay would be that of the man standing in the exact centre of the line. It is still just an average, but it is a better representation of 'normal' pay for both genders. In the imaginary society I just sketched, the *median* pay gap would be basically zero.

In reality, the median pay gap is not zero. The ASHE data shows that the median pay for a woman working full-time is £12.84 per hour. The median pay for a man working full-time is £14.25. Even if we use a better measure of the average, women still earn a full 10% less than men.

Equal pay for equal work?

By focusing on the hourly pay of people who work full-time, we've ruled out the possibility that the gender pay gap is purely the result of more women working part-time. By using the median instead of the mean, we've also ruled out the idea that it is entirely produced by men infesting the very uppermost rungs of the earnings ladder. Is this enough to demonstrate that the gender pay gap is real?

From one perspective, the answer is obviously yes. On average, we've found that women earn substantially less than men – even after taking into account the factors we've discussed. If this is all you mean by 'gender pay gap', then clearly it is not a myth. However, many discussions

---

*   Justifying their use of the mean, the Fawcett Society argue that 'an important part of the gender pay gap is that women are less likely to be in the highest paid and most senior positions. We think that this inequality matters and should be measured in the pay gap statistics'. This is a reasonable point. However, the language the Fawcett Society use around the gender pay gap makes the use of the mean problematic. Discussions of 'the average woman' strongly imply that the pay gap is something that exists between most men and women. As the imaginary example shows, the median does a much better job of actually demonstrating this.

Fun with definitions

Here are a few words that sound like they mean basically the same thing: income, earnings, pay, wage, salary. In stories about money (including stories about the gender pay gap), the media often uses these words interchangeably. Journalists are taught that using the same word over and over again is bad writing. So rather than repeat the word 'pay' twenty times, they mix it up. The problem is that, when you are dealing in statistics, seemingly minor differences in language can fundamentally change the story. Here are some definitions for common money words:

- **Income** refers to all the money someone receives, regardless of its source. For example, let's say that last year you had a couple of part-time jobs, but you also received some government welfare and won some money on the horses. This would all count towards your total *income* for the year.

- **Earnings** means money you get from working and not from any-where else. So the money you got from the government, or from gambling (or from investments, or from an inheritance, or from any source that isn't paid work) doesn't count: economists call money from these sources 'unearned income'.

- **Pay** is basically the same as earnings. The difference is really one of perspective. Talking about earnings places the emphasis on you, the earner. Talking about pay emphasises your employer(s), the pay-er(s). Compare 'What did you earn least year?' to 'What were you paid last year?'.

- **Salary** and **wages** are specific *types* of pay. Wages are money you get for performing a specific task or for working a certain number of hours. For example, for working in a call centre, your wages might be £10 per hour, or £20 for every 100 calls. If you are paid a salary, on the other hand, your pay will be based on a contract rather than on an exact account of your hours or productivity. Most 'white-collar' office workers receive salaries rather than wages. They are paid a fixed amount per month to do something general (like 'manage an office', or 'be a graphic designer'), rather than a variable amount depending on how many hours they work or how many graphics they design. People who are paid a salary are sometimes described as being members of the 'salariat'.*

These definitions are not just pointless semantics. They make a big difference to the statistics. For example, the average *income* of a household in the UK (before tax) is around £41,000. Average household *earnings* on the other hand (again, before tax) are around £26,000. If you confuse the two, you might end up thinking that people are much richer (or poorer) than they actually are.

---

*   The word 'salary' derives from the Latin *salarium*, which itself derives from *sal*, the Latin for 'salt'. I used to think this was because Roman soldiers were paid in salt (salt being rare and valuable at the time). But apparently, this is another one of those things that is often repeated without there being much evidence that it's actually true.

---

of the pay gap go beyond this. Arguments on both sides imply that an important part of gender pay inequality is unequal pay for equal work – women being paid less than men for doing the same jobs. Suggestions that women are 'working for free' for a portion of the year encourage this reading of the issue – as do calls for policies to prevent pay discrimination. For example, a common rationale for pay transparency policies is that they will allow female employees to recognise when they are being paid less than male colleagues working in the same roles.

There are many ways in which pay differences could arise between men and women doing the same jobs. For example, let's say Jane and John are both working as office managers in a large firm. John goes to his bosses and asks for a raise. They admire his go-getting chutzpah and the way he's taken charge of his team, so they give him one. Jane goes to ask for the same raise. They find her request a bit aggressive and demanding, and her team find her 'too bossy'. Besides, she's in her thirties, so she'll probably have a baby soon and won't be able to put in the hours like John will. Alternatively, maybe Jane, who was brought up to think that women shouldn't be too pushy, never asks for the raise in the first place. We return a few years later to find that John is being paid considerably more than Jane, despite both still having the same job title.

There is no denying that scenarios like this do happen.* The question for us is whether they happen *often enough* to play a significant role in producing the overall gender pay gap. The alternative possibility is that unequal pay for equal work is actually relatively rare, and that the gender pay gap is instead mostly driven by men and women having different kinds of jobs. Many better paid professions are male-dominated; whereas many lower paid occupations are more often done by women. For example, men with a university degree are more likely than similarly qualified women to pursue jobs in technology and finance; whereas the reverse is true for teaching and social work. Similarly, among the jobs available to people with few educational qualifications, higher paid factory work is predominantly done by men, and lower paid retail and service work is more often done by women. Within most workplaces, men are also more

---

*   They seem to be particularly common in the creative industries, where pay structures are less formalised.

likely than women to hold senior roles. By themselves, these patterns would be enough to produce a large gender difference in average pay.

From this perspective, 'the average man' earns more than 'the average woman' almost exclusively because 'the average man' works in a higher paying profession (and is also more likely to hold a senior role); *not* because women tend to be paid less for the same work.

One way to determine if this is true is to look at whether the gender pay gap still exists when we only compare men and women who are doing the same jobs. So let's try to do this using the ASHE data.

The ASHE breaks down jobs in two different ways – by industry and by occupation. Industry describes the type of organisation you work for. Occupation describes the type of work you do. For example, if your job was keeping the books for a small chain of shops selling humorous underwear, your industry would be 'Retail (clothing)' and your occupation would be 'Accountant'.

We'll start with industry – are women generally paid less than men who work in the same industry? The ASHE records industry using the Standard Industrial Classification system (SIC for short). This system, which is used around the world, classifies every possible workplace according to a four-digit code. The first two digits give a general idea, and the next two get more specific. For example, if you knew someone worked somewhere with a SIC code beginning '82' you would know that they worked in some sort of 'human health activity'. If you knew that the next two digits were '23' you would know they worked at a dentist's office.

The ASHE data breaks down men and women's average earnings by industry at both the two- and four-digit levels. Ideally, if we're trying to get at 'equal work', we want the more specific level right? So, for example, the spreadsheets show that women who work full-time in the 'retail sale of books in specialised stores' (in other words, women who work in bookshops) earn a median average of £7.84 per hour. By comparison, men who work in bookshops earn an average of £8.58 per hour. A small, but substantial, gender pay gap.

However, here is where we hit a big problem with the data. By the standards of most surveys, the ASHE, with its sample of almost 200,000 respondents, is *huge*. But of these 200,000 people, how many of them specifically work in bookshops? Fifty? Twenty? Five? However many it is, it's unlikely to give us a reliable estimate of what's going on in every bookshop in the country.

Let's say there are 10 bookshop workers in the sample: 5 women and 5 men. The 5 men are where we get the £8.58 average. This is an *estimate* (think back to Chapter 3) of what every male bookshop worker in the UK earns. How confident can we be that this estimate is even close to correct? The answer is 'not very'. The same goes for the estimated pay of female bookshop workers. And if we can't be confident that the estimates are accurate, then we can't be confident of the size (or even the direction) of the bookshop worker pay gap. Maybe male bookshop workers earn a bit more than female ones. Maybe they earn a *lot* more. Or maybe a lot less. We just can't be sure.

This is an inevitable problem of relying on survey data. The more specific we try to make our comparisons, the smaller the groups of people we end up looking at. Any differences we see between these tiny samples are a very uncertain indication of what's going on in reality.

The same issue arises if we look at occupation rather than industry. Ideally, we might want to compare men and women in very specific occupations – for example, the spreadsheets show that male CEOs earn a (median) average of £49.33 per hour, compared to £35.59 for female CEOs. However, again, there are only a few CEOs of either gender in the survey. This problem would get even worse if we wanted to compare men and women in the same occupation *and* industry.

To make sure we end up with reasonably accurate estimates, we're going to have to keep our analysis at the level of broad occupations and industries. This is what I've done in Table 10.1 (for the sake of space, this table does not include every possible industry and job in the data, just a selection).

In every occupation and industry in this table, men earn more than women on average. This is suggestive. However, it's not clear that either of the breakdowns in the table represents a good measure of 'equal work'. It is entirely possible that the pay gap within, for example, financial services, arises not because women are being paid less for doing the same work, but because women are more likely to occupy lower paid roles. For instance, if they work at a bond trading outfit they may be more likely to work in a 'back-office' support role than on the trading floor where the money is made. The story is similar if we look at other occupations. For example, female corporate managers may earn less than male ones primarily because they work at different sorts of companies (smaller companies, or companies in less profitable sectors). The limitations of the data mean we can't rule out these possibilities. And since there currently isn't a better source of data out there (at least not for the UK), there's not much more that we (or anyone else) can do.

Though this may not seem like a particularly satisfying conclusion, we have actually taken some significant steps here. At the outset, all we knew was that some people said the gender pay gap was a big problem, and that other people said it was a myth. Now we know that (1) the overall gender pay gap exists even if you look only at the median pay of full-time workers, and (2) that a pay gap is still visible even when you look within similar industries and similar jobs. This is progress! However, it is not the end of the story …

Table 10.1 Median full-time hourly pay of UK workers in selected industries and occupations

	Median hourly pay of full-time workers (2016)		Pay Gap
	Men	*Women*	
INDUSTRY			
Financial services (except insurance and pensions)	£25.70	£16.54	36%
Computer programming	£20.44	£16.63	19%
Legal and accounting	£19.31	£14.45	25%
Advertising and market research	£18.77	£15.61	17%
Education	£17.89	£15.63	13%
Human health	£16.80	£14.56	13%
Social work (without accommodation)	£12.47	£9.53	24%
Manufacture of food products	£10.83	£9.34	14%
Retail trade (except of motor vehicles)	£10.41	£9.19	12%
Food and beverage service	£8.40	£8.00	5%
OCCUPATION			
Corporate managers and directors	£23.35	£20.22	13%
Teaching and educational professionals	£23.10	£21.37	7%
Health professionals	£20.47	£17.33	15%
Protective service occupations	£17.37	£16.96	2%
Skilled metal, electrical, and electronic trades	£13.50	£12.29	9%
Administrative occupations	£11.89	£11.15	6%
Customer service occupations	£10.39	£10.23	2%
Caring personal service occupations	£9.46	£8.95	5%
Textiles, printing, and other skilled trades	£9.18	£8.73	5%

Source: Annual Survey of Hours and Earnings

Is the gender pay gap caused by sexism?

In the previous section, we looked for evidence that women were being paid less than men for equal work. We weren't able to answer this question satisfactorily with the available data. However, we are obviously not the first people to try to solve this particular puzzle.

Earlier in the chapter I mentioned an article in *The Economist* magazine which argued that the gender gap is almost non-existent if you look at men and women who are doing the same jobs. The figures cited in this article didn't come from the ASHE. They came from a study conducted by a recruitment consultancy company called Korn Ferry. The Korn Ferry study compared men and women who worked for the same employers, performing the same roles at the same level of seniority. In most European countries they found only very small gender differences in pay. In the UK, for example, they found that women make 'just 1% less than men who have the same function and level at the same employer'.

Many commentators have cited these results as proof that the gender pay gap is entirely the result of men and women doing different kinds of work, and therefore nothing to do with pay discrimination. Others have gone further to claim that this study (and others like it) *prove that the gender pay gap has nothing to do with sexism at all.*

Both of these claims are problematic. However, in this section we are going to focus on the second, more extreme claim. Even if we accept Korn Ferry's results as proof that equal pay for equal work is largely a reality (though there are plenty of reasons we shouldn't do this)* does this mean that sexism has no role to play in producing the gender pay gap?

It's not about sexism

If men and women who do the same jobs are largely paid the same, then any overall differences in average pay must be because women are more likely to end up in lower paid kinds of work. The question then becomes *why* this happens.

Critics of the 'myth' of the gender pay gap argue that men and women tend to pursue different types of jobs because they have naturally different aptitudes and preferences. Women prefer (and may be better at) jobs that involve human relationships; whereas men prefer (and may be better at) working with abstract systems. It just so happens that 'systems' jobs (which include many jobs in finance and technology) tend to pay better

---

* Neither *The Economist* nor Korn Ferry themselves provide much in the way of detail about how the study was conducted. *The Economist* reports that the study included data from 8.7 million employees worldwide – which is a lot. But we don't know how this 8.7 million was spread across the various countries in the study. We also don't know what kinds of companies they worked for. Was this data from a representative slice of different types of organisation, or was it just from large firms (Korn Ferry appear to deal mostly with recruitment for big multinational corporations)? Crucially, we also have no idea how 'same level' or 'same function' were defined. Did the men and women have exactly the same job title, or was there some wiggle room – and if so, how much? Without this information, we have no real idea of what the Korn Ferry results actually mean.

than 'human relationship' jobs. This difference in preferences and abilities might affect grand decisions, such as whether to go into teaching or engineering, but also more specific choices, such as between corporate law (higher paid, more likely to be done by men) and family law (lower paid, more likely to be done by women); or between orthopaedic surgery (higher paid, male-dominated) and paediatrics (lower paid, more often done by women).

Women's choices outside the workplace may also have an effect. Women, it is argued, tend to place a greater priority on family life than on getting ahead. They are therefore less willing to stay late at the office, or to put themselves forward for promotions or additional responsibilities. Importantly, they are also more likely to choose to take time out to have children. Together, these decisions tend to make women less likely to rise to senior positions.

So to sum up: women are attracted to jobs in areas that tend to be lower paid. Their prioritisation of child-rearing and family life also means they are less likely to move into senior roles. It's not about sexism – it's all about women's choices.

It is about sexism

Differences in preferences and abilities are clearly not the only potential explanation for the fact that women are more likely to end up in lower paid jobs. First, a narrow focus on women's personal choices ignores the existence of sexist discrimination at the stage of hiring and promotions. Women may not be paid less for doing the same jobs. However, sexist prejudices may prevent them from having an opportunity to do the same job in the first place. Many people hold sexist stereotypes about what men and women are good and bad at (the argument outlined in the previous section is *based* on such stereotypes). For example, studies have found that employers (particularly in male-dominated fields) tend to perceive female job applicants as nicer, but less competent than their male counterparts.* Potential female employees are also viewed as being less committed to their careers due to their probable family responsibilities. Research has shown that stereotypes like these do have an impact on decisions relating to hiring and promotion, especially in fields like science and technology.

Another major potential disruption to women's career progression is children. Spending extended periods working reduced hours, or being out of the labour market completely, sets back women's careers substantially. But aside from what is biologically necessary at the earliest stages of a child's life, why are women more likely to take time out than men?

---

* This is true even when the employers are reviewing fake CVs in which the only difference between the candidates is the gender of the applicant.

Critics of the gender pay gap idea often frame this as being a free choice. However, it is difficult to argue that the choice is *entirely* free, given that it takes place in a society which strongly expects women to be the primary caregivers. This expectation is also often explicitly reinforced by policies around maternity and paternity leave.

The question of free choice is also relevant to the issue of women's career preferences. From an early age, children's aspirations are not formed in a gender-neutral vacuum. They are guided by society's expectations. This can be subtle – Jane's parents reinforce her perception that she is 'good with people', while her nascent interest in computers is treated as a curiosity. Or it can be overt – Jane's teacher tells her she should expect to do worse than John in science because he's a boy, and boys are just better at that sort of thing. Gendered expectations and stereotypes like this can manifest in any number of ways as children make their way through education and then out into the workforce.*

And one final route through which sexism may play a role is in the value society places on different kinds of work. What if instead of asking 'why do women choose lower paid occupations?', we ask 'why do occupations mostly done by women tend to pay less?'. What a particular job pays is not solely determined by the invisible, infallible hand of the market. What employers are willing to pay care workers, machine operators, teachers, and engineers is not solely a product of supply and demand. It is also informed by what people consider certain kinds of work to be 'worth'. And society has generally tended to view 'women's work' as less valuable. For example, it is difficult to explain why janitorial work often pays better than housekeeping without accounting for the fact that janitors tend to be men and housekeepers tend to be women.

Historic patterns of pay in different professions bear out this notion. A comprehensive study conducted in the USA found that, as the proportion of women within a specific occupation increases, average pay levels tend to drop.[3] For example, between 1950 and 2000, design work went from being a male-dominated profession to a female-dominated one. Over the same period, the average wage of a designer dropped by 34%. Similarly, these five decades saw biological science become an increasingly female profession, and at the same time saw the average pay of biologists drop by 18%. The reverse is also true. For example, in the early days of computer programming, most coders were low-paid women. However, as the profession attracted more men, wages rose dramatically.

Taken together, these explanations represent clear ways in which the gender pay gap could be a manifestation of societal sexism, *even if direct pay discrimination (unequal pay for the same role) is rare or even non-existent.*

---

*   This is necessarily a very superficial summary of the issue. I recommend Cordelia Fine's excellent book *Delusions of Gender* if you are interested in knowing more.

The verdict

So which of these arguments is right? If you think back to Chapter 7, you can see that this is fundamentally a **causal** question. We are trying to figure out if the gender pay gap is *caused* by sexism, or by women's choices. Unfortunately, what the lessons of Chapter 7 also show is that this is not a question we can answer with the data we have. This data can tell us that women tend to end up in lower paying jobs than men. What it can't tell us is *why*.

If we wanted definitive proof in one direction or another, we would ideally want to do an experiment. We would take a sample of boys and girls at an early age and control every aspect of their lives except their biological sex. We would need to make sure that their abilities and career aspirations developed without any gendered social pressures. No helpful aunts, well-meaning teachers, or even books or TV shows pushing them towards an idea of 'girl jobs' and 'boy jobs'. We would also need to make sure that whenever our participants applied for a job or a promotion, sexist stereotypes played no role in the selection process. Finally, we would need to make sure that our girls and boys did not absorb any gendered expectations about child-rearing (and that any policies around parental leave were entirely gender-blind). Then, and only then, could we come close to definitively ruling out sexism (or free choice) as a potential explanation for gender pay differences.*

In the real world, we have to settle for less direct evidence – for attacking the problem from the edges. For example, we could look at evidence from studies of how young children respond to gender stereotypes; or of how male and female brains respond to different sorts of tasks or stimuli; or of how gender bias affects the evaluation of male and female job applicants. I don't have the space here to go into this evidence in detail.** All I will say is that the more research we do, the fewer differences there seem to be in the way men and women are wired. Allied to this is clear evidence of the countless ways, big and small, that men and women are exposed to sexist expectations and beliefs. Given these facts, my general feeling is that sexism has a large role to play in producing the gender inequalities we see in the world. However, you will have your own ideas, and the issue is far from settled.

Writing up the results

We've done our research the best we can with the data available to us. Now, to save other people the hassle of going through this whole process themselves, we should write it up and publish it. We could do this as a

---

*   Though, we still would not have accounted for the societal undervaluation of female-dominated professions. For that we would have to travel back in time and purposefully skew the gender balance of a random set of occupations.

** Once again, Fine's *Delusions of Gender* is a good introduction to this research.

blog post, a podcast, a research report, or we could even pitch it as an article to a newspaper or a magazine. All of these different outlets require different approaches. For example, if you are intending to speak to a general audience, you can't assume they will be familiar with all the underlying concepts and technical jargon. But whatever your intended audience, your fundamental goal should be the same: to communicate your results clearly and honestly – to be transparent about what you did and what you found, and about what your numbers prove and what they don't.

IMRaD

One way to make sure that you are reporting your results clearly and transparently is to maintain a clear separation between (1) what you did and what you found, and (2) any speculation about what your findings might mean. Your numbers are like pristine white t-shirts in the laundry – you don't want your theories and suppositions getting in there and polluting them, like an errant red sock.

So in the case of our gender pay gap analysis, we would first want a self-contained section describing our handling of the data: where we downloaded the spreadsheets, which measure of pay we are focusing on (median hourly pay), what definitions we are using (for example, of occupation and industry), and so on. A sensible title for this section would be 'Methods' or 'Methodology'.

Next, we would need another section describing exactly what we found: What was the overall gender pay gap? What was the gap in each of the different industries and occupations? This section we would probably want to call 'Results'.

Finally, we can have a section where we discuss what our results might mean. This section should be clearly separated from the straightforward report of our findings. Here we are a little more free to speculate. With reference to theories other authors have suggested, we can go through some possible explanations for why we found what we found. We can also discuss what implications our findings might have, for example for government or corporate policy. Because this section is devoted to discussing our results, we'll call it the 'Discussion'.

Before we call it a day, it's probably sensible to go back to the beginning and add a section where we set up the research. We can't assume that everyone reading our report is familiar with all the ins and outs of the gender pay gap issue. So in this section we'll provide the background and context people will need to understand what we did and what we found, along with why the research is important. We should probably also summarise what previous research has found on the same topic. Have people before us tried to answer the same question, or a similar one? What did *they* find in their studies? These two components (the background and the literature review) will make up the 'Introduction' to our study.

If these headings sound familiar to you, it's because we've just invented the 'IMRaD' structure – the standardised structure used by almost all modern scientific reports, whether they are about physics, psychology, politics, criminology, or any other subject. I learned this structure at school as just 'the way you are supposed to do things' – but, as you can see, it actually exists for a good reason.

In the earliest days of science, when academic journals had titles like: *Philosophical Transactions: Giving Some Account of the Present Undertakings, Studies, and Labours of the Ingenious in Many Considerable Parts of the World*,* people used to write about their experiments in the same way they would write a letter about their summer holiday. Here is an example of an early scientific report on the subject of the electric eel:

> *To John Walsh, ESQ.*
>
> *As the electric eel has lately engaged the public attention, and yours in particular, I have taken the liberty of sending you some experiments which I made on that fish ... Besides by my own superficial acquaintance with the subject of electricity, of which I am very conscious, there are other circumstances that may help to apologize for the imperfect state in which these experiments appear. The eel, being sickened by the change of climate, its owner refused to let us take it out of the water for the purpose of making experiments*
>
> *...*
>
> *On touching the eel with one of my hands, I perceived such a sensation in the joints of my fingers as I received on touching a prime conductor or charged phial ... On touching the eel more roughly, I perceived a similar effect in my wrist and elbow ...*[4]

Letters like this, though delightful, are difficult to follow. Crucial methodological details are mixed in with details of the author's travel arrangements; important results end up in footnotes attached to long passages of speculation.

Academic publishers realised they needed to constrain these rambling dialogues into some sort of coherent structure. Ideally this structure would allow the reader to quickly identify, first, exactly what the researchers did, and second, exactly what they found. Many different systems were tried over years. However, in the 20th century the IMRaD structure, which helpfully keeps theory and conjectures confined to the introduction and the discussion, is the one that stuck.

---

* This is the title of the first ever scientific journal, published in 1665 by the Royal Society. It is still going strong today under the slightly less cumbersome title of the *Philosophical Transactions of the Royal Society.*

The fundamental principle when publishing scientific research is transparency. But what does transparency actually *mean*? Perhaps the easiest way to understand it is by its absence. What does our write-up look like when we are *not* trying to be transparent?

How to lie with true statistics

Why might we want to avoid being transparent about our results? The reason will almost always be that we have a particular message to sell, and that a full accounting of our results would not do a great job of selling it.

Let's say we work for a feminist campaign organisation.* Our current campaign is focused on getting the government to pass legislation to end pay discrimination (in other words, to stop women from getting paid less for equal work). We want to use the statistics we got from the ASHE to help support this campaign.

Our first step is to give an overall figure for the size of the gender pay gap. The bigger this gap seems to be, the more impact it's going to make. We *could* therefore use the mean annual salary figures from the beginning of this chapter. These figures show that the average woman earns just 62% of what the average man earns. This would make for a good, shocking headline. The trouble is that it would also be pretty easy to criticise. All it would take would be for someone to point out that our number does not take into account the obvious difference between people working full-time and part-time.

To avoid this critique, we'll use the annual salary for full-time workers. That gives us a smaller number than the overall difference, but it's much harder to 'debunk'. We won't use the hourly pay difference, even though this is arguably a better figure, because it gives us a smaller and therefore less headline-worthy pay gap. For the same reason we'll stick to using the mean rather than the median – trusting that most people won't have the statistical expertise to unpick the mean/median distinction.

The transparent thing to do in this situation would have been to report a variety of different estimates of the gender pay gap, along with a commentary on why they are different. However, this would muddy the waters of the message we are trying to convey. So, for our purposes, it is better to just select the biggest number. This process is called <u>cherry-picking</u>, and it is an extremely popular way of lying with statistics. Almost any statistical analysis will produce a lot of different numbers bearing on the same question. Some of them will do a better job of selling a particular story than others. Cherry-picking means reporting

---

*   This is an entirely hypothetical example and is not based on the activities of any particular feminist organisation. The Fawcett Society, for example, (problematic framing aside) are very clear about how they calculate their gender pay gap numbers, and about what these numbers do and don't say.

the ones that tell the story you want to tell, and dropping the ones that don't. This is a very easy way to craft a misleading message (see the box below for more on why cherry-picking is such a big problem).

Next, our campaign is about pay discrimination, so we want to convey the idea that women are paid less for equal work. One way to do this would be to say that, even for women working in the same jobs, the gender pay gaps are large. Our results show that this is true if we define 'same jobs' very broadly (as being in the same general occupation or industry). However, if we don't clarify exactly what we mean by 'same jobs', then hopefully people won't notice the problem with this (see Chapter 4 for more examples of this trick in action). Here we could also do another bit of cherry-picking – by selecting some of the largest pay gaps by occupation or industry to serve as illustrative examples. For example, in finance women earn 40% less than men,* so we would choose this as an example rather than the food and drink service industry, where the gap is 'only' 17%. In terms of occupation, we would choose health professionals (a 35% gap) over customer service workers (a 12% gap).

The final step in our pitch is to tell a causal story. We want people to come away with the idea that the pay gap is entirely caused by sexism, and not by other processes. Of course, our results show only that there is a gap, and that the gap exists within broad industries and professions. They don't allow us to come down on one side or the other as to what causes this gap to exist. But we don't need to point that out. Instead we can transition straight into talking about how legislation is needed to solve pay discrimination, thereby strongly implying that *this* is the primary cause of the pay gap we have identified.

Put this all together and we get something like this:

Official Statistics Show that British Women are Still Staggeringly Underpaid

*Our analysis of the latest government figures shows that the average woman in the UK is paid **25% less** than the average man.*

The statistics show that women working full-time earn an average salary of £29,053 (before tax), compared to an average salary of £37,893 for men.

*This difference translates to a full **90 days** of unpaid work put in by women up and down the country every year.*

*Our analysis shows that women are paid substantially less than their male colleagues working in the **same jobs**. For example, women in finance are paid an astonishing **40% less** than their male*

---

* Remember we are using the mean annual pay figures here, so the gap is larger than it is in the table we produced earlier.

*counterparts. The gap is almost as large for female health profession-
als, who earn a massive 35% less than men in the same line of work.*

*New legislation is required to make sure employers pay their male
and female employees fairly. Forcing companies to be fully transparent with their employees about how much everyone is paid will
encourage women to seek equal pay for equal work, helping to close
the yawning pay disparity highlighted by our analysis.*

None of the statistics in this statement are false. They have all been
derived, unchanged, from a legitimate source. But I hope you agree that
this statement does not give a full and honest representation of what our
analysis of the ASHE data actually showed.

Of course, we could take exactly the same approach from the other
side of the debate. If we wanted to argue that the gender pay gap is a
myth, we could go through essentially the same process, but making
the opposite decisions. Instead of cherry-picking the largest numbers, we
pick the smallest. Rather than using the figures for broad occupations,
we use the most specific comparisons (conveniently failing to mention
the problem of small sample sizes). Instead of saying the gap is caused
by sexism, we say it is caused by women's choices. The same underlying
data; a completely different story.

Cherry-picking

It might not be immediately obvious to you why 'cherry-picking' is such
a sin. After all, the numbers you are reporting are real. You're not making them up – you are just selecting the ones that tell a particular story.

As evidence against this position, consider the following question:
From just seeing someone's Instagram or Facebook feed, how confident would you be that you really knew how their life was going?
I imagine the answer is 'not very'. Most people's Facebook and Instagram
posts are a carefully curated (cherry-picked) selection of the best parts
of their lives: achievements, holidays, photogenic dinners and parties.
Even if each post is individually true, by cherry-picking the good while
omitting the bad, someone who is actually pretty miserable can seem
like they are winning at life. Given enough material, selective editing
allows you to craft whatever story *you* want to tell.*

This is as true in statistics as it is on Instagram. By purposefully
selecting only a few numbers out of many, you can tell almost any story
you like. Let's say, for example, you want to prove that playing violent
video games causes people to behave more aggressively in real life.
You gather a sample of people in the lab and you get them to play a
violent game for a couple of hours (your control group watches a violent action movie on TV). In this experiment, you measure aggression in

three different ways: a questionnaire and two behavioural tasks (people's willingness to play an unpleasantly loud sound into a competitor's headphones, or to deliver a minor electric shock through an electrode attached to their finger).

When you get your results back, they're a mixed bag. When looking at two of the three measures, there is no difference between the experimental group and the control group. But for the other measure, there is a difference. The real, unedited story here is that the majority of your results suggest no effect of violent video games on aggressive behaviour. But by cherry-picking only the measure which *did* seem to show an effect, you can tell a very different story. If the two measures that didn't 'work' conveniently go missing in your final report, then the audience is going to take away the clear message that violent video games do make people more aggressive.

This is why cherry-picking is simultaneously so common and so dangerous. It's incredibly easy to do – you just leave out the things that don't fit the case you're trying to make – while also being extremely difficult to detect. Unless someone was there with you while you were doing the analysis, how can they spot what you left out?

This is a hypothetical example, but cherry-picking exactly like this has done enormous damage in the real world. For some truly devastating examples, I recommend Ben Goldacre's book *Bad Pharma*, which illustrates numerous cases in which cherry-picking in the pharmaceutical industry has literally killed people.

---

* This is the fundamental principle that makes reality TV both (1) possible as a form of entertainment, and (2) an oxymoron.

How to use statistics to tell the truth

Being honest should be easy. Surely it's being *dis*honest that takes effort? But in order to be honest about our research, we have to overcome a very human desire – the desire to shape facts into a story that supports what we already believe.

It's rare for anyone to start a piece of research with a completely open mind. Especially when it comes to the big debates in society, everyone has some pre-existing ideas. But being a good researcher means being open to the possibility that these ideas will be challenged. Your analysis should proceed on that basis. Don't just do the safe sums that you're sure will give you the answer you want. Do the scary ones that you're worried will shake your existing beliefs. In fact, the more frightened you are that your results will disrupt something you really want to believe, the more likely you are to be doing good research. If, on the other hand, you're perfectly certain of what the results will be before you start, then you are not really doing research at all.

In a court of law, the prosecution puts forward the best case it can that the defendant is guilty. If there is a fact that doesn't help their story, they leave it out. It's up to the defence to bring up these details, to use them to tell a different story in which the defendant is innocent. When you are writing about research, it's tempting to think like the prosecution – to leave out details that don't quite work; that confuse your story and make your conclusions less clear-cut. But the job of a researcher is very different to the job of a prosecutor. You are not out there to reach a particular conclusion, but to find the truth. This means you have to act as both prosecution and defence – offering every detail that might be relevant, so the jury is equipped to decide what actually happened.

In other words, your default position should be one of radical transparency. Put everything out there: exactly where you got your data from, exactly what definitions you are using, exactly what calculations you did, and *all* the numbers you got back. Think of the world as your maths teacher: they need to be able to check your work. The internet makes this very easy, even if you are constrained by the limited space of a press-release or a newspaper article (or a university assignment). If you are using publicly available data, you can hyperlink to it directly. If you don't have space to describe your methodology in detail, write it up in a blog post and link to that. Better yet, upload the spreadsheet with all your calculations, and link to that too.

If these ideas make you uncomfortable, then that's a hint that you might not have been as honest with your write-up as you could have been. For example, if I was behind the analysis I described in the previous section, I would feel *very* uncomfortable sharing all my workings. I would be worried that the reader would see that (for example) hourly pay yields a smaller gap than annual, or that my definition of 'same occupation' is a lot broader than I made it seem.

***

Most of the examples in this book have been of bad statistics: statistics which, whether intentionally or not, tell stories about the world that aren't actually true. It would be very easy to turn this into a general cynicism about numbers – statistics are just so easy to manipulate that I really shouldn't trust any of them. This would be a mistake. Statistics are a tool like any other. They have the power to deceive, but they also have an incredible power to do good. When research is approached openly, as an act of discovery, rather than as a way to prove a point; when results are reported honestly and transparently – then statistics can do amazing things. They can give us insights into how the world really works. They can uncover injustice and help us find ways to address it. They can help us reach solutions to age-old problems. It's not an exaggeration to say that they can help us make the world a better place. So yes, be on the lookout for dodgy numbers. Be sceptical. Be critical. But don't close your mind to the possibility of finding something real.

Summary

The truth is out there. The data used by academics and other researchers to answer the big questions is often publicly available for free, allowing us to investigate these questions ourselves.

Start with the question, not the answer. Research should be carried out with the intention of finding something out. If you start with the answer you want, and then work backwards to try to prove it, you are not conducting genuine research.

Data and methods should be chosen or rejected based on whether they provide a better or worse chance of finding the truth, not on whether they provide a better or worse chance of giving you the answer you were looking for.

Let it all hang out. Methods and results should be reported honestly and transparently. Don't cherry-pick. Be open about everything you did and everything you found. Give the reader all the information they need to make up their own minds.

 ## Terminology used in this chapter

IMRaD: An acronym representing the standard structure of a scientific report. It stands for **Introduction** (setting up the context of the research and what is already known on the topic), **Methods** (what you did), **Results** (what you found), and **Discussion** (what you think your findings *mean*).

Cherry-picking: Purposefully reporting results which fit the story you want to tell, while failing to report results which contradict or complicate this story.

 ## Seeing beyond the headlines

When it comes to numbers, it's not only other people's bullshit you have to watch out for. To paraphrase Richard Feynman, you must also avoid fooling yourself – and you are the easiest person to fool. Here are three questions to ask to help make sure that doesn't happen:

1. HAVE YOU BEEN HONEST WITH YOURSELF ABOUT THE RESULT YOU WANT?

It's rare for anyone to start a piece of research with a completely open mind. There are almost always things we want to find, and things we'd definitely prefer not to find. Be honest with yourself about what those are.

2. HAVE YOUR METHODOLOGICAL DECISIONS BEEN SELF-SERVING?

Quantitative research involves lots and lots of small decisions – about how to measure things, about what comparisons to make, about what data points to include or exclude ... the list goes on. This means it's often very easy to come up with legitimate-sounding reasons to ditch or tinker with an unwanted result. 'That country shouldn't have been in the analysis in the first place', 'the mean actually makes more sense than the median here ... '. Don't let yourself be persuaded. This is a slippery slope, so best not start down it at all. Go back to the first question: Are you making these arguments because they objectively make sense? Or are you making them because they allow you to find what you wanted to find in the first place?

3. HAVE YOU TRIED TO PROVE YOURSELF WRONG?

Don't just accept your first result. Put yourself in the position of someone who is convinced that your conclusions are completely wrong. Think about what they would do to try and overturn your findings – then do it. Be the defence as well as the prosecution.

Example

CLAIM	HONEST ABOUT THE RESULT WE WANT?	SELF-SERVING DECISIONS?	TRIED TO PROVE OURSELVES WRONG?	VERDICT
The average woman is paid 25% less than the average man	YES. Clear that we wanted the biggest gap possible	YES. Decisions made on the basis of what would produce the most attention grabbing number	NO. No attempt to change result	Bad research – worked backwards to get the result we wanted

Exercises for Chapter 10

Below are three research questions that can be addressed using publicly available data. Choose a question that interests you.

Following the same process as we went through with the gender pay gap, try to use relevant data to answer the question (some relevant sources are suggested).

Write a blog post explaining (transparently) what you did and what you found.

QUESTION 1: In the USA, is gun violence more common in states with fewer restrictions on gun ownership?

It would seem to make sense that gun violence would be more common in states where guns are more readily available. However, is this really the case?

Suggested data sources:

Academics at the Boston University School of Public Health keep a publicly available database on state gun laws called the 'State Firearm Law Database' (you can find the link to the database on this book's companion website).

The FBI Uniform Crime Reports provide statistics on the numbers of crimes committed with different types of weapons (you can find the link to these reports on this book's companion website).

Alternative question:

You may also be interested in answering the question of whether mass-shootings are more common in states with fewer gun laws, or in states which lack specific restrictions (for example, on the purchase of assault weapons). There are a variety of databases which use different definitions of what constitutes a mass-shooting. It's up to you which you think it is most sensible to use. Make sure you read the methodological notes carefully.

QUESTION 2: Are millennials less tolerant of political difference than previous generations?

Many political commentators have expressed concern that 'millennials' are less willing than previous generations to listen to ideas with which they disagree. For example, much has been written about the practice of 'no-platforming' – of preventing people with problematic ideas (for example, ideas that might be considered racist, sexist, homophobic, or transphobic) from speaking from a particular platform (for example, a university event).

But are millennials really more censorious than previous generations?

Suggested data sources:

Researchers in many countries conduct regular surveys which ask people about their feelings on important social issues. Many of these surveys include questions on free speech and censorship. For example, for many years the US General Social Survey (GSS) has included questions on whether a variety of groups should be allowed to teach or to 'speak in your community' (there is a link to this survey on this book's companion website). Similar questions are asked in the Australian Survey of Social Attitudes, and in attitudes surveys in other countries around the world. Data from many of these survey (including the US GSS) is publicly available online.

QUESTION 3: Did hate crimes increase in 2016?

In 2016 and 2017 a number of commentators suggested that events such as Brexit and the election of Donal Trump would lead to an increase in the number of hate crimes towards minority groups. Does the data suggest that this actually occurred? If so, were any specific groups particularly strongly affected?

Suggested data sources:

Government agencies in many countries (including the FBI in the USA and the Home Office in the UK) collect data on the number of hate crimes committed in a given year (you can find links to such data on this book's companion website).

---

www.macmillanihe.com/devries-critical-statistics

 ONLINE RESOURCES AVAILABLE

Go to the book's companion website for further examples, data, links, and other useful resources.

👁 Seeing beyond the headlines

Each of the preceding chapters has had its own 'Seeing beyond the headlines' toolbox, listing things to look out for when interpreting statistics. Here I've attempted to distil these lists down into a single, handy set of questions to ask of any number:

1. **IS THE NUMBER AN ESTIMATE BASED ON A SAMPLE?**
   If it is, is the sample a good one? Is it big enough? Is it likely to be biased towards a particular type of person?

2. **WHAT IS BEING MEASURED?**
   What concept is the number supposed to be capturing? How is this concept defined? What is actually being measured 'on the ground' (e.g. through a survey question)? How well does the measure match the concept?

3. **IS THE NUMBER AN AVERAGE?**
   If so, what type of average: mean, median, or mode? Is this average likely to be an accurate representation of what's 'normal' for the population? Regardless, remember that all averages are summaries that conceal a lot of variation.

4. **IS THE NUMBER A RAW COUNT?**
   If so, would a percentage be more appropriate? If a comparison is being made between populations of two different sizes, the answer is definitely yes.

5. **IS THE NUMBER A PERCENTAGE?**
   If so, has it been calculated correctly?

6. **IS THE NUMBER A RISK?**
   If so, has the baseline risk information been provided?

7. **IS A CAUSAL CLAIM BEING MADE?**
   If so, what evidence is being presented to support the idea that X really causes Y? What alternative explanations might there be for X and Y being related? What efforts have been taken to rule out these explanations – for example, through an experiment, a natural experiment, or a regression model?

8. **ARE NUMBERS BEING PRESENTED IN THE FORM OF A GRAPH?**
   If so, what type of graph is it? What quantities are being represented and by which visual elements? Is the visualisation telling the story of the data accurately?

9. **IN WHAT CONTEXT HAS THE NUMBER BEEN PLACED?**
   Does this context appear to have been selected to make the number look big or small? Would another context change your impression of whether the number was big or small?

10. **IS THIS A NUMBER YOU HAVE PRODUCED YOURSELF?**
    If so, have you tried hard enough to avoid biasing it in favour of the result you wanted? Have you been transparent in reporting exactly how the number was worked out?

NOTES

Chapter 1

1. Smith, M. (2015). No, 1 in 5 British Muslims doesn't have sympathy with ISIS – here's why'. *Mirror* (online), 23 November [retrieved 7 March 2018]. Available at: http://www.mirror.co.uk/news/uk-news/no-1-5-british-muslims-6882598#comments-section.

2. https://twitter.com/hashtag/1in5muslims?lang=en.

3. Survation. New Polling of British Muslims. *Survation Blog*, 20 November 2015 [retrieved 7 March 2018]. Available at: http://survation.com/new-polling-of-british-muslims/.

4. Iqbal, S. (2015). The Syria-bound schoolgirls aren't jihadi devil-women, they're vulnerable children. *The Guardian* (online), 24 February [retrieved 6 March 2018]. Available at: https://www.theguardian.com/commentisfree/2015/feb/24/syria-bound-schoolgirls-arent-jihadi-devil-women-theyre-vulnerable-children.

5. Anonymous. (2005). I conducted the Sun's '1 in 5 Muslims' poll and was shocked by how it was used. *VICE*, 24 November [retrieved 6 March 2018]. Available at: https://www.vice.com/en_uk/article/vdxqwx/i-conducted-the-muslim-poll-the-sun-jihadi-sympathy.

6. Independent Press Standards Organisation. *Decision 09324-15: Muslim Engagement and Development (MEND)* v. *The Sun*. IPSO, 17 February 2016 [retrieved 6 March 2018]. Available at: https://www.ipso.co.uk/rulings-and-resolution-statements/ruling/?id=09324-15.

7. Cushion, S., Lewis, J., & Callaghan, R. (2017). Data journalism, impartiality and statistical claims. *Journalism Practice, 11*(10), 1198–1215.

8. Cameron, D. (2015). The Conservatives have become the party of equality. *The Guardian* (online), 26 October [retrieved 6 March 2018]. Available at: https://www.theguardian.com/commentisfree/2015/oct/26/david-cameron-conservatives-party-of-equality.

9. Washington Post Staff. Transcript: Bernie Sanders's full speech at the 2016 DNC. *Washington Post,* 26 July 2016 [retrieved 6 March 2018]. Available at: https://www.washingtonpost.com/news/post-politics/wp/2016/07/26/transcript-bernie-sanderss-full-speech-at-the-2016-dnc/.

10. New York Governor's Office. (2016). Video, Photos & Rush Transcript: Governor Cuomo Announces Official Opening of New Silvercup Studios Film & TV Production Facility in the Bronx. New York Governor's Office, 17 August [retrieved 6 March 2018]. Available at: https://www.governor.ny.gov/news/video-photos-rush-transcript-governor-cuomo-announces-official-opening-new-silvercup-studios.

11. The Labour Party. The Conservative's Six Years of Failure on Housing. *Labour Party General Secretary* [retrieved 6 March 2018]. Available at: https://www.ucatt.org.uk/files/publications/Local%20elections%20Housing%20campaign%20pack.pdf.

12. Day, J. (2005). Pantene panned by ASA for misleading claims. *The Guardian* (online), 11 May [retrieved 6 March 2018]. Available at: https://www.theguardian. com/media/2005/may/11/advertising.asa.

13. American Cancer Society. (2017). *Tobacco and Cancer Fact Sheet.* American Cancer Society Inc. [retrieved 6 March 2018]. Available at: https://www.cancer.org/ content/dam/cancer-org/cancer-control/en/booklets-flyers/tobacco-and-cancer-fact-sheet.pdf.

14. Sattelmair, J., Pertman, J., Ding, E.L., Kohl, H.W., Haskell, W., & Lee, I.M. (2011). Dose response between physical activity and risk of coronary heart disease: A meta-analysis. *Circulation, 124*(7), 789–795.

15. The Onion. (2012). 42 million dead in bloodiest Black Friday weekend on record. *The Onion,* 26 November [retrieved 6 March 2018]. Available at: http://www. theonion.com/article/42-million-dead-in-bloodiest-black-friday-weekend-30517.

16. BBC News. (2011). Implanon: 600 pregnancies despite contraceptive implant. *BBC News* (online), 5 January [retrieved 6 March 2018]. Available at: http://www. bbc.co.uk/news/health-12117299.

17. Goldacre, B. (2011). Putting a number in its context. *Badscience.net,* 8 January [retrieved 6 March 2018]. Available at: http://www.badscience.net/2011/01/ putting-a-number-in-its-context/.

18. Trussell, J. (2004). Contraceptive failure in the United States. *Contraception, 70*(2), 89–96.

19. Drobnic Holan, A. (2015). All Politicians Lie. Some Lie More Than Others. *New York Times* (online), 11 December [retrieved 6 March 2018]. Available at: https://www.nytimes.com/2015/12/13/opinion/campaign-stops/all-politicians-lie-some-lie-more-than-others.html.

20. Solon, O. (2016). Facebook's failure: Did fake news and polarized politics get Trump elected. *The Guardian* (online), 10 November [retrieved 6 March 2018]. Available at: https://www.theguardian.com/technology/2016/nov/10/facebook-fake-news-election-conspiracy-theories.

21. Silverman, C., Strapagiel, L., Shaban, H., Hall, E., & Singer-Vine, J. (2016). Hyper-partisan Facebook pages are publishing false and misleading information at an alarming rate. *Buzzfeed News,* 20 October [retrieved 6 March 2018]. Available at: https://www.buzzfeed.com/craigsilverman/partisan-fb-pages-analysis.

22. National Association of Colleges and Employers (NACE). (2016). Job Outlook 2016: The attributes employers want to see on new college graduates' resumes. *NACE* [retrieved 6 March 2018]. Available at: http://www.naceweb.org/career-development/trends-and-predictions/job-outlook-2016-attributes-employers-want-to-see-on-new-college-graduates-resumes/;

23. Tariq, V., & Durrani, N. (2009). Every student counts: Promoting numeracy and enhancing employability. *MSOR Connections, 9*(1), 7–11; Durrani, N., & Tariq, V. N. (2012). The role of numeracy skills in graduate employability. *Education+Training, 54*(5), 419–434.

Chapter 2

1. Lipton, E. (2014). Lobbyists, bearing gifts, pursue Attorneys General. *New York Times,* 28 October [retrieved 6 March 2018]. Available at: https://www.nytimes. com/2014/10/29/us/lobbyists-bearing-gifts-pursue-attorneys-general.html.

2. Kiel, P., & Waldman, A. (2015). The color of debt: How collection suits squeeze black neighborhoods, *ProPublica,* 9 October [retrieved 6 March 2018]. Available at: https://www.propublica.org/article/debt-collection-lawsuits-squeeze-black-neighborhoods.

3. Centers for Disease Control (CDC). (2016). New data show continuing opioid epidemic in the United States. CDC Media Relations, 16 December [retrieved 6 March 2018]. Available at: https://www.cdc.gov/media/releases/2016/p1216-continuing-opioid-epidemic.html.

4. Pressat Wire. (2016). Naked ambition: Why nudist holidays are now on the cards for half of Brits. *Pressat Wire,* 10 August [retrieved 6 March 2018]. Available at: http://www.pressat.co.uk/releases/naked-ambition-why-nudist-holidays-are-now-on-the-cards-for-half-of-brits-8d38ab555ebcc79d5e6e6ba30604f5e1/.

5. Fenwick Elliott, A. (2016). Naked ambition! More than HALF of Brits would go nude on holiday … and men are twice as willing. *Mail Online,* 3 August [retrieved 6 March 2018]. Available at: http://www.dailymail.co.uk/travel/travel_news/article-3721861/More-HALF-Brits-nude-holiday-according-Lastminute-com-survey.html.

6. Roberts, S. (2016). Beach bums! As over HALF of Brits admit they'd strip off on holiday … here are 10 of the best nudist beaches in the world. *The Sun* (online), 4 August [retrieved 6 March 2018]. Available at: https://www.thesun.co.uk/living/1554941/as-over-half-of-brits-admit-theyd-strip-off-on-holiday-here-are-10-of-the-best-nudist-beaches-in-the-world/.

7. Thistlethwaite, F. (2016). Nudist beaches not the BUTT of the joke anymore: Search for naked-friendly up 50%. *Express* (online), 6 August [retrieved 6 March 2018]. Available at: http://www.express.co.uk/travel/articles/696545/Nudist-beaches-find-naked-sunbathing-UK-britain.

8. BT News. (2016). Time to get naked as more than half of Brits would consider adding nudism to their holiday. *BT.com*, 3 August [retrieved 6 March 2018]. Available at: http://home.bt.com/news/features/time-to-get-naked-as-more-than-half-of-brits-would-consider-adding-nudism-to-their-holiday-11364077317218.

9. Davies, N. (2009). *Flat Earth News*. London: Vintage Books.

10. Lewis, J., Williams, A., Franklin, B., Thomas, J., & Mosdell, N. (2008). *The Quality and Independence of British Journalism*. Report. University of Cardiff [retrieved 6 March 2018]. Available at: https://orca.cf.ac.uk/18439/1/Quality%20%26%20Independence%20of%20British%20Journalism.pdf.

11. Alpert, L.I., & Marshall, J. (2015). Bezos takes hands-on role at *Washington Post*. *Wall Street Journal* (online), 20 December [retrieved 6 March 2018]. Available at: https://www.wsj.com/articles/bezos-takes-hands-on-role-at-washington-post-1450658089.

12. Meyer, R. (2016). How many stories do newspapers publish per day. *The Atlantic* (online), 26 May [retrieved 6 March 2018]. Available at: https://www.theatlantic.com/technology/archive/2016/05/how-many-stories-do-newspapers-publish-per-day/483845/.

13. Lewis, J., Williams, A., & Franklin, B. (2008). A compromised fourth estate? UK news journalism, public relations and news sources. *Journalism Studies, 9*(1), 1–20.

14. Pew Research Center Journalism & Media Staff. (2010). *How News Happens*. Report. Pew Research Center, 11 January [retrieved 6 March 2018]. Available at: http://www.journalism.org/2010/01/11/how-news-happens/.

15. Forde, S., & Johnston, J. (2013). The news triumvirate. *Journalism Studies, 14*(1), 113–129.

16. Bohannon, J. (2015). I fooled millions into thinking chocolate helps weight loss. Here's how. *io9,* 27 May [retrieved 6 March 2018]. Available at: https://io9.gizmodo. com/i-fooled-millions-into-thinking-chocolate-helps-weight-1707251800.

17. Russia Today (RT). (2016). 1 Christian killed for their faith every 6 minutes in 2016 – study. *RT,* 29 December [retrieved 6 March 2018]. Available at: https:// www.rt.com/news/372184-christians-killed-faith-study/.

18. Le Miere, J. (2017). Christians were 2016's most persecuted religious group: Study. *Newsweek* (online), 1 January [retrieved 6 March 2018]. Available at: http:// www.newsweek.com/christians-2016-most-persecuted-religious-group-537413.

19. Williams, T.D. (2017). Report: 90,000 Christians killed for their faith in 2016. *Breitbart,* 1 January [retrieved 6 March 2018]. Available at: http://www.breitbart. com/national-security/2017/01/01/report-90000-christians-killed-faith-2016/.

20. MSN. (2017). 90,000 Christians killed for their faith last year. *MSN.com,* 2 January [retrieved 5 August 2017]. Available at: https://www.msn.com/en-us/news/ video/group-90000-christians-killed-for-their-faith-last-year/vp-AAlOf2C.

21. Le Miere, J. (2016). A Christian killed every 6 minutes in 2016. *Yahoo News,* 30 December [retrieved 6 March 2018]. Available at: https://uk.news.yahoo.com/ christian-killed-every-6-minutes-145134269.html.

22. Fox News. (2017). OUTRAGEOUS: Study: 90k Christians were killed for their faith in 2016. *Fox News insider,* 12 January [retrieved 6 March 2018]. Available at: http://insider.foxnews.com/2017/01/12/study-christianity-persecuted-around-world-90k-martyred-2016.

23. Haverluck, M.F. (2016). Half billion Christians can't express faith, 90k killed in 2016. *One News Now,* 29 December [retrieved 6 March 2018]. Available at: https://www.onenewsnow.com/persecution/2016/12/29/half-billion-christians-cant-express-faith-90k-killed-in-2016.

24. Smith, S. (2016). 90,000 Christians killed in 2016, 1 every 6 minutes: Study. *The Christian Post,* 30 December [retrieved 6 March 2018]. Available at: http://www.christianpost.com/news/90000-christians-killed-in-2016-1-every-6-minutes-study-172464/.

25. Senator Ted Cruz. (2017). Facebook, 4 January. https://www.facebook.com/ SenatorTedCruz/posts/1095766203869012.

26. Center for the Study of Global Christianity. (2016). *Status of Global Christianity, 2017, in the Context of 1900–2050.* Report. Center for the Study of Global Christianity at Gordon-Conwell Theological Seminary [retrieved 6 March 2018]. Available at: http://www.gordonconwell.edu/ockenga/research/documents/ StatusofGlobalChristianity2017.pdf.

27. Radio Vaticana. (2016). Persecuzioni anticristiane. Introvigne: 90 mila uccisi nel 2016. *Vatican Radio,* 26 December [retrieved 6 March 2018]. Available at: http:// it.radiovaticana.va/news/2016/12/26/persecuzioni_anticristiane_2016_circa_ 90_mila_uccisi/1281180.

28. Alexander, R. (2013). Are there really 100,000 new Christian martyrs every year? *BBC News* (online), 12 November [retrieved 6 March 2018]. Available at: http:// www.bbc.co.uk/news/magazine-24864587.

29. Cushion, S., Lewis, J., & Callaghan, R. (2017). Data journalism, impartiality and statistical claims: Towards more independent scrutiny in news reporting. *Journalism Practice, 11*(10), 1198–1215.

30. Greenslade, R. (2012). More PRs and fewer journalists threatens democracy. *The Guardian* (online), 4 October [retrieved 6 March 2018]. Available at: https://www.theguardian.com/media/greenslade/2012/oct/04/marketingandpr-pressandpublishing.

31. McChesney, R.W. (2012). Farewell to journalism? Time for a rethinking. *Journalism Studies, 13*(5–6), 682–694.

32. Greenberg, J. (2014). Carly Fiorina: 70% of world's poor are women. *PolitiFact PunditFact,* 15 January [retrieved 6 March 2018]. Available at: http://www.politifact.com/punditfact/statements/2014/jan/15/carly-fiorina/carly-fiorina-70-worlds-poor-are-women/.

Chapter 3

1. http://interactive.news.sky.com/Robots_Tabs_FULL.pdf.

2. Tranter, B., & Booth, K. (2015). Scepticism in a changing climate: a cross-national study. *Global Environmental Change, 33,* 154–164.

3. Maxwell, A. (2015). *Adult Criminal Court Statistics in Canada, 2013/14.* Canadian Centre for Justice Statistics [retrieved 6 March 2018]. Available at: http://www.statcan.gc.ca/pub/85-002-x/2015001/article/14226-eng.pdf.

4. Koblin, J. (2016). 'Game of Thrones' finale draws record ratings. *New York Times,* 28 June [retrieved 6 March 2018]. Available at: http://www.nytimes.com/2016/06/29/arts/television/game-of-thrones-finale-draws-record-ratings.html.

5. Ipsos MORI. (2016). The perils of perception and the EU. *Ipsos MORI,* 9 June [retrieved 6 March 2018]. Available at: https://www.ipsos-mori.com/research-publications/researcharchive/3742/The-Perils-of-Perception-and-the-EU.aspx.

6. IFOP (Institut français d'opinion publique). (2014). L'observatoire Européen de l'infidélité: la France est-elle la patrie de l'infidélité? *IFOP,* 27 February [retrieved 6 March 2018]. Available at: http://www.ifop.com/?option=com_publication&type=poll&id=2535.

7. Vasel, K. (2016). Couples are spending more than ever to get hitched. CNN Money, 6 April [retrieved 6 March 2018]. Available at: http://money.cnn.com/2016/04/05/pf/average-wedding-costs/.

8. Rampell, C. (2017). A chilling study shows how hostile college students are toward free speech. *Washington Post,* 18 September [retrieved 6 March 2018]. Available at: https://www.washingtonpost.com/opinions/a-chilling-study-shows-how-hostile-college-students-are-toward-free-speech/2017/09/18/.

9. Hite, S. (2005). *The Hite Report: A Nationwide Study of Female Sexuality.* New York: Seven Stories Press.

Chapter 4

1. BBC News. (2017). Sweden to Trump: What happened last night? *BBC News* (online), 19 February [retrieved 6 March 2018]. Available at: http://www.bbc.co.uk/news/world-us-canada-39020962.

2. LBC Radio. (2017). Nigel Farage: 'Malmo is now the rape capital of Europe'. *LBC Radio,* 20 February [retrieved 6 March 2018]. Available at: http://www.lbc.co.uk/radio/presenters/nigel-farage/nigel-farage-malmo-sweden-rape-capital-of-europe/

3. https://data.unodc.org/.

4. Swedish Crime Prevention Council (Bra). (2012). Allt polisanmaler nar de utsatts for brott. *Bra,* 6 November [retrieved 6 March 2018]. Available at: https://www.bra.se/nytt-fran-bra/arkiv/press/2012-11-06-allt-fler-polisanmaler-nar-de-utsatts-for-brott.html.

5. Swedish Crime Prevention Council (Bra). (2015). Kortanalys 7/2015. *Bra* [retrieved 6 March 2018]. Available at: https://www.bra.se/download/18.31d7fffa1504-bbffea044822/1447769941578/2015_Skjutningar+2006+och+2014.pdf.

6. University of Pittsburgh. (2017). *More Social Connection Online Tied to Increasing Feelings of Isolation.* News release. University of Pittsburgh Schools of the Health Sciences, 6 March [retrieved 6 March 2018]. Available at: http://www.upmc.com/media/NewsReleases/2017/Pages/primack-smu.aspx.

7. Primack, B.A., Shensa, A., Sidani, J.E., Whaite, E.O., yi Lin, L., Rosen, D., Colditz, J.B. Radovic, A., & Miller, E. (2017). Social media use and perceived social isolation among young adults in the US. *American Journal of Preventive Medicine, 53*(1), 1–8.

8. Boutwell, B.B., Nedelec, J.L., Winegard, B., Shackelford, T., Beaver, K.M., Vaughn, M., Barnes, J.C., & Wright, J.P. (2017). The prevalence of discrimination across racial groups in contemporary America: Results from a nationally representative sample of adults. *PloS One, 12*(8), e0183356.

9. https://www.cdc.gov/healthyyouth/data/yrbs/index.htm.

10. Coates, T. (2016). Hillary Clinton was politically incorrect, but she wasn't wrong about Trump's supporters. *The Atlantic* (online), 10 September [retrieved 6 March 2018]. Available at: https://www.theatlantic.com/politics/archive/2016/09/basket-of-deplorables/499493/.

11. Flitter, E., & Kahn, C. (2016). Exclusive: Trump supporters more likely to view blacks negatively – Reuters/Ipsos poll. *Reuters,* 28 June [retrieved 6 March 2018]. Available at: http://www.reuters.com/article/us-usa-election-race-idUSKCN0ZE2SW.

12. Ingraham, C. (2015). The most racist places in America, according to Google. *Washington Post* (online), 28 April [retrieved 6 March 2018]. Available at: https://www.washingtonpost.com/news/wonk/wp/2015/04/28/the-most-racist-places-in-america-according-to-google/.

13. Chae, D.H., Clouston, S., Hatzenbuehler, M.L., Kramer, M.R., Cooper, H.L., Wilson, S. M., Stephens-Davidowitz, S.I., Gold, R.S., & Link, B.G. (2015). Association between an internet-based measure of area racism and Black mortality. *PloS One, 10*(4), e0122963.

Chapter 5

1. Rayner, G., & Swinford, S. (2017). Corbyn's tax raid would take Britain back to the 1950s. *Daily Telegraph,* 17 May.

2. McMahon, T., Kohler, N., & Stobo Sniderman, A. (2012). How Canadian are you? *Maclean's* (online), 28 June [retrieved 6 March 2018]. Available at: http://www.macleans.ca/news/canada/how-canadian-are-you/.

3. Oremus, W. (2015). The Wedding industry's pricey little secret. *Slate,* 19 March [retrieved 6 March 2018]. Available at: http://www.slate.com/articles/life/weddings/2013/06/average_wedding_cost_published_numbers_on_the_price_of_a_wedding_are_totally.html.

4. Holodny, E. (2015). Americans plan to celebrate Christmas like it's 2007. *Business Insider UK,* 18 November [retrieved 6 March 2018]. Available at: http://uk.businessinsider.com/americans-plan-to-spend-more-this-christmas-2015-11.

Chapter 6

1. http://dx.doi.org/10.4232/1.12661.
2. O'Niell, E. (2012). Frank Lautenburg says gun violence claimed more American lives in U.S. than in Iraq and Afghanistan. *PolitiFact New Jersey,* 6 August [retrieved 6 March 2018]. Available at: http://www.politifact.com/new-jersey/statements/2012/aug/06/frank-lautenberg/frank-lautenberg-says-gun-violence-claimed-more-am/.
3. Goldberg, M.S. (2014). Updated Death and Injury Rates of U.S. Military Personnel During the Conflicts in Iraq and Afghanistan. *Congressional Budget Office Working Paper Series,* 2014–08.
4. Fourkala, E.O., Burnell, M., Cox, C., Ryan, A., Salter, L.C., Gentry-Maharaj, A., Parmar, M., Jacobs, I., & Menon, U. (2014). Association of skirt size and postmenopausal breast cancer risk in older women: a cohort study within the UK Collaborative Trial of Ovarian Cancer Screening (UKCTOCS). *BMJ Open, 4*(9), e005400.
5. Goldacre, B. (2008). You are 80% less likely to die from a meteor landing on your head if you wear a bicycle helmet all day. *Badscience.net,* 15 November [retrieved 6 March 2018]. Available at: http://www.badscience.net/2008/11/you-are-80-less-likely-to-die-from-a-meteor-landing-on-your-head-if-you-wear-a-bicycle-helmet-all-day/.
6. Oppenheim, M. (2017). 22 million Americans support neo-Nazis, new poll indicates. *The Independent,* 22 August [retrieved 6 March 2018]. Available at: http://www.independent.co.uk/news/world/americas/us-neo-nazi-support-american-public-charlottesville-white-supremacists-kkk-far-right-poll-a7907091.html.
7. Brown, A. (2013). Assisted suicide poll shows support among majority of religious people. *The Guardian* (online), 30 April [retrieved 6 March 2018]. Available at: https://www.theguardian.com/society/2013/apr/30/assisted-suicide-poll-religious.

Chapter 7

1. Lucas, M., Mirzaei, F., Pan, A., Okereke, O.I., Willett, W.C., O'Reilly, É.J., Koenan, K., & Ascherio, A. (2011). Coffee, caffeine, and risk of depression among women. *Archives of internal Medicine, 171*(17), 1571–1578.
2. Jacobson, R.M., & Feinstein, A.R. (1992). Oxygen as a cause of blindness in premature infants: 'autopsy' of a decade of errors in clinical epidemiologic research. *Journal of Clinical Epidemiology, 45*(11), 1265–1287.
3. Twenge, J.M. (2017). Have smartphones destroyed a generation. *The Atlantic,* September [retrieved 6 March 2018]. Available at: https://www.theatlantic.com/magazine/archive/2017/09/has-the-smartphone-destroyed-a-generation/534198/.
4. Duncan, G.J., Boisjoly, J., Kremer, M., Levy, D.M., & Eccles, J. (2005). Peer effects in drug use and sex among college students. *Journal of Abnormal Child Psychology, 33*(3), 375–385.

5.   Miller, M., Azrael, D., & Hemenway, D. (2002). Rates of household firearm ownership and homicide across US regions and states, 1988–1997. *American Journal of Public Health, 92*(12), 1988–1993.

6.   Vigen, T. (2015). *Spurious Correlations*. New York: Hachette Books.

7.   Howard, M. (2010). Study confirms that Fox News makes you stupid. *Alternet,* 14 December [retrieved 6 March 2018]. Available at: https://www.alternet.org/story/149193/study_confirms_that_fox_news_makes_you_stupid.

Chapter 8

1.   Diaz, J. (2012). Holy F*ck, the New iPad has a gigantic 70-percent larger battery. *Gizmodo,* 15 March [retrieved 6 March 2018]. Available at: https://gizmodo.com/5893738/holy-fck-the-new-ipad-has-a-gigantic-70-percent-larger-battery.

2.   Lauzen, M. (2017). *It's a Man's (Celluloid) World: Portrayals of Female Characters in the Top 100 Films of 2016.* Center for the Study of Women in Television and Film.

3.   Tufte, E.R. (2001). *The Visual Display of Quantitative Information.* Cheshire, CT: Graphics Press.

4.   Mann, M.E., Bradley, R.S., & Hughes, M.K. (1999). Northern hemisphere temperatures during the past millennium: Inferences, uncertainties, and limitations. *Geophysical Research Letters, 26*(6), 759–762.

5.   Pearce, F. (2010). Controversy behind climate science's 'hockey stick' graph. *The Guardian* (online), 2 February [retrieved 6 March 2018]. Available at: https://www.theguardian.com/environment/2010/feb/02/hockey-stick-graph-climate-change.

6.   Qiu, L. (2015). Chart shown at Planned Parenthood hearing is misleading and 'ethically wrong'. *PolitiFact,* 1 October [retrieved 6 March 2018]. Available at: http://www.politifact.com/truth-o-meter/statements/2015/oct/01/jason-chaffetz/chart-shown-planned-parenthood-hearing-misleading-/.

7.   Pickett, K., & Wilkinson, R. (2010). *The Spirit Level: Why Equality Is Better for Everyone.* London: Penguin Books.

8.   Daly, M. (2016). Exclusive: New conviction data tells us how the UK sells drugs. *VICE,* 2 February [retrieved 6 March 2018]. Available at: https://www.vice.com/en_uk/article/dp5npk/foi-uk-drug-conviction-ethnicity-282.

9.   Gelman, A. (2011). (Worst) graph of the year. *Andrewgelman.com,* 17 September [retrieved 6 March 2018]. Available at: http://andrewgelman.com/2011/09/17/worst-graph-of-the-year/.

Chapter 9

1.   Hudson, J. (2016). Five facts about 'black oppression' Colin Kaepernick needs to know. *Breitbart,* 2 September [retrieved 6 March 2018]. Available at: http://www.breitbart.com/sports/2016/09/02/five-facts-about-black-oppression-colin-kaepernick-needs-to-know/.

2.   Neyfakh, L. (2016). Should the media downplay the new murder spike? *Slate,* 27 September [retrieved 6 March 2018]. Available at: http://www.slate.com/articles/news_and_politics/crime/2016/09/how_to_think_about_the_fbi_s_2015_crime_statistics.html.

3. Davies, C., & Neate, R. (2017). Queen's income rises to £82m to cover cost of Buckingham Palace works. *The Guardian* (online), 27 June [retrieved 6 March 2018]. Available at: https://www.theguardian.com/uk-news/2017/jun/27/queens-income-rises-to-82m-to-cover-cost-of-buckingham-palace-works.

Chapter 10

1. Jacobson, L. (2013). Rep. John Duncan Jr. says 90 percent of felons grew up in fatherless households. *PolitiFact,* 18 April [retrieved 6 March 2018]. Available at: http://www.politifact.com/truth-o-meter/statements/2013/apr/18/john-duncan/rep-john-duncan-jr-says-90-percent-felons-grew-fat/.
2. Economist Data Team. (2017). Are women paid less than men for the same work? *The Economist* (online), 1 August [retrieved 6 March 2018]. Available at: https://www.economist.com/blogs/graphicdetail/2017/08/daily-chart.
3. Levanon, A., England, P., & Allison, P. (2009). Occupational feminization and pay: Assessing causal dynamics using 1950–2000 US census data. *Social Forces, 88*(2), 865–891.
4. Williamson, H. (1775). Experiments and observations on the gymnotus electricus, or electrical eel. *Philosophical Transactions of the Royal Society, 65,* 94–101.

INDEX